US Health
A Failed System

A Threat to Society and the Economy

LYKOURGOS LIAROPOULOS

US Health: A Failed System – A Threat to Society and the Economy
Copyright © 2016 Lykourgos Liaropoulos
Cover image: © Niyazz | Adobe Stock
ISBN-13: 978-1-910370-92-6 (Stergiou Limited-Assigned)
ISBN-13: 978-1-540543-51-6 (CreateSpace-Assigned)
ePub ISBN-13: 978-1-910370-89-6 (Stergiou Limited-Assigned)
Published by Stergiou Limited
Suite A, 6 Honduras Street
London EC1Y 0TH
United Kingdom
Email: publications@stergioultd.com
URL: http://stergioultd.com

Digital Edition

CONTENTS

PREFACE

I left the US in 1974, after eleven wonderful years there. First a student, then a researcher in the State Government in Michigan. As an academic, in Greece, I continued to have a strong interest in the country to which I owe my best and formative years. Being a "political animal," I followed the political scene. What struck me most were the lines of voters in the 2012 presidential election. I had never seen such a huge number of really fat, almost obese, people together. I remember wondering, What is happening to this country? Among the things that make the US health system dangerous, none is more disturbing than what I call its "institutional indifference" for the health of Americans. [1]

Change must happen in American health, but the question is, what change and how? The recent Obamacare experience, after the Clinton attempt in 1993, should teach politicians and the American public a lesson. The core element of the Clinton National Health Insurance plan was an enforced mandate for employers to provide coverage to their employees. The reaction at the time came from many—conservatives, libertarians, the health insurance industry—but mainly, from small business. They killed it before it was born.

The Affordable Care Act (ACA), fifteen years later, puts the burden of private health insurance on individuals, with the government chipping in. Obamacare, with the Supreme Court stamp, works so far, but still millions are without insurance. At the same time, the ineffectiveness of the health-care system in terms of the health of Americans, its gross inefficiencies resulting in huge costs, its inequity coupled with increasing income inequality, and, as revealed lately, its unsustainability, leave much to be desired.

The main point in this book is that the "gradual creep" to universal coverage and national health insurance, which started timidly with the ACA, must be completed, as America can no longer afford the present alternative. One fifth of GDP spent in one sector alone should be a matter not for academic debate but for serious economic policy scrutiny. To spend three trillion dollars to support the health care and insurance industries while Americans get fatter, sicker, and with a shorter life expectancy than elsewhere in the developed world, is not something to be proud of. Nor are employers happy when their competitiveness suffers due to no fault of their own. Politics be damned, America deserves an efficient, effective, equitable, and affordable health system. This book is about what and how.

---

1 This may change, but not for health reasons. In its October 24, 2015 issue, *The Economist* wonders on the cover page "Too Fat to be an American Soldier?" Besides many other problems that now make it difficult for the Army to find new recruits, a certain Lieutenant Colonel Tony Parilli is quoted as saying, "a bigger problem is that America is obese."

INTRODUCTION

"Good health is a blessing. But how countries structure their health-care system—and their society—makes a huge difference in terms of outcomes. America and the world pay a high price for excessive reliance on market forces and an insufficient attention to broader values, including equality and social justice."

—*Joseph Stiglitz, Nobel Laureate in Economics*

The 2000 World Health Organization (WHO) World Health Report[1] was groundbreaking. It ranked 191 health systems from all member countries, suggesting three main goals a health system should primarily aim at: 1) **Good health**: making the health status of the entire population as good as possible across the whole life cycle, 2) **Responsiveness**: responsibility to people's expectations of respectful treatment and client orientation by health providers, and 3) **Fairness in financing**: ensuring financial protection for everyone, with costs distributed according to one's ability to pay. In every respect the performance of the US health system, then and today, leaves much to be desired.

Despite the "usual" methodological objections,[2] the WHO study created a stir. For the first time, US excellence in health care was "officially" challenged, causing a debate, starting with a seminal article in *Health Affairs* in 2001.[3] It presented data from the Organization for Economic Cooperation and Development (OECD) and the WHO on the performance of health care systems in 29 industrialized countries in 1998. The authors compared performance in the United States with other industrialized countries for selected indicators in 1960, 1980, and 1998. On most indicators the US's relative performance had declined since 1960, and, more important, on none had it improved. Another article followed in 2004, again in *Health Affairs*.[4] The title was "US Health Care Spending in an International Context," but the subtitle was much more telling: "Why is US spending so high, and can we afford it?"

This could be the title of this book, except that the situation is much worse. For the seven GDP percentage points[5] by which health expenditure exceeds that of other OECD countries, the US displays awful health statistics. The debate on the relative performance of various health systems caused major comparative studies both in the US and abroad. In 2011, the Bureau of Labor Education of the University of Maine published a paper titled *The US Health Care System: Best in the World, or Just the Most Expensive?*[6] According to the authors, the second is the correct answer. Three years later, the 2014 Commonwealth Fund Report concluded:[7]

1 The World Health Report 2000—Health Systems: Improving Performance (Geneva: WHO, 2000).
2 http://content.healthaffairs.org/content/20/3/10.full
3 http://content.healthaffairs.org/content/20/3/219.short
4 http://content.healthaffairs.org/content/23/3/10.full.pdf+html
5 Projected to reach 10 percent by 2020.
6 http://umaine.edu/ble/files/2011/01/US-healthcare-system.pdf
7 http://www.commonwealthfund.org/publications/fund-reports/2014/jun/mirror-mirror

"The United States health care system is the most expensive in the world, but this report and prior editions consistently show that the US underperforms relative to other countries on most dimensions of performance. Among the 11 nations studied in this report . . . the US ranks last, as it did in the 2010, 2007, 2006, and 2004 editions. Most troubling, the US fails to achieve better health outcomes than the other countries, and, as shown in the earlier editions, the US is last or near last on dimensions of access, efficiency, and equity. In this Report, the United Kingdom ranks first, followed closely by Switzerland."

The American health-care system is not easily analyzed in the manner used by the WHO, the OECD, or other organizations who have conducted large comparative studies of health system performance. The reason is that the main philosophical and political pillars on which the US health system stands are quite different from the way healthcare is viewed in the rest of the developed world. For some, this might be expected, since the philosophical foundation of a given society and its politics are related. This is not entirely true however, since values and ethics are not necessarily uni-directional. It is true that the American ethic bows to the principle of equal opportunity, and since all people "are created equal," one cannot exclude the "right to health care" for those that cannot afford it. On the other hand, politics everywhere are a compromise between various interests which are not always ethical. One of the chapters in this book has the somewhat provocative title "Politics and Morals are Strange Bedfellows."[8]

It is said that a crisis often also carries an opportunity. Wisely perhaps, both words in Chinese are expressed by the same ideogram. The "fake and forced" political crisis which arose of the need to manage a genuine debt-ceiling crisis in 2013 should teach Americans a lesson about the current health crisis, even though it is not yet officially recognized as such. The same ideology and political forces which then used the "budget limit" for political profit are responsible for the fact that America spends twice as much as other developed western countries to run a much worse health system. These forces, at the time, nearly brought America to its knees and the world economy to a standstill. It is not surprising that in the summer of 2011, *The Economist* considered health reform as one of the two issues[9] which "will decide the outcome of the 2012 presidential election."[10] It happened then and it may also happen in 2016.

I believe that the US health system is simply no longer sustainable in its present form. The monstrous expenditure, projected to reach almost 20% of GDP by 2020—for no apparent health gain—will soon force major political decisions. We claim that America should find a new stand on health care, worthy of its stature in the world. For many reasons, health is considered a social stabilizer. Our view, however, is not based on ethical ideals but on something the American society can easily understand and accept. Pure, unadulterated self-interest can show the road to reform, which, as we claim in this book, must obey four imperatives.

The Societal Imperative

Social stability becomes important when a country has exhausted its limits for growth in terms of vital area or economic expansion opportunities. As long as the US had a frontier to conquer, the motto "Go West, young man" was a potent harbinger of progress and social evo-

---

8 See Part C.
9 The other one being, of course, jobs.
10 *The Economist*, August 6th 2011.

lution. When vast expansion and growth opportunities became scarcer, however, the need for social stability and equitable distribution of the benefits of growth became a social imperative. In Europe, this happened earlier with the "nanny state" first appearing as social security in 1895 Bismarck's Germany. The same may be said of China at the end of the 20th century. In America, this imperative was first but timidly recognized in the 20th century with the major Social Security reforms of the '30s and the '60s. It is even more evident now, when the limits to growth acquire new dimensions, including the threat to the environment.

The Moral Imperative

A certain degree of equity is required in every society, if not for ethical or moral reasons, but for reasons of survival. It is not essential or even desirable that all members of society enjoy the same standard of living. It is essential, however, that they all have equal access to food and shelter, to which one might add basic medical care. The moral imperative behind the Affordable Care Act was that no American should have to do without health insurance coverage, even if they could not afford it. No modern society can be successful if people suffer or die early of preventable disease or because of lack of care in a dysfunctional health system.

The Economic Imperative

Inefficiency in business or other private economic affairs is punished by the market, and it concerns the perpetrator, be it a firm or an individual. Inefficiency in public affairs, however, concerns all of us, wherever we live, and when punished, the punishment is to all, guilty or not. Health care, even in America, absorbs a considerable portion of public funds and an even greater share of private resources. It affects the public debt, and it diverts resources from other productive uses—such as education, research, environmental protection, infrastructure development, even defense. In a three trillion dollar sector, 30% inefficiency means waste of one trillion dollars, more taxes, less growth, and fewer jobs. In this book we maintain that efficiency gains alone can finance the expansion of health care coverage and health insurance for all Americans.

The Political Imperative

Health care is a rising concern for many in America. It is the rallying point for those who consider health care an essential right, and not a commodity sold and bought on the market. It is also a concern for business and its competitive position in a globalized environment. The Affordable Care Act experience showed that the expansion of public health insurance coverage is useful and increasingly popular. The opponents are getting more strident and, therefore, less effective. The imperative for greater public involvement in the regulation and financing of health care through national health insurance is becoming increasingly clear, even to politicians.

Complete health reform is absolutely essential simply because America can no longer afford the present course. The purpose of this book is to offer an international perspective, to facilitate understanding of the forces at work, and to suggest a way out of the present conundrum. That it is written by a foreigner should not be a disadvantage, but, rather, an attempt to bring another view to a very complicated universal problem which has known better solutions elsewhere.

PART A

AMERICAN HEALTH CARE:
A NON-PERFORMING SYSTEM

INTRODUCTION

A NON-PERFORMING HEALTH SYSTEM

The US is the country with the most (257) Nobel Laureates, seventy of whom come from the field of medicine. Many scientific discoveries and medical innovations have come out of American laboratories and health research centers, and many of its hospitals are of top quality, both technologically and scientifically. Organizations, such as the Food and Drug Administration (FDA), the Centers for Disease Control and Prevention (CDC), the National Institutes of Health (NIH) and others set world standards of quality. It is inconceivable that a new drug may be sold in the United States and in the rest of the developed world unless it is "FDA approved". The European Center for Disease Control (ECDC) is only a few years old, whereas the CDC in the US was founded in 1946. If the cure for cancer is ever found, it will, in all probability, be developed in an American laboratory.

Health care is, indeed, one of the sectors in which America should be a world leader. And yet, in the beginning of 2007, *The Economist*, the oldest and leading economic and political weekly in the world, and by its own admission a conservative magazine, used the following words to describe the American health care "crisis":

> *"If you had to sum up the problems of American health care in two words, they would be "cost" and "coverage". The country spends 16% of its GDP on health, twice the average of other rich economies. Yet, a sixth of the population lacks medical coverage. ... That so many people should be without medical coverage in the world's richest country is a disgrace. It blights the lives of the uninsured, who suffer by being unable to get access to affordable care at an early stage. And it casts a shadow of fear well beyond, to America's middle classes, who worry about losing not just their jobs, but also their health care benefits. It is also grossly inefficient. Hospitals are forced, by law, to help anyone who arrives in the emergency room. Since those without insurance coverage usually cannot pay for that care, the bill is passed on to everyone else, driving up premiums. Higher premiums, in turn, swell the ranks of the uninsured." [1]*

On November 15, 2015, again, *The Economist* described the American health system with the paragraph below:

> *"AMERICA remains the world's most profligate spender on health care, according to a report published on November 4th by the OECD, a club of 34 rich countries. In 2013 the United States spent, on average, $8,713 per person—two and a half times as much as the OECD average. Yet the average American dies 1.7 years earlier than the average OECD citizen. This longevity gap has grown by a year since 2003. Americans have the same life expectancy as Chileans, even though Chile spends less than a fifth of what America spends on health care per person."*

It is sad but true that the average American is worse-off than the average European, Canadian, or Australian if luck would put him/her in the unfortunate position of seeking health care in America. Even sadder is that Americans don't even know that they pay twice as much to get half the quantity and quality of health care compared to their rich counterparts elsewhere. The main reason is that health care is bought and sold in a "free health market," and is financed to a large extent by private health insurance. As in every country, the health system develops in a manner reflecting the national value system and the beliefs of the average citizen as expressed by its politics and institutions. Especially in developed democracies, the health system cannot but be in harmony with the national "mood," if such a notion exists. In that sense, it is indeed a paradox that the American health system is such a failure, as conceived not only by observers abroad but also in America. This paradox needs explaining, but not justification, and is the major theme in this book. Before we pass judgment in such a summary way, however, let us first see what a health system is and what Americans could or should expect from it.

What is a Health System and Why Do We Need One?

"...a health system is the ensemble of all public and private organizations, institutions and resources mandated to improve, maintain or restore health. Health systems encompass both personal and population services, as well as activities to influence the policies and actions of other sectors to address the social, environmental and economic determinants of health." [1]

A country's health system could be a matter of national pride in international comparisons. It may be a claim of achievement by the government or of opprobrium by the opposition. It is a business opportunity, a major source of employment, and a drain on public and private money. It could be a reflection of the ethical armature of a society, although it is not often discussed as such, except, perhaps, in Britain. Above all, it is a major political issue, especially around election time. Alas, in America, it is also a very expensive business.

The question of what we gain for the money spent in health care should be a major concern to individuals, political parties, and the society as a whole. Unfortunately, the questions of what a health system is, what it does, how it works and for whom, how much it costs and why, and who pays for it, are often secrets, well kept by "experts" of various disciplines, affiliations, and loyalties. It is thus difficult for laymen to find their way around, when it matters most, which is on their way to the ballot box.

As recorded in public opinion polls, the American health system is not a success story for the average citizen. This is reflected in public opinion polls and statistics measuring population health levels in the developed world. The American system is not responsive to the needs of its customers while absorbing one-fifth of the nation's GDP. The first chapter of this Part A is devoted to an analysis of health expenditure in the US and the reasons why it has risen so much. In the course of the last fifty years, a substantial body of literature has dealt with health system performance. The major aspects studied are the three E's: efficiency (including per capita expenditure), effectiveness (including quality of care), and equity (including financial protection). The three E's are the main issues an informed citizen should always raise when discussing the

---

1 Definition adopted at The WHO Ministerial Conference held in Tallinn, Estonia in 2008, under the title theme: "Health Systems for Health and Wealth."

health system. Three simple definitions will help.

- *Efficiency:* "Is the money spent by me, by my insurance company (public or private), or by my government the least possible for the given quantity and quality of care? In other words, are the providers of care mindful of the cost, or are they simply profit maximizers?

- *Effectiveness:* "Is the quantity and quality of care I receive adequate and suitable to the prevention of disease and the protection and maintenance of my health and that of my family? If we include the proviso "for the money spent," we are talking about *cost-effectiveness,* another side of efficiency.

- *Equity:* "Is the financial burden, in terms of taxes and/or employment contributions for running the system, distributed fairly? Does the cost of care relative to my ability to pay prevent me from accessing necessary health services?"

These three questions are relevant regardless of whether the health system is privately run and financed for profit, as in America, or publicly financed and run as a public service as, say, in the UK. In a privately run health system, the *electorate* must ask only these three questions, especially at election time. In a public health system, administered by a national or regional government, there is a fourth question which must be answered. The topic of the *sustainability* of the health system in relation to the economy has appeared lately in the international discussion. This is mainly concerned with whether the resources required for running the health system will or can be available in the long run. This implies, of course, that the society recognizes that a *sustainable* health system is a responsibility of the government, like other services covered by public funds, such as education, justice, defense, and public safety.

The method chosen for the financing of the health system, the incidence of the burden, and the method chosen for the collection and disbursement of the funds is, therefore, a very important political question for governments in the developed world. Politicians in the US, on the contrary, seem, so far, less concerned with the total cost of health care than with the incomes and profits produced in the "health industry". Health care and health services are a matter of personal or, at best, professional responsibility, not very different from all other economic activity, such as choosing and buying a home or a car. The fallacy and the real consequences of this have not yet "sunk in" for the *body politic* in the US. Hopefully by election time in November 2016 it will play a more central role. Our point in Chapter A-5 is that in a market-dominated system such as the American, the government ignores the question of sustainability at its peril. Whether expenditure on health care can keep rising according to the whims of the "health market" will soon be a major political issue. There are, after all, many other competing uses for the "health dollar," in any advanced society, including money privately spent. The 20% of GDP expenditure for health, which the new American president will face in 2017, is simply unacceptable, unaffordable, and unsustainable. Unfortunately, so far, not many seem to care.

References
[1]   The Economist, Jan 11th 2007, "Sensible Medicine from the States."

A-1: HEALTH IN THE US IS A (VERY) COSTLY BUSINESS

"The first myth about the American Health System is that it is failing. In reality, it is succeeding, but in a very expensive way."

—Henry Mintzberg, Professor at McGill University, Harvard
Business Review, October, 2011.

It is indeed curious that America spends almost twice as much for health care as other developed economies. Many Americans do not seem to know this, and if they do, they do not seem to mind. One can say the same for expenditure on defence, but Americans consider world supremacy and national safety as worthwhile. There is enough historical evidence on the importance of strong defence and even of world leadership. On the contrary, one wonders whether Americans think the same about their health dollar, or, in fact, whether they know much about it. After all, many think the American health system is the best in the world. Figure A1-1 tells the first part of an interesting story. Beginning in 1980, America and twelve other wealthy Organization for Economic Cooperation and Development (OECD), countries started from a roughly equal position, spending between seven and nine percent of their Gross Domestic Product (GDP) for the health of their people. Since then, health expenditure in America rose fast during the Reagan years, remained stable during the Clinton presidency in the last decade of the 20th century, then "went through the roof," especially during the first Bush presidency, and remained stable during the first Obama presidency. This remarkable "partisan divide" is interesting and we should keep it in mind from now on. At the same time, the rest of the "rich" world seems to follow a much more moderate course in line with rising incomes, medical and technological progress, and economic cycles as, for example, in 2007.

Figure A1-1. Total Health Expenditure as percent of GDP, selected OECD countries, 1980-2013

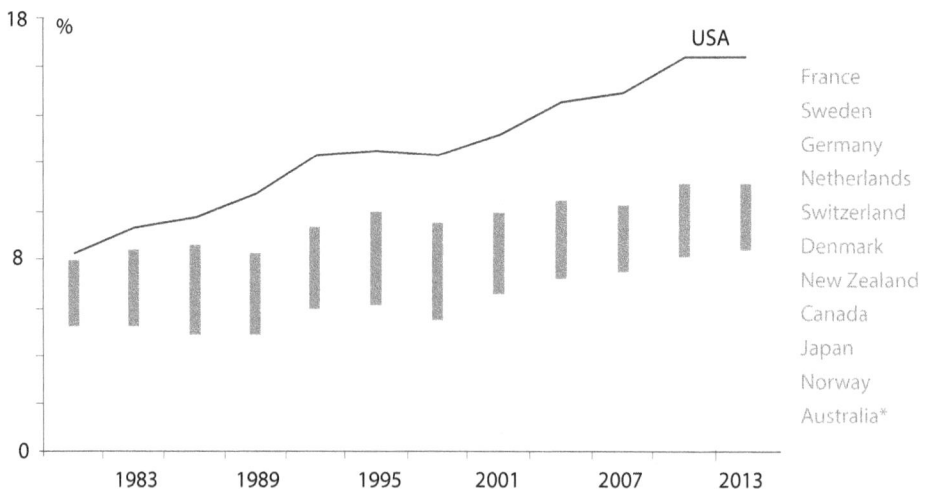

Source: OECD Health Data.

The money to finance this expenditure in all countries comes from a variety of sources, private and public, and is collected through a variety of mechanisms. Government taxes, employer-employee voluntary or mandatory insurance contributions, and philanthropic and local government institutions all contribute to the health dollar, pound, or euro. Expenditure increases as medical knowledge and technology produces more and better health, and growing wealth in all societies allows this increase, as with many other goods and services. Only one country stands out in the share of income devoted to health care. In 33 years, the US has managed to devote twice as big a share of GDP to the health-care industry (approaching the 20% range) as the other countries under review, all of which are democratic societies with elected governments and wide social protection networks, who manage with almost half as much.

The OECD consists of 34 of the most economically advanced countries in the world. According to OECD data,[1] the United States spent $8,454 per capita on health care in 2012, more than double the OECD average of $3,440 and 37% more than Switzerland, the second highest-spending country. In 2012, 16.4% of the US economy was devoted to health care, compared with 8.8% in the average OECD country and 11.0% in second-placed Switzerland. Table A1-1 below summarizes the performance of the health sector in the US in the 23 years from 1990 to 2013, compared to 28 OECD countries and 16 EU countries, most of which are OECD countries as well.

Table A1-1 is dramatically explicit. In the almost quarter century since 1990, the US increased its health expenditure fastest, even though it started from a much higher level. Although the total amount of resources spent on health in the US as a percent of GDP is double that spent by European countries, Europeans seem to be getting twice as much of a "bang" for their pounds or euros compared to what Americans get for their dollars. In the rest of the book and especially in Part A, we will examine this "bang" much more closely. In what follows here, we will only mention some of the main facts.

Table A1-1. Health-Care Costs in the Developed World, 1990-2013.

	Total Health Expenditure as % of GDP							% Change
	1990	1995	2000	2005	2010	2012	2013	
US	11.29	12.54	12.53	14.57	16.40	16.41	16.40	45.3
OECD*	6.48	7.17	7.45	8.35	9.10	9.12	9.24	42.6
EU*	6.50	7.34	7.42	8.43	9.18	9.29	9.33	43.5

Source: OECD Health Data.
*For the purpose of comparability over time we used the 28 OECD countries and the 16 EU counties reporting data to the OECD database after 1990.

Health Care Expenditure–Basic Facts and Sources

Below we list, without discussing, certain key facts on health expenditure in America and the sources from which the information is derived.[2]

- National health-care expenditures are paid by: households (28%), private businesses (21%), state and local governments (16%), and the federal government (27%). Another

---

1 The OECD Health Database is the largest and most complete set of fairly comparable countries, as opposed to the WHO database. Although some data exist for 2013, 2012 is the year for which the dataset is complete and suitable for meaningful comparisons.

2 NHE Fact Sheet 2013, the Medicare and Medicaid Actuary Office.

8% come from other sources. *Centers for Medicare & Medicaid Services.*

- Seventy-five percent of all health-care dollars are spent on patients with one or more chronic conditions, many of which can be prevented, including diabetes, obesity, heart disease, lung disease, high blood pressure, and cancer. *Health Affairs.*

- Half of health-care spending is used to treat just 5% of the population. *Kaiser Family Foundation, May 2012.*

- Since 2001, employer-sponsored health coverage for family premiums has increased by 113%. *Kaiser Family Foundation, May 2012.*

- As of 2009, health spending in the US was about 90% higher than in many other industrialized countries. The most likely causes are higher prices, more readily accessible technology, and greater obesity. *Kaiser Family Foundation, May 2012.*

Why Does America Spend so Much on Health?

Economists break health spending into two parts: quantity, which includes the number of providers, visits to health-care providers, and the resources used, and price, that is the remuneration of providers. In terms of quantity, OECD data indicate that the United States has far fewer doctors and doctor visits per person compared with the OECD average; in hospitalizations the United States ranks well below the OECD average and is roughly comparable in terms of length of hospital stays. The intensity of service delivery is a different story: the United States uses more of the newest medical technologies and performs several invasive procedures (such as coronary bypasses and angioplasties) more frequently than the average OECD country. In terms of price, the OECD concludes that "there is no doubt that US prices for medical care commodities and services are significantly higher than in other countries and a key determinant of health spending."

Unlike most markets for consumer services in the United States, the health-care market generally lacks transparent market-based pricing [1]. Patients cannot comparison-shop for medical services based on price, as medical service providers do not typically disclose prices prior to service. Government-mandated critical care and government insurance programs like Medicare also impact market pricing of US health care. According to The New York Times, "the United States is far and away the world leader in medical spending, even though numerous studies have concluded that Americans do not get better care." [2].

One of the reasons why the US health-care system is so expensive may be high prices. Although the OECD data do not compare prices of medical care, studies have found that the United States pays higher prices for medical care than countries such as Canada and Germany. American general practitioners, specialists, and nurses are the highest paid among OECD countries. Health professionals in wealthier countries earn higher salaries than in poorer countries but, even accounting for this, health professionals in America are paid significantly more than the national GDP would predict (for example, specialists are paid approximately $50,000 more than would be expected, based on international experience). On the other hand, many US health-care professionals begin their careers later and with substantially more educational debt than in other OECD countries. For example, in 2006, 62% of new medical school graduates had educational debt exceeding $100,000 [3].

Economists say that the main reason for high costs in the US is the ever-expanding use of expensive kinds of diagnosis and treatment, such as new drugs, diagnostic tests, imaging methods, and surgical procedures. However, physicians in most other advanced countries have access to virtually the same resources. They simply use them less and more appropriately. This difference is partly explained by a higher proportion of specialists in the US who rely more on expensive technical procedures for their livelihood, and in general are much more highly paid than primary care physicians. This is one reason why primary care doctors are now in short supply (see Chapter D-4). The American College of Physicians attributes much of the high cost of the health system to a relative excess of well-paid specialists and a lack of primary care doctors.

There is much greater financial incentive in the US to overuse technology, since health insurers pay doctors and clinical facilities most of what they charge for such services. In most countries with universal coverage and national health insurance, the government, one way or another, controls remuneration rates and determines how medical expenses are reimbursed. The income of health-care providers from technical services is therefore more modest. Finally, relatively more practicing physicians, especially in primary care, in those countries, are paid on a salary basis, and relatively more hospitals (where most advanced technology is concentrated) are controlled by government budgets. This limits the overuse of expensive technology.

A very important but overlooked reason for the high health expenditures in the US is that, more than in any other advanced country, large parts of the system are owned by investors and the entire system behaves like a profit-driven industry [4]. The commercialization of the health system dates back a few decades, and its consequences are profound. Investors now own about 20 percent of non-public general hospitals, almost all specialty hospitals, and most freestanding facilities for ambulatory patients, such as walk-in clinics, imaging centers, and ambulatory surgical centers. These medical-care businesses, like other businesses, need profits to satisfy their investors, and for this purpose they use marketing and advertising, directed at physicians and the general public. At the same time, electronic record-keeping is ever more complicated and expensive due to the fact that all these providers are, one way or the other, linked to many private insurers competing against each other and due also to the complexity of the American health-care system [5].

What do Americans get for the money they spend on health? Does the United States get corresponding value from the money spent on health care? The available data do not always provide clear answers. For example, among OECD countries, the US has shorter-than-average life expectancy and higher-than-average mortality rates. Does this mean that the US system is inefficient in light of what is spent on health care? Or does it reflect the greater prevalence of certain diseases in the United States (the US has the highest incidence of cancer and AIDS in the OECD) and less healthy lifestyles (the US has the highest obesity rates in the OECD)? These are some of the issues that confound international comparisons. We will say more on this in Chapter A-3.

Research comparing the quality of care has not found the US superior overall, either. Nor does the US population have substantially better access to health resources, even putting aside the uninsured. Although the US does not have long wait times for non-emergency surgeries, unlike some OECD countries, Americans find it more difficult to make same-day doctor's appointments when sick and have the most difficulty getting care during nights and weekends [6]. They are also most likely to delay or forgo treatment for some expensive ailments because of the high cost of the required treatment.

Another Look at Health Costs

There are those who do not think the cost of health in the US is too high. They are usually advocates of the view that health care is just a commodity or like any other economic activity. The fact that health costs constitute twice the share of GDP than in other wealthy countries is, according to this view, not really a problem, since the health industry produces employment, income, and wealth. In a comparison between 1958 and 2012, Chris Conover, a contributor to Forbes, [7] takes this view to extremes. He found a paper by a Michigan University economist that compared the cost of home appliances in 1959 and 2012 in terms of the "time cost," which is the cost of labor time needed to produce a washer-dryer combination in 1959 and 2012 [8]. Conover used this method to calculate health costs for 1958 and 2012. Deflating per capita health expenditure according to the hours required to pay for the per capita health expenditure in 1958 and in 2012, the author concludes that the price of health care in 2012 has fallen to one-fourth the price in 1958.[3]

Lest anybody have doubts, Conover concedes that *"health care in 2012 is vastly different and greatly improved compared to what it was in 1958."* Nevertheless, he uses the exercise as an opportunity to "sing the song of the market." He goes on, *"In general, private markets tend to produce steadily lower prices in real terms (e.g. in worker times costs) and steadily rising quality."* And he concludes with the refrain, *"If we were willing to rely more on markets in medicine, we might be able to harness the superior ability of Americans to find good value for the money to produce results more similar to other goods."* The message is clear. It is actually worth somebody's time to look up this *Forbes* article just to see the extent to which champions of the "health market" will stress an argument if it suits their cause. In Part C we come back to the issue of ideology and politics and the way these concepts warp the health policy debate in the US

Thankfully, most experts would agree that the main problem with the American Health Care system is its very high cost. The US has experienced rapid growth in the last three decades and health expenditure is soon expected to reach or exceed three trillion dollars. The rate of price increases in health care at seven percent a year, or three times the rate of inflation, has continuously outpaced that of the overall price index over this period. Yet, a considerable number of Americans (almost 30 million in 2015) are still without health insurance. As the 2016 presidential election draws nearer, protection against the often catastrophic cost of health care will probably again be a major issue, but it should now be second to the concern about cost inflation. Apart from other problems such as access to care, equity, quality of care, and affordability of insurance coverage, which are discussed in detail in the rest of Part A, it is painfully clear that health spending at three trillion dollars, or 20% of GDP is unsustainable for long. Issues of national importance such as the federal deficit, the national debt, [9] and the defence budget—not to mention environmental protection, and infrastructure renovation—become difficult to manage because of failings in health care alone. Quite simply, health care is increasingly becoming the leviathan that threatens the future of the American society in more ways than one. It has become an issue mired in political controversy, although it should be above politics in the traditional sense (see Part C). It has to do with the future of America itself, and even with stability in the rest of the world. We will say more on this in Chapter E-3.

---

3 If someone finds this a methodological leap, I should mention that the author in the Forbes article used a by-line under his name "I explode myths that pervade the health policy debates." Such modesty is worth mentioning and the rest follows.

References

[1]   Rosenberg T. Revealing a health care secret: The price. *The New York Times* [newspaper on the Internet]. 31st July 2013 [cited: 7th June 2016]. Available from: http://opinionator.blogs.nytimes.com/2013/07/31/a-new-health-care-approach-dont-hide-the-price/?_r=0

[2]   Rosenthal E. The $2.7 trillion medical bill. *The New York Times* [newspaper on the Internet]. 30th June 2013 [cited: 7th June 2016]. Available from: http://www.nytimes.com/2013/06/02/health/colonoscopies-explain-why-us-leads-the-world-in-health-expenditures.html

[3]   Peterson CL, Burton R. *US health care spending: Comparison with other OECD countries*. RL34175. Cornell University ILR School, Washington, 2007.

[4]   Relman A. The health reform we need & are not getting. *The New York Review of Books* [website on the Internet]. 2nd July 2009 [cited: 7th June 2016]. Available from: http://www.nybooks.com/articles/archives/2009/jul/02/the-health-reform-we-need-are-not-getting/

[5]   Jayanthi A, Ellison A. 8 hospitals' finances hurt by EHR costs. Becker's Hospital [website on the Internet]. 23rd May 2016 [cited: 7th June 2016]. Available from: http://www.beckershospitalreview.com/finance/8-hospitals-finances-hurt-by-ehr-costs.html

[6]   Peterson CL, Burton R, Eds. *The US health care spending: Comparison with other OECD countries*. New York: Nova Science Publishers, Inc. 2008.

[7]   Conover C. The cost of health care: 1958 vs. 2012. Forbes [magazine on the Internet]. Pharma & Healthcare, 22nd December 2012 [cited: 7th June 2016]. Available from: http://www.forbes.com/sites/chrisconover/2012/12/22/the-cost-of-health-care-1958-vs-2012/

[8]   Perry MJ. Appliance shopping: 1959 vs. 2012. American Enterprise Institute [website on the Internet]. 21st December 2012 [cited: 7th June 2016]. Available from: http://www.aei.org/publication/appliance-shopping-1959-vs-2012/

[9]   Auerbach AJ, Burc RD, Harris BH, Eds. *Federal health spending and the budget outlook: Some alternative scenarios* [monograph on the Internet]. Boston: Brookings 2014 [cited: 7th June 2016]. Available from: http://www.brookings.edu/~/media/events/2014/04/11%20health%20care%20spending/federal_health_spending_budget_outlook_auerbach_gale_harris.pdf

A-2: THE HEALTH SYSTEM IS NOT EFFICIENT

To be efficient is to produce the most output with the least use of resources, and, therefore, the least cost. Efficiency is a basic concept at the heart of economic science and the driving force in all national economies, including those that do not follow the capitalist doctrine. After 1989, even the last bastions of socialist economies adopted efficiency as a guiding principle, including, otherwise still communist, China [1]. To be efficient is the essence of "making money," which is what the capitalist system is all about. But, efficiency is essential even in activities that are not profit seeking, such as public health provision. Efficiency in a market economy is promoted by free competition which, at least in theory, rewards the most efficient producers and discourages inefficient methods of production. In this chapter, we discuss the issues of efficiency and competition and the role they play in the context of the health care market, as it is shaped in the United States.

"Health Economics" as an Academic Discipline

The importance of the health-care system in the national economy became apparent half a century ago, both in Europe and in America. So apparent, in fact, that health economics, as a distinct academic field, appeared in the 1960s, first in the UK and soon afterwards in the US. It is defined as a *"division of economics focused on evaluating scarcity in health care systems. Health economics seeks to identify problem areas in a health care system and propose solutions for pressing issues by evaluating all possible causes and solutions"* [2]. It is interesting to follow the evolution of health economics as an academic discipline in the two countries that shared a language and an economic, political, and philosophical tradition—the US and Britain.

Spending roughly ten per cent of national income on one sector alone is important. Even more so when this sector consumes twice that share of GDP, compared to other countries. It is not surprising that health economics as an academic discipline has known increasing attention, along with the development of health systems mainly in developed countries. In the sense that applied science deals with relevant societal values and problems, one might expect the subject to evolve accordingly. However, one characteristic title is *"The Origins and the Evolution of Health Economics: a discipline by itself? Led by economists, practitioners or politics?"* [3]. The question, posed in 2007 by an author from Portugal, implies that health economics may not be a *bona fide* academic discipline after all, but, rather, an area concerning those who pay or profit from the money spent on health care. Not surprisingly, the direction of the discipline took a different course in the two countries that mainly produced relevant scientific work.

In the UK, during the 60s, the British already enjoyed the benefits of the National Health Service (NHS). The NHS, funded entirely by the government budget, competed with other publicly run sectors, such as defense, education, transport, etc. The health economics literature, therefore, mainly dealt with the effect of the "health economy" on public finances, namely the share of national income that went into the administration of state-provided health care. In that respect, the production and delivery of health care goods and services had to be as efficient as possible, because it was tied directly to society's welfare. Most developed countries in the rest of the world share this concern about the resources the health sector absorbs in terms of public and private expenditure.

Most, except one, that is. In the US, health and the delivery of health care was, and still is, looked at strictly as an economic activity *within* a sector. Mainly a for-profit business, health care is subject to economic analysis just as all other sectors in the economy. As a result, efficiency was of interest only in specific health markets, but not in the health system as a whole. In other words, hospitals needed to be efficient as profit-making entities, but they did not have to be cost-effective in terms of the cost to society. Whether PTCA or CABG was used in a specific patient treatment was of little significance as long as they were both profitable. PTCA could be performed in just a few hours, it was non-invasive, it used fewer resources, and it was more effective. On the contrary, CABG, as a major operation, carried more risk, and required a much longer hospital stay at a higher cost to the system. This, however, was of no economic consequence to the hospital administrator, as long as it was profitable to the hospital.[1]

As a result, American health economists view national health care expense at 20% of GDP as perfectly normal, just as defense specialists would not mind a similar share going to their major "industry" as long as it provided economic activity, employment, and profits.[2] On the other hand, health economists are quite adept at developing and willing to propose efficiency and profit-enhancing mechanisms to health-care providers and insurers. The development of Diagnosis-Related Groups, or DRGs, back in 1974 is a good example. When Fetter et al. [4] proposed a measure of hospital output which "adjusted" for differences in hospital case-mix and, hence, resource use and cost for different patient groups by age, sex, and case complexity, it was only done for the purpose of reimbursing hospitals by Medicare, Medicaid, and private insurance.[3]

This, of course, is a short-sighted view which makes no economic sense. America, just as any other country, has many other needs to finance from public and private sources to afford such inefficiency. Perhaps recognizing this, a presumably unbiased evaluation of American health system efficiency was undertaken in the 2007 Congressional Report. It contained a comparative study between the US and the OECD countries. Below we include some of the main conclusions from the report [5]. Although somewhat dated, the results are relevant today and the conclusion of the report is intriguing. After documenting the huge health bill that the US spends every year, it concludes:

> "...however, research comparing the quality of care has not found the United States to be superior overall. Nor does the US population have substantially better access to health care resources, even putting aside the issue of the uninsured. Although the United States does not have long wait times for non-emergency surgeries, unlike some OECD countries, Americans found it more difficult to make same-day doctor's appointments when sick and had the most difficulty getting care on nights and weekends. They were also most likely to delay or forgo treatment because of cost."

If we compare the United States with the OECD countries, we see that there are many things which cannot be explained simply by the fact that America is a rich country. In fact, there are some things which one would not expect for a country as rich as America. For example, the US

---

1 I do not imply that improper treatment was used. I simply refer to the direction of economic incentives.
2 Especially as all who make a profit are willing to "subsidize" suitable "scientific analyses" by health economists.
3 My Ph.D. dissertation, at Michigan State University in 1972, was probably a forerunner, with only nine distinct patient categories, or case-types, compared to the 458 originally proposed by Fetter. It was titled, very characteristically, "A Measure of Productive Efficiency with Application in Incentive Reimbursement for Hospital Care."

shows fewer hospital admissions and doctor visits than the average OECD country. The US also has only 2.9 hospital beds per 1000 population, three quarters the OECD average of 4.8. Practicing physicians per 1000 population at 2.5 are well below the OECD average of 3.2. Only the number of nurses per population is roughly the same as the OECD average.

On the other hand, the United States has a higher than average number of staff and nurses per hospital bed, while the length of hospital stays is the same as the OECD average. With 76.8 % of hospital beds in privately-owned hospitals, the US is second only to Korea and way above the 27.4 average for all OECD countries. On average, one might say that in terms of hospital resource utilization, the picture is one of efficient operation. But the verdict on efficiency is much more complicated. For example, the United States in 2004 spent $2,668 per capita on outpatient care, three-and-a-half times the OECD average. In most OECD countries, visits to general practitioners outnumber visits to specialists, but not in America. The United States also performs far more heart procedures per population than the average OECD country, and also an above-average amount of organ transplants per capita, but does not perform more of *all* *t*ypes of surgical procedures. These are only two indications that the American health system works in a manner quite different from that of other wealthy countries. The main reason is the way the system is organized and the per-verse system of incentives put to work by the market system, as we discuss in Chapter C-2.

Table A2-1 below lists the most indicative aspects of health system performance by which one may examine the efficiency of the American health system. The main health resources, the extent to which they are utilized, the per capita expenditure on the three main health services, and some health "outputs" are listed for the US, Canada, the UK, France, and Germany. We also show the OECD median, and the rank of the relevant US statistic in the 34 OECD countries.[4]

TABLE A2-1. Health Care Resources, Service Utilization, and Expenditure, 2013.

		US	CANADA	UK	FRANCE	GERMANY	OECD median	US RANK
RESOURCES	Doctors per 1000 population	2.5	2.5	2.7	3.1	4.0	3.2	28/34
	Hospital Beds per 1000 population	2.9	2.6	2.8	6.3	8.3	4.2	26/34
	Nurses (practising) per 1000 population	11.1[1]	9.4	8.1	9.3[1]	12.9	8.8	13/34
	MRI units per million population	35.4	8.8	6.0	9.4	n/a	11.3	2/29
	CT scanners per million population	43.4	14.6	7.8	14.5	n/a	17.7	3/30
	PET scanners per million population	52.0[2]	1.2[2]	0.5[3]	1.4	n/a	1.3	2/30
	Health and Social Work-force (% of Labor Force)	13.6	12.4	13.5	12.7	12.3	10.5	7/34

---

4   For a more detailed analysis of the comparative performance of 14 health systems around the world, see Mossialos et al. [6]

		US	CANADA	UK	FRANCE	GERMANY	OECD median	US RANK
SERVICE UTILIZATION	Hospital discharges per 100,000 population	12,549[4]	8320[2]	12,901	16,633	25,224	16,205	25/34
	Doctors consultations per capita	4.0[4]	7.7[2]	5.0[5]	6.4	9.9	6.4	27/34
	MRI exams per 1000 population	106.9	52.8	n/a	90.9	95.2[5]	51.2	2/23
	CT exams per 1000 population	240.4	131.5	n/a	192.8	117.1[5]	131.5	2/23
	PET exams per 1000 population	5.0	2.0	n/a	n/a	n/a	2.3	4/15
	Cholecystectomy (total procedures per 100,000 population)	307[8]	208.9[2]	139.3[2]	195.1	244.4	185.5	2/30
	Cancer cases diagnosed per 100,000 population[2]	318.0	295.7	272.9	303.5	283.8	283.5	5/34
HEALTH STATUS	Potential years of life lost (years lost/100,000 population, aged 0-69 years)	4628.8[4]	3006.6[7]	3037.1	3338[7]	2988.6	3037.1	6/33
	Life expectancy after 65 (years)	19.2	20.2	19.7	21.4	19.6	19.8	25/34
EXPENDITURE PER CAPITA	Hospital expenditure per capita, current prices, current PPPs (US$)	1578.7	727.5	n/a	1170.4	1334.8	956.0	4/30
	Outpatient expenditure per capita, current prices, current PPPs (US$)	4297.1	1306.6	n/a	797.3	1102.4	995.7	1/31
	Pharmaceutical expenditure per capita, current prices, current PPPs (US$)	1034.4	761.4	366.9[6]	622.1	678.3	497.6	1/33

Source: OECD Health Data.
[1] Professionally active nurses, [2] Data for 2012, [3] Data for 2005, [4] Data for 2010, [5] Data for 2009, [6] Data for 2008 [7] Data for 2011 [8] Data for 2006.

The Role of Medical Technology

America uses a lot of medical technology, but it does not use it efficiently, as shown in Table

A2-2. The United States has a much greater supply of advanced technological equipment than other OECD countries, with nearly twice as many CT scanners per capita as the OECD average and three times as many MRI machines.

TABLE A2-2. Diagnostic Imaging Supply and Use, 2013.

	Magnetic Resonance Imaging		Computed Tomography		Positron Emission Tomography	
	MRI machines per million population	MRI exams per 1000 population	CT scanners per million population	CT exams per 1000 population	PET scanners per million population	PET exams per 1000 population
Australia	13.4	27.6	53.7	110	2.0	2.0
Canada	8.8	52.8	14.7	132	1.2[a]	2.0
Denmark	-	60.3	37.8	142	6.1	6.3
France	9.4	90.9	14.5	193	1.4	-
Japan	46.9[b]	-	101.3[b]	-	3.7[b]	-
Netherlands	11.5	50.0[b]	11.5	71[b]	3.2	2.5[a]
New Zealand	11.2	-	16.6	-	1.1	-
Switzerland	-	-	36.6	-	3.5	-
United Kingdom	6.1	-	7.9	-	-	-
United States	35.5	106.9	43.5	240	5.0[a]	5.0
OECD median	11.4	50.6	17.6	136	1.5	-

a2012, b2011.
Source: OECD Health Data 2015.

Technology can play an important role in minimizing overall health costs by improving efficiency and reducing mistakes. One of the most commonly cited goals that could be spurred by increased investment is the shift to electronic medical records. Though critics worry about privacy, digitizing patient records achieves a number of ends at once: It cuts paper costs and also reduces the likelihood of errors in prescriptions and in the transfer of data between hospitals—flaws that can cause medical errors and prompt the need for expensive ongoing care. More importantly, the healthcare industry in the US lags in information technology (IT), spending not only less than its competitors internationally, but also less than other industries domestically. Ten years ago, the average company outside the health industry was found to spend seven times as much as US health-care companies on information technology, and companies in some wealthier industries like banking spend up to twenty times as much. US competitors abroad have also consistently outspent the US government on healthcare IT investment. To illustrate, we present below a Table from a 2006 study supported by the Commonwealth Fund [7].

	US	Australia	Canada	Germany	Norway	UK
Initial year of national IT effort	2006	2000	1997	1993	1997	2002
Expected year of complete implementation	2016	Undefined	50% by 2009	2006	2007	2014
Estimate of total investment (as of 2005)*	$125M	$97.9M	$1.0B	$1.8B	$52M	$11.5B
Total investment per capita (as of 2005)**	$0.43	$4.93	$31.85	$21.20	$11.43	$192.79

*In US dollars. Exchange rates as of September 2005: 1 USD = 1.31 AUD, 1.19 CAD, 0.80 EURO, 6.21 NOK, 0.54 GBP.
** In US dollars. Per capita is based on 2003 population numbers from the Organization for Economic Cooperation and Development (OECD).
Source: Adapted from G. F. Anderson et al., "Health Care Spending and Use of Information Technology in OECD Countries," *Health Affairs*, May/June 2006 25(3):819–31.

Pharmaceuticals

The United States spends more on prescription drugs per capita than any other OECD country and consumes more prescription drugs than most OECD countries. The United States paid more for brand name drugs but less for generic drugs than other OECD countries. One of the major categories are antibiotics. The National Action Plan for Combating Antibiotic-Resistant Bacteria set a goal of reducing inappropriate outpatient antibiotic use by 50% by 2020, but the extent of inappropriate outpatient antibiotic use is unknown. One recent study estimated the prescribing rates of outpatient oral antibiotic, by age and diagnosis, and the portions of antibiotic use that may be inappropriate in adults and children in the United States. Using the 2010-2011 National Ambulatory Medical Care Survey and National Hospital Ambulatory Medical Care Survey, annual numbers and population-adjusted rates of ambulatory visits with oral antibiotic prescriptions by age, region, and diagnosis in the US were estimated. The study found that in 2010-2011, there was an annual antibiotic prescription rate per 1000 population of 506. Of these only 353 antibiotic prescriptions were likely appropriate, something that points to the need for guidelines for outpatient antibiotic prescription and use [8].

Another example of high pharmaceutical consumption and cost is cancer care. According to a recent comparative study, the United States had a $32.6 billion net positive return from cancer drug spending in 2014 in terms of survival and quality of life. However, it consistently outspent other countries and obtained less of a return to health per cancer drug dollar spent, suggesting that there is an opportunity to improve value in the US oncology drug market [9]. Similar efficiency gains can be obtained throughout the pharmaceutical market.

Price Variations among States and Cities

Inasmuch as price variations in health services among countries are to be expected, it is interesting that similar variations have been observed among states and cities in the US. Using a national multi-payer commercial claims database containing allowed amounts, a very recent study examined variations in the prices for 242 common medical services in forty-one states and the District of Columbia [10]. Ratios of average state prices to national prices ranged from a low of $0.79 in Florida to a high of $2.64 in Alaska. Two- to threefold variations in prices were identified within some states and Metropolitan Statistical Areas. When trying to compare prices among 242 services, researchers found wide variations. The question that remains for researchers, policy makers, and health care leaders is, Why do prices for the same service differ markedly across distances of only a few miles and what amount of that difference is justifiable? The question clearly points to the influence of the market in shaping prices. The relative strength of the medical profession, business interests of medical providers, and the private insurance market clearly produces results which could not exist in regulated markets, such as in most advanced countries in the world where health care is an essential human right, not a mere commodity as all others.

Inefficient Production and Delivery of Health Care

Being efficient is being competitive in national or international markets. In private markets for goods and services, producing and delivering at low cost is essential. In this sense, where health care is produced and delivered by a government, efficiency may be less of a concern, as the cost of producing health services is a matter of legal arrangements or ethical judgment. In the health area minimum standards of quality, consumer protection, and access to services are of the essence, because they have to do with safety, outcomes, and patient satisfaction. When it comes to the health system, therefore, efficiency has to do less with wages, prices, and the organization of resources and more with the extent and the quality of services a health system offers.

For example, until fairly recently, at the end of last century, China's health system was a disgrace. As a command economy, China, for many decades, opted for few, underpaid, undertrained, and poorly distributed health care personnel. The question of efficiency did not even arise, as it did not arise in most countries in their early stages of development. In the new century, however, China is developing its health system rapidly, and remarkably for a communist country, it relies heavily on the private market for this development, while it also establishes a wide social insurance net [11].

In many ways health system efficiency is more important for countries where the government or the public sector plays an important role, for example, by offering universal health coverage through national health insurance. As this concerns the funding of the system, inefficient production and delivery means wasting public funds. In America, on the contrary, a strong government role in health care production, delivery, and financing is considered bureaucratic and, by definition, wasteful and inefficient. However, the opposite seems to be the case—a thing often conveniently overlooked. In America, administrative costs account for 25 percent of total US hospital spending. A recent study compared these costs across eight nations. The US had the highest administrative costs, while Scotland and Canada, two countries with national health insurance, had the lowest. The study showed that reducing US per capita spending for hospital administration to Scottish or Canadian levels would have saved more than $150 billion in 2011 [12]. Most pundits blame the complexity of private health insurance for this monstrous inefficiency, as we will see below.

An Extremely Inefficient Insurance System

America spends a lot on the administration of its system, mainly because of the reliance on a complicated private insurance system. It is telling that spending on the administration of health-care delivery and insurance cost $465 per person in the United States in 2004. This figure was seven times the OECD median.[5] As far back as 2006, Nobel Economist Paul Krugman wrote in *The New York Times* [13]:

> *"Medicare spends only 2 cents out of every dollar for administrative costs, leaving 98 cents for medical care. By contrast, private Insurance companies spend only around 80 cents of each dollar in premiums on medical care; much of the remaining is spent denying insurance to those who need it."*

Some individuals are covered by both public and private health insurance. For example,

---

5 See the summary and conclusions of the 2007 Congressional Report. It is interesting that the paragraph in which this extremely important and telling datum, on the inefficiency of managing health care in America, is the shortest in the whole report. Only two lines written for the most negative aspect of the US health-care system. Let us not forget, however, that a Congressional Report is addressed first and foremost to the members of Congress. As such, it is an extremely political document.

many Medicare beneficiaries purchase private supplemental "Medigap" policies to cover additional services and cost-sharing. Private insurers, in general, pay rates to providers that are higher than the rates paid under public programs, particularly Medicaid, leading to wide variations in payment rates among payment sources and in revenues among providers, depending on their payer mix and market power. Private insurance is mainly responsible for the health-care cost inflation. Even efficiency improvements do not serve to reduce the cost of health care. Instead, they are used to increase profitability. The introduction of electronic medical records and the expansion of the relevant industry funded by extensive government intervention is characteristic, as presented in a *New York Times* extensive report, written in 2013 [14].

References

[1]   Zhang Jianhua. DEA Method on Efficiency Study of Chinese Commercial Banks and the Positivist Analysis from 1997 to 2001. *Journal of Finance* [via Internet webpage] [cited: 7th June 2016]. Available from: http://en.cnki.com.cn/Article_en/CJFDTOTAL-JRYJ200303002.htm

[2]   InvestorWords [homepage on the Internet]. WebFinance. What is health economics? Definition and meaning; [cited: 7th June 2016]. Available from: http://www.investorwords.com/7952/health_economics.html#ixzz3kexMGoSg

[3]   Rebelo LP, Ed. The origins and the evolution of health economics: a discipline by itself? Led by economists, practitioners or politics? Working paper on economics. No.: 16/2007. University of Porto, Faculty of Economics and Management, Portugal, 2007.

[4]   Fetter R, Shin Y, Freeman J, Averill R, Thompson J. Case mix definition by diagnosis-related groups. *Medical Care* 1980; 18 (Suppl 2):1-53.

[5]   Peterson CL, Burton R. US health care spending: Comparison with other OECD countries. RL34175. Cornell University ILR School, Washington, 2007.

[6]   Mossialos E, Wenzl M, Osborn R, Anderson C. *International profiles of health care systems,* 2014. Publication No.: 1802. Sponsored by The Commonwealth Fund. New York, 2015.

[7]   Anderson GF, Frogner BK, Johns RA, Reinhardt UR. Health care spending and use of information technology in OECD countries. *Health Affairs.* 2006; 25(3):819-31.

[8]   Fleming-Dutra KE, Hersh AL, Shapiro DJ, *et al.* Inappropriate antibiotic prescriptions among ambulatory care visits, 2010-2011. *JAMA* 2016; 315(17):1864-73.

[9]   Salas-Vega S, Mossialos E, Cancer drugs provide positive value in nine countries, but the United States lags in health gains per dollar spent. *Health Affairs.* 2016; 35(5):813-23.

[10]   Newman D, Parente ST, Barrette E, Kennedy K. Prices for common medical services vary substantially among the commercially insured. *Health Affairs.* 2016; 35(5):923-27.

[11]   Deloitte Touche Tohmatsu Limited [webpage on the Internet]. 2015 health care outlook: China. [cited: 7th June 2016]. Available from: http://www2.deloitte.com/content/dam/Deloitte/global/Documents/Life-Sciences-Health-Care/gx-lshc-2015-health-care-outlook-china.pdf

[12]   Himmelstein DU, Jun M, Busse R, et al. A comparison of hospital administrative costs in eight nations: US costs exceed all others by far. *Health Affairs*. 2014; 33(9):1586-94.

[13]   Krugman P. Insurance horror stories. The New York Times [newspaper on the Internet]. 22nd September 2006 [cited: 7th June 2016]. Available from: http://www.nytimes.com/2006/09/22/opinion/22krugman.html?_r=0.

[14]   Creswell J. A digital shift on health data swells profits in an industry. *The New York Times* [newspaper on the Internet]. 15th August 2014 [cited: 7th June 2016]. Available from: http://www.nytimes.com/2013/02/20/business/a-digital-shift-on-health-data-swells-profits.html?nl=todaysheadlines&emc=edit_th_20130220

A-3: THE SYSTEM IS NOT EFFECTIVE

"If the United States could reduce amenable mortality to the average rate achieved in the three top-performing countries, there would have been 101,000 fewer deaths per year by the end of the study period" [1].

Health is what people all over the world wish each other most often when they raise a glass of wine. It is "salud," "a votre santé," "to your health," that we wish our friends. It is not wealth or good fortune. In every language there is probably a phrase like "*health is the most important thing in life.*" In Greece, when a baby is to be born and the parents are asked about their preference for the baby's gender, the answer, now part of the folklore, is "*it does not matter, as long as it is healthy.*" These attitudes have been part of the societal value system over many generations. In this sense, they must represent a true account of what a society considers really important.

And yet, it is also often said that we realize how precious health is only when we lose it. Disease often has its roots in genetic factors for which we can (still) do very little. It is common, however, for people to live dangerously or adopt lifestyles they know are harmful to their health. It is easy to find people who delay visiting their doctor, postpone their check-ups, or forget their pills. For irresponsible behavior, one can only blame the individual. It is not unusual, however, that ill health or disability may be due not to personal failing but to the failure of the health system, which is there not only to cure and rehabilitate the damage caused by illness, but also to prevent negligent, dangerous, or unhealthy behavior or lifestyles.

For many years, the main criticism directed at the American health system was that 50 million Americans were left without private insurance coverage, because they could not afford it. There are studies that point out the difference in public satisfaction and other quality and access indicators in which the US system seems to be lagging behind, not only European countries, but also Canada, Australia, and New Zealand [2]. This was the reason for the political and societal attraction of "Obamacare," and probably the reason why it passed the test in the Supreme Court.

Although a major problem, this is not the only problem with health care in America. Eleven years ago, in 2005, a six-country Commonwealth Fund international survey found that one-third of patients with health problems in the US report medical, medication, or test errors—the highest rate of any nation. Assessing health care access, safety, and care coordination in Australia, Canada, Germany, New Zealand, the United Kingdom, and the US, the survey found that while no one nation was best or worst overall, the US stood out for high error rates, inefficient coordination of care, and high out-of-pocket costs leading to barriers to accessing care [3]. The American health system, in other words, is anything but effective.

What is an Effective Health System?

Effectiveness is the degree to which a certain activity, aiming at a certain result, achieves a desired goal. Health care has the prevention of illness and the restoration of health as its stated goals. The degree to which a national health system, a public health program, a hospital, a primary health center, or a doctor's office achieve the desired and measurable results is the litmus test for their success. A modern health system should pursue such goals and its success in attaining them is the measure of effectiveness.

The first and most important goal certainly has to do with the health of the American people. Many indices are used to describe and rate this composite variable, each with special reference to the social, economic, and cultural characteristics in each society. In 2000 the WHO issued its new Healthy Life Expectancy Rankings [4]. The results for the US were rather disappointing. In what follows we include some indicative comparative data on the health of Americans and the risk factors facing the US population in the first decade of this century. We also list the sources for the interested reader.

Infant Mortality

- Approximately 30,000 infants die in the United States each year. The infant mortality rate, the risk of death during the first year of life, is related to the underlying health of the mother, public health practices, socioeconomic conditions, and the availability and use of appropriate health care for infants and pregnant women. Infant mortality is considered an important indicator of the health of a nation. In 2005, the United States ranked 30th in infant mortality. Singapore has the lowest rate with 2.1 deaths per 1000 live births, while the United States has a rate of 6.9 deaths per 1000 live births. *Sources: CDC and National Center for Health Statistics, 2008, and CDC, NCHS Data Brief, Number 23, November 2009.*

- The main cause contributing to the high infant mortality rate in the United States is the very high percentage of preterm births. One in eight births in the United States was preterm, an increase of 36% since 1984. *Source: CDC, NCHS Data Brief, Number 23, November 2009.*

Life Expectancy

- Life expectancy at birth in the United States is an estimated 78.49 years, which ranks 50th compared to other countries. *Source: CIA Factbook (2011).*

- Lack of health insurance is associated with 44,789 deaths per year in the United States. *Source: Harvard Medical School Study,* American Journal of Public Health, *December 2009.*

- People without health insurance had a 40 percent higher risk of death, being unable to obtain necessary medical care compared to those with health insurance. *Source: Harvard Medical School Study,* American Journal of Public Health, *December 2009.*

Population Risk Factors

Compared to other OECD countries, the United States has a lower than average proportion of elderly population, and lower than average rates of smoking and drinking. On the other hand, Americans consume more calories and sugar per capita—156 pounds of sugar per person per year, compared with 99 pounds in the average OECD country. As a result, 34% of Americans in 2004 were overweight and an additional 32% were obese. Obesity is associated with a 77% increase in consumption of medications and a 36% increase in inpatient and outpatient spending.

That these population risk factors are taking an increasing health toll, due to factors outside what is considered the domain of health care, is painfully apparent but also documented by research results, reported by two Princeton economists, Angus Deaton[1] and Anne Case [5]. Analyzing health and mortality data from the Centers for Disease Control and Prevention and from other sources, they concluded that rising annual death rates of poorly educated white Americans are driven not by the big killers like heart disease and diabetes but by an epidemic of suicides and afflictions stemming from substance abuse, alcoholic liver disease, and overdoses of heroin and prescription opioids. The analysis by Dr. Deaton and Dr. Case may offer the most rigorous evidence to date of the causes and implications of a development that has been puzzling demographers in recent years: the declining health and fortunes among this group . In middle age, they are dying at such a high rate that they are increasing the death rate for the entire group of middle-aged white Americans. This is the most vigorous proof that health care is not to be left only to the market, as we will discuss later.

Health Outcomes

As mentioned earlier, health-care has the prevention of premature death as one of its main goals. Ellen Nolte and Martin McKee, in 2008, compared trends in *"deaths considered amenable to health care before the age of seventy-five,"* between 1997–2003 for the US and eighteen other industrialized countries. They reported an increase in avoidable deaths by 100,000 in the US. Such deaths account, on average, for 23 percent of total mortality under age seventy-five among males and 32 percent among females. Amenable mortality in all countries during the 5-year period declined 16 percent on average. The United States was an outlier, with a decline of only 4 percent. The authors conclude that this cost is 101,000 more deaths per year.

The fact that the American health system is not effective is not due to a lack of resources except, perhaps, for the shortage of physicians, as shown in Table A3-1 following.

Table A3-1. Health Care Resources, Service Utilization, and Expenditure, 2013.

		US	CANADA	UK	FRANCE	GERMANY	OECD median	US RANK
RESOURCES	Doctors per 1000 population	2.5	2.5	2.7	3.1	4.0	3.2	28/34
	Hospital Beds per 1000 population	2.9	2.6	2.8	6.3	8.3	4.2	26/34
	Nurses (practising) per 1000 population	11.1[1]	9.4	8.1	9.3[1]	12.9	8.8	13/34
	MRI Units per million population	35.4	8.8	6.0	9.4	n/a	11.3	2/29
	CT Scanners per million population	43.4	14.6	7.8	14.5	n/a	17.7	3/30
	PET Scanners per million population	52.0[2]	1.2[2]	0.5[3]	1.4	n/a	1.3	2/30
	Health and Social employment (% Labor Force)	13.6	12.4	13.5	12.7	12.3	10.5	7/34

---

1 Winner of the 2015 Nobel Memorial Prize in Economic Science.

		US	CANADA	UK	FRANCE	GERMANY	OECD median	US RANK
SERVICE UTILIZATION	Hospital Discharges per 100,000 population	12,549[4]	8,320[2]	12,901	16,633	25,224	16,205	25/34
	Doctors consultations per capita	4.0[4]	7.7[2]	5.0[5]	6.4	9.9	6.4	27/34
	MRI Exams per 1000 population	106.9	52.8	n/a	90.9	95.2[5]	51.2	2/23
	CT Exams per 1000 population	240.4	131.5	n/a	192.8	117.1[5]	131.5	2/23
	PET Exams per 1000 population	5.0	2.0	n/a	n/a	n/a	2.3	4/15
	Cholecystectomy (total procedures per 100,000 population)	307[8]	208.9[2]	139.3[2]	195.1	244.4	185.5	2/30
	Cancer cases diagnosed per 100,000 population[2]	318.0	295.7	272.9	303.5	283.8	283.5	5/34
HEALTH STATUS	Potential years of life lost (years lost/100,000 population, aged 0-69 years)	4628.8[4]	3006.6[7]	3037.1	3338[7]	2988.6	3037.1	6/33
	Life expectancy after 65 (years)	19.2	20.2	19.7	21.4	19.6	19.8	25/34
EXPENDITURE PER CAPITA	Hospital expenditure per capita, current prices, current PPPs (US$)	1 578.7	727.5	n/a	1 170.4	1 334.8	956.0	4/30
	Outpatient expenditure per capita, current prices, current PPPs (US$)	4 297.1	1 306.6	n/a	797.3	1 102.4	995.7	1/31
	Pharmaceutical expenditure per capita, current prices, current PPPs (US$)	1 034.4	761.4	366.9[6]	622.1	678.3	497.6	1/33

Source: OECD Health Data.
[1]Professionally Active Nurses, [2]Data for 2012, [3]Data for 2005, [4]Data for 2010, [5]Data for 2009, [6]Data for 2008 [7]Data for 2011 [8]Data for 2000.

Table A3-2. Select Population Health Outcomes and Risk Factors, 2013.

	HEALTH OUTCOMES			RISK FACTORS			
	Life expectancy at birth, 2013[a]	Infant mortality per 1000 live births, 2013[a]	Amenable mortality per 100,000 inhabitants, 2013[f]	Percent of population (aged 65+) with 2 or more chronic conditions, 2014[b]	Obesity rate (BMI>30), 2013 [a,c]	Percent of population (aged 15+) who are daily smokers, 2013[a]	Percent of population aged 65+
Australia	82.2	3.6	57[g]	54	28.3[c]	12.8	14.4
Canada	81.5[e]	4.8[e]	77[g]	56	25.8	14.9	15.2
Denmark	80.4	3.5	93.9	-	14.2	17.0	17.8
France	82.3	3.6	72.8	43	14.5[d]	24.1[d]	17.7
Germany	80.9	3.3	106.8	49	23.6	20.9	21.1
Japan	83.4	2.1	-	-	3.7	19.3	25.1
Netherlands	81.4	3.8	86.5	46	11.8	18.5	16.8
New Zealand	81.4	5.2[e]	79[g]	37	30.6	15.5	14.2
Norway	81.8	2.4	86.5	43	10.0[d]	15.0	15.6
Sweden	82.0	2.7	92.6	42	11.7	10.7	19.0
Switzerland	82.9	3.9	70.4	44	10.3[d]	20.4[d]	17.3
UK	81.1	3.8	108.1	33	24.9	20.0[d]	17.1
USA	78.8	6.1[e]	96[g]	68	35.3[d]	13.7	14.1

[a] Source: OECD Health Data, 2015.
[b] Includes: hypertension or high blood pressure, heart disease, diabetes, lung problems, mental health problems, cancer, and joint pain/arthritis. Source: Commonwealth Fund International Health Policy Survey of Older Adults, 2014.
[c] DEN, FR, NETH, NOR, SWE, and SWIZ based on self-reported data; all other countries based on measured data.
[d] 2012.   [e] 2011.
[f] Source: Eurostat Database, 2016.
[g] 2006–07 World Health Organization (WHO) mortality data; Canada data from 2002–03.

Quality of Health Care

In terms of quality of health care, a five-country study (the US, Canada, the UK, Australia, and New Zealand) found that each of the five countries had the best and worst health outcomes on at least one measure, but no country emerged as a clear quality leader [6]. For example, the US had the highest breast cancer survival rate but the lowest kidney transplant survival rate. The same study found that Americans were most likely to report receiving specific recommended preventive services for diabetic and hypertensive patients, but were most likely to complain that their doctor did not spend enough time with them and did not have a chance to answer all their questions.

Wait Time

The United States is one of eight countries in which wait times for elective surgery are reported as low. In a recent survey [6], a quarter to a third of respondents in Canada, the UK, and Australia reported waiting more than four months for a non-emergency procedure, compared with only 5% of Americans. In terms of doctor visits to primary care physicians, a five-country survey found that Americans had the greatest difficulty getting care during nights and weekends and were the most likely to forgo care because of cost [6]. Wait time is probably one of the few success stories in American health care, but probably among the costliest.

Health and "Public Health"

Every organized society assigns the essential functions or activities which protect the well being of the population to distinct public services and sectors. To protect the country we have the armed forces. To protect internal peace and security we have the police and the judicial system. To offer elementary basic education to our children we have public libraries and public education. To preserve and protect our health we have the public health system.[2] Although the US is considered an organized society, it differs from other countries in this last respect. It is difficult to speak of the "American public health system," let alone to describe it in an unambiguous way. Perhaps the most telling point is the one raised recently by Thomas R. Frieden, director of CDC and a world-class expert on public health [7].

> *"Although there has sometime been distrust and disrespect between the health care and public health fields,[8] they are inevitably and increasingly interdependent; maximizing potential health gains is a defining challenge for both fields."*

It is interesting that Dr. Frieden talks of "distrust and disrespect" between the health care and public health fields. It is as if the two fields belong to or serve two different "masters." And, in fact, this is the actual case, especially in America. Health care belongs in the domain of the market, where the main driver is profit. Public health depends on political commitment to invest in prevention and control. There is no "money to be made" in fighting obesity or smoking. Indeed, one might say quite the opposite.[3]

---

2 There is a certain ambiguity in the term "public health." Many think it refers to clean water, sanitation, vaccinations, and other such activities which belong in the *public sphere*. For others, public health encompasses all health-related activities available to all, i.e. what we here call a "health system," which is implicitly considered to be not only in the public sphere, but also a publicly financed and administered service.

3 The American airlines are about face this reality in a painful way. A bill is making its way through Congress which will force airlines to increase minimum seat-width and leg room. Both dimensions were reduced after 1970 with the deregulation of the airline industry, in order to increase profitability. Since then, the average person has become 32 pounds heavier and quite a bit taller. This presents risk of thrombosis and embolism, while making evacuation in case of danger quite cumbersome. The bill in Congress is a "public health measure."

Health System Performance

The United States has the third-highest percentage of the population reporting their health status as being "good," "very good," or "excellent." However, the United States has below-average life expectancy and high mortality rates. The United States has the third-highest rate of deaths from medical errors and the highest infant mortality rate among the eight countries that report this metric similarly. Such measures are often limited by differing measurement methodologies. They may also reflect fundamental population differences (in underlying health, for example) rather than differences in countries' health-care systems. In any case, they point out weaknesses in American health outcomes, for which the health system must find the appropriate answers.

Research [6] comparing the quality of care has not found the United States to be superior overall. The OECD data and other research provide some insight as to why health care spending is higher in the United States than in other countries, although many difficult research issues remain. This report presents some of the available data and research and concludes with a summary of study findings.

Table A3-3. Selected Health System Performance Indicators for 11 Countries.

Indicator (#below)	Australia	Canada	France	Germany	Netherlands	New Zealand	Sweden	Switzerland	UK	US
1. Access	16%	13%	18%	15%	22%	21%	6%	13%	4%	37%
2. Quality of care	19%	21%	13%	16%	20%	22%	20%	9%	8%	22%
3. Coordination	19%	25%	20%	16%	18%	15%	16%	11%	13%	27%
4. Health results	57	n/a	55	76	66	79	61	n/a	83	96
5. Public opinion[1]	48%	42%	40%	42%	51%	47%	44%	54%	63%	25%
6. Public opinion[2]	9%	8%	11%	10%	5%	8%	10%	7%	4%	27%

1. Access - Experienced access barrier because of cost during the past year, 2013.
2. Quality of care - Experienced medical, medication, or lab tests error in the past 2 years.
3. Coordination - Experienced coordination problems with medical tests/records in the past 2 years.
4. Health results - Avoidable deaths/mortality amenable to health care deaths per 100,000 population.
5. Public opinion1 - Public view on health system: *"Works well, minor changes needed,"* 2013.
6. Public opinion2 - Public view on health system: *"Needs to be completely rebuilt,"* 2013.
Source: Table adopted from Table 3 in Mossialos et al. *International Profiles of Health Care Systems, 2014,* The Commonwealth Fund, January 2015.

Table A3-3 above summarizes the main and most recent findings on the effectiveness of health systems in 11 major high-income countries around the world. These countries have many cultural, institutional, economic, and political similarities with the US. It is remarkable, however, that as far as health care is concerned, there is considerable divergence in access to care, effectiveness in terms of amenable deaths, and public satisfaction. It is not surprising, therefore, that half as many Americans as citizens in other countries think their health system "works well, minor changes are needed" or that three times as many think it "needs to be completely rebuilt." As usual, the majority is right.

Access to Care

Research evidence suggests that access to health care is the key influential factor for improved population health outcomes and health care system sustainability. Although the importance of addressing barriers in access to health care across European countries is well documented, little has been done to improve the situation. This is due to different definitions, approaches, and policies, and partly due to persisting disparities in access within and between European countries. Research evidence suggests that access to health care is the key influential factor for improved population health outcomes and health care system sustainability. To bridge this gap, the Patient Access Partnership (PACT) developed (a) the '5As' definition of access, which details the five critical elements (adequacy, accessibility, affordability, appropriateness, and availability) of access to health care, (b) a multi-stakeholder approach for mapping access, and (c) a 13-item questionnaire based on the 5As definition in an effort to address these obstacles and to identify best practices. These tools are expected to effectively contribute to addressing access barriers in practice, by suggesting a common framework and facilitating the exchange of knowledge and expertise, in order to improve access to health care between countries and within the European Union.

An Uncomfortable Truth about Effectiveness

The failure of the American health system is nowhere more apparent than in the situation with obesity in the country. Obesity is one of the biggest drivers of preventable chronic diseases and health-care costs in the United States. Currently, estimates for these costs range from $147 billion to nearly $210 billion per year. In addition, obesity is associated with job absenteeism, costing approximately $4.3 billion annually, and with lower productivity while at work, costing employers $506 per obese worker per year.

Adult obesity now exceeds 30% of the population in 20 US states. In 2014, the rates of obesity surpassed 35% in three states—Arkansas (35.9%), West Virginia (35.7%) and Mississippi (35.5%). Twenty-two states have rates above 30%, 45 states are above 25%, and every state is above 20%. Arkansas has the highest adult obesity rate at 36%, while Colorado has the lowest at 21%, according to an annual report released by Trust for America's Health, a Washington, D.C. health policy group, and the Robert Wood Johnson Foundation, a nonprofit organization dedicated to public health. The data show that 23 of 25 states with the highest rates of obesity are in the South and Midwest.

This is a dramatic shift from previous generations. In 1980, no state had a rate above 15%, and in 1991, no state had a rate above 20%. Today, more than 30% of adults and nearly 17% of 2- to 19-year-olds are obese. Americans are drinking more bottled water and diet beverages and (at least) say they are exercising more frequently than before the Great Recession. But they're also eating more products such as butter and salt, and are spending more time sitting in their cars commuting to and from work. Last year, the average American eating alone consumed a snack food as a meal 191 times, up from 167 times in 2011, equating to billions more snacks (and calories) every year. American health care is not only dangerous for Americans, it is also financially non-viable as well.

Cost-Effectiveness

Being ineffective is bad enough; doing it at great cost is even worse. What does the United States get for the money it spends on health? Does the US get corresponding value from the money it spends on health care? The available data often do not provide clear answers. For example, among OECD countries, the United States has shorter-than-average life expectancy and higher-than-average mortality rates. Does this mean that the US system is ineffective in light of what is spent on health care? Or does this reflect the greater prevalence of certain diseases in the United States (the highest incidence of cancer and AIDS in the OECD), which would "justify" higher per capita expenditure. Finally, are there less healthy lifestyles (the United States has the highest obesity rates in the OECD)? These are issues that confound international comparisons.

Cost-effectiveness is a corollary measure of effectiveness related to the cost at which a certain output, result, or outcome was achieved. In other words, the years after age 70 for which a population is still alive and in good health is a measure of effectiveness, but whether the result is achieved at twice the cost compared to another country is not inconsequential. To put it another way, spending a lot on health may be a choice a society may wish to make, but it is doubtful that it should accept this choice if the results in terms of health and welfare are not proportional to the welfare gained by competing uses of the funds. It is in this respect that the US fails miserably. Not only does it perform worse than many other countries with comparable economic, political, and societal characteristics, but it also spends much more money in the course of this failure. Figure A3-1 below is quite convincing.[4]

Figure A3-1. Life Expectancy Compared to Health-Care Spending from 1970 to 2013, in the US and the Next 19 Wealthiest OECD Member Countries by Total GDP.

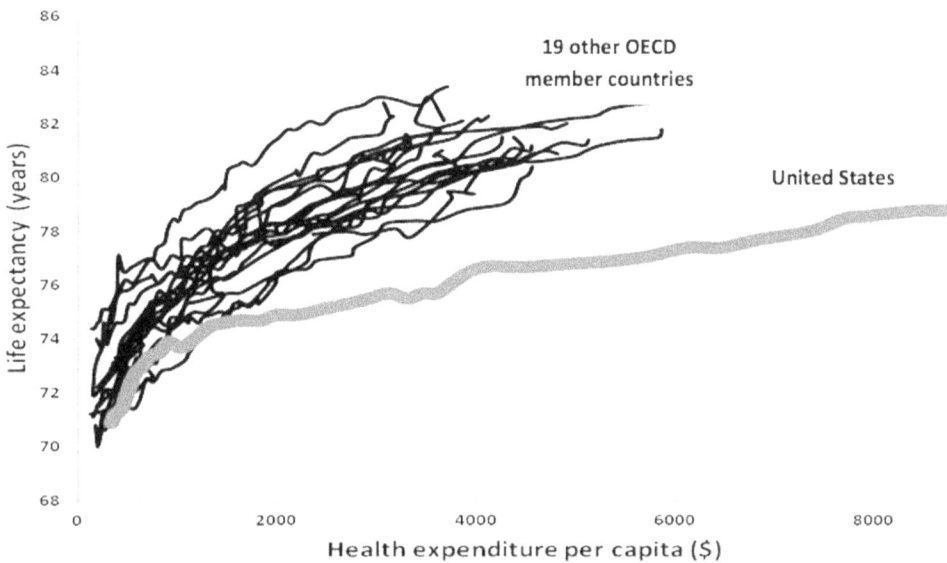

In forty years, America managed to gain almost eight years in overall life expectancy while increasing per capita health expenditure by almost five times. The 19 wealthiest OECD counties managed to do almost four times as well, gaining twice as many years on average, by spending almost half the money. What is even more interesting, however, is that the real gains in life expectancy in the US are almost totally disconnected from the money spent. The first 4 years were gained at a cost of little over $1,000 per capita. The next four years required more than $6,000. On the contrary, in other countries, the health system seems to produce a much bigger "bang" for the, euro, yen, or Canadian dollar used. Cost-effectiveness, in other words, is not something America can brag about, at least not in health care.

---

4   Figure A3-1 does not show the 19 countries separately, mainly for technical reasons. The reader is reminded, however, that the OECD includes the wealthiest countries in the world.

References

[1]   Nolte E, McKee CM. Measuring the health of nations: Updating an earlier analysis. *Health Affairs.* 2008; 27(1):58-71.

[2]   Davis K, Stremikis K, Squires D, Schoen C, Eds. Mirror, mirror on the wall. How the performance of the US health care system compares internationally [monograph on the Internet]. Washington: The Commonwealth Fund 2014 [cited: 7th June 2016]. Available from: http://www.commonwealth-fund.org/~/media/files/publications/fund-report/2014/jun/1755_davis_mirror_mirror_2014.pdf

[3]   Schoen C, Osborn R, Huynh PT, Doty M, Zapert K, Peugh J, Davis K. Taking the pulse of health care systems: Experiences of patients with health problems in six countries. *Health Affairs.* 2005; W5:509-525.

[4]   WHO Press Release. *Japan number one in new 'Healthy Life' system.* 4th June 2000 [cited: 7th June 2016]. Available from: http://www.photius.com/rankings/healthylife.html

[5]   Kolata G. Death rates rising for middle-aged white Americans, study finds. *The New York Times* [newspaper on the Internet]. 4th November 2015 [cited: 7th June 2016]. Available from: http://www.nytimes.com/2015/11/03/health/death-rates-rising-for-middle-aged-white-americans-study-finds.html?emc=edit_th_20151103&nl=todaysheadlines&nlid=12129446&_r=0

[6]   Peterson CL, Burton R. US health care spending: Comparison with other OECD countries. RL34175. Cornell University ILR School, Washington, 2007.

[7]   Frieden TR. The future of public health. *New England Journal of Medicine.* 2015; 373(18):1748-54.

[8]   Fee E, Brown TM. The unfulfilled promise of public health: déjà vu all over again. *Health Affairs.* 2002; 21(6):31-43.

A-4: THE HEALTH SYSTEM IS NOT EQUITABLE

"Of all the forms of inequality, injustice in health is the most shocking and inhumane."

—*Martin Luther King, Jr.*

The terms equity and equality are sometimes used interchangeably, leading to confusion. While related, there are important distinctions between the two concepts. This is especially true in understanding health policy and health systems. **The search for equity** is providing people *what they need* to enjoy full, healthy lives. **Equality**, in contrast, means ensuring that everyone *gets the same things* in order to enjoy full, healthy lives. It sounds like the same thing, but it is not, and the difference often is a source of major misunderstanding.

Like equity, **equality** aims to promote fairness and justice, but it can only work if everyone *starts from the same place* and needs *the same things*. This seems like a rather obscure distinction, but, in charting health policy, the difference is huge. Equity is giving *all the people* the health education they need to understand that smoking will make them ill. Equality is to make sure that all people have equal access to lung surgery when they fall ill. Inequity is to tolerate a health-damaging environment for some Americans.[1] Inequality is to deprive some people of necessary medicines because of the cost.

The perennial question of health system performance obscures a cost, which, although not expressed in dollars and cents, puts enormous strain on society. It is the cost of being ill, or, rather, its reverse, "the price of being well."[2] A central point in this discussion is the variety of factors responsible for ill health, paramount among which seems to be the degree of inequity and inequality in a society. In a widely cited 1992 paper, Whitehead defined health inequities as *"differences in health that are unnecessary, avoidable, unfair and unjust"* [1]. What distinguishes equity from equality in health is, therefore, the market. When what we need when ill is bought and sold in the market, the implications of constantly increasing income inequalities are clear. That a part of the US population was (and still is) effectively without insurance coverage was the moral and practical justification for the Affordable Care Act (ACA), the most important equity-promoting intervention in health in the last few decades, and perhaps, in American history. To quote from a 2014 study [2]:

> *"The inequity of the US health care system is particularly troubling. The difference in health care experiences between people with below-average and above-average incomes will need to be monitored over time to determine whether further steps to improve cov-*

---

1   As with the water in Flint, Michigan, a topic that received painful national attention during the Clinton-Sanders Primary debate in March 2016.

2   The title of an article in *The Economist*, p. 55, August 30, 2008.

erage, especially for those at the lowest end of the income range, are needed. Although Americans at both ends of the income spectrum were more likely than their counterparts in other countries to report financial barriers to care, it is the substantially worse experience provided to people with below-average income that most seriously undermines the overall performance of the US health care system."

The inequity of the American health-care system is particularly troubling. According to a 2013 Commonwealth Fund survey of adults in eleven high-income countries, the US ranks last on measures of financial access to care as well as of availability of care on nights and weekends [3]. Uninsured people are particularly likely to report encountering barriers to care. In this sense, we have a serious limitation of freedom in society.

On Equity, Equality, and Freedom

Equity is the state where people are equal in the eyes of the law, or in regard to their rights. In this sense, equity is synonymous to *social justice* and quite distinct from *altruism*. In a seminal book on equity in health, the authors note that, while altruism is a matter of preference, i.e. a person derives pleasure (or utility) from its exercise, equity is not, since the person cannot influence or impose it [4]. Equity, in other words, is external to the individual as an *intrinsic value of society*. In the health sector, for example, equity means equal rights for access to health services, relatively equal burden in the financing of health, and a guarantee that all citizens have an equal right to health protection.

Equality is a state where certain attributes are equal in value. When the American Constitution states, however, that "all men are created equal," it implies a state of equity, or equality in terms of human rights and opportunities.[3] Most, if not all, modern democratic societies have equity built into their constitutions. They guarantee, in one way or the other that their citizens have equal rights, and the more progressive societies strive for a least a modicum of equal opportunities for their citizens. But, does equity lead to equality? Or is there another value, the pursuit of which runs contrary to the realization of equality?

In reality, neither equity nor equality are central objectives or guiding principles in American politics. They are much more so in Europe, where a tradition of state intervention, through taxation and other active social programs ensures at least a degree of equity. In America, instead, we see strong forces leaning towards freedom at the expense of equity. Of the two yardsticks used by economists to judge the performance of health care systems—equity and efficiency—the latter has dominated cross-country comparisons. It is perhaps for this reason that the study of health policy and health economics has taken precedence over public health [5].

In what follows we will have many occasions to ask ourselves whether the time has come for America to look for a different health policy. Perhaps our interest should turn more to equality and equity, while looking for efficiency and value for money in health. As these objectives are met, the time will come to discuss an even more important objective close to the heart of Americans. The quest for *freedom,* one might say, is in the American DNA. It is, however, time to ask

---

3   After all, the American Constitution was influenced heavily by the work of Voltaire and, especially, Jean Jacques Rousseau, the father of the "Social Contract" and the Age of Humanism.

an important question as we discuss health care. Is it possible to imagine *that better and more health might actually mean more, not less, freedom*? This is a political question which must, at least, be discussed in America. So far, the main "argument" against health reform and especially of the ACA is that it "limits freedom." And one of the many arguments used is that "equal care" is only good for "left-leaning Europe."[4]

It is here that one may put to rest the "fears" of our American friends. Europe in the 21st century is very different from post-war Europe about to build the "nanny state" Republicans in the US abhor. There are voices now in Europe that speak about the "Voiceless Left." Having solved its issues with democracy and prosperity, the Left in Europe has lost its "vital space." The political parties left and right no longer speak of equality but of the "effectiveness of the welfare state."[5] This is something that should interest Americans and especially American politicians more than anything else. After all, as we saw in Chapter A-3, the American health system is anything but effective.

To return to the notion of freedom and equality, as discussed by Ronald Dworkin [6], there is freedom "from" and freedom "to." Freedom "from" is freedom from hunger, oppression, and poverty. It is a passive definition of freedom stating what man should not be in danger of.[6] Freedom "to" is an active definition of freedom. It implies the freedom to live anywhere, to conduct business, to acquire and own property, and, in general all the human rights to develop one's personality and achieve its full potential, including religious and sexual freedom.

Is there a conflict between these two notions of freedom? Is my right to be rich consistent with your right for a just wage or free health care? For many years we were accustomed to thinking that there is a trade-off between freedom and equity. Freedom to develop one's full potential implies the inherent possibility of inequality, as one is free to develop perhaps at the expense of others. Conversely, equity, a central ideal of certain socialist societies during the last century, was seen as a state worth pursuing, even at the expense of certain freedoms. A look at Scandinavian countries' experience may be instructive. For the last 50 years, they have constantly been moving to greater equality and, at the same time, more freedom, in both senses mentioned above, at least in comparison with other OECD countries [7]. We must, therefore, look for a positive relationship between equality, equity, and freedom. After all, I suppose we would all agree that all three notions are positively related with the welfare of society, which, by default, is our ultimate goal, no matter where we live or what our political inclinations are.

Inequality and Health: The Two Don't Mix

The big picture appears when we look at the equity-health nexus even closer. For the past twenty years, research has linked health status with income, class, or wealth inequality [8]. Wilkinson has argued forcibly that the reality, sometimes even the perception, of inequality in itself breeds poor health. This is the second part of the "chicken and the egg" argument, and the most disturbing. A society where social and economic inequality is widely experienced is a sick

---

4 At least in popular "trash sites" http://www.bullshitexposed.com/scandinavian-socialism-debunked/
5 The interested reader might look for Ronald Dworkins' interview by the Italian *La Republica*, on January 7, 2004.
6 It is interesting to note in this regard that even in the United States "freedom from" is not as guaranteed as we might think. In a recent survey among 168 countries by Journalists Without Borders, an NGO, the US ranked in the unenviable 119th position in 2005, down from the 17th position in 2002.

society where ill health is increasingly a reality. People get sick because they perceive themselves as belonging to a "separate, disadvantaged group." They lack information, they adopt negative health habits and behavior, and they belong to what we will call the "health desperados" of our times. Lower class status, as perceived by them, makes preoccupation with their health secondary to other concerns. It is very difficult to make a poor person with low self-esteem aware of the risks of obesity when other (seemingly) more urgent problems occupy their daily concerns and worries.

Inequity in health due to income inequality is one of the most important challenges facing modern societies, as inequality in health outcomes appears to be more acute in social groups characterized by acute income inequality. It has been shown that people living in conditions of social exclusion run more than twice the risk of suffering from major illness or even premature death [9]. The investigation of the relationship between poverty and health has been the subject of research, especially in the United Kingdom. An important and well documented study, more than 20 years ago, showed that the risk of death among the poorest socioeconomic groups is 2½ times greater than that of the highest group, which shows much higher utilization of health services [10].

Although the exact relationship between income inequality and mortality or health status remains obscure, inequity in health is definitely due to reduced access to health care. This is certainly related to lack of health insurance. A much more sinister form is the prevalence of poor health among the lower income groups or population groups who belong to certain social classes. Even in societies where equity as a value is not considered a primary objective (as in the US), the idea that inequity in access to health care may result in lower life expectancy or higher morbidity or mortality is, or should be, abhorrent.

There is also the reverse relationship: bad health results in economic and social inequality. A person who is ill or disabled cannot hold a job and often suffers serious income loss. For example, bad dental hygiene may cause serious employment problems. Recent research results in Greece showed that 26% of the people do not use the available preventive services because they cannot afford them.

Health care is, in a way, an engine for income redistribution. This works in two ways, going in opposite directions. When health care financing is through a progressive tax system (as in most of the European countries), we have redistribution from the fewer rich to the many. At the same time, we should not forget that the health sector employs resources amounting to 8-10% of GDP.[7] This expenditure is also income for the suppliers of health care. To the extent, therefore, that a health system is privatized, we have a concentration of enormous resources in relatively few individuals providing health care. If this power is used primarily to produce profits rather than good health care, there is a problem with the society which allows this reverse income and wealth redistribution.

Equity and Equality in Health Outcomes

Science and the art of medicine have one accepted (evidence based) solution to each health problem or condition. The extent to which the solution is available to all, irrespective of economic and social status, measures "equity in health" in a society. What we need to avoid, there-

---

7 The argument is much more germane to the US where health expenditure is twice as high.

fore, is the prevalence of poor health in certain population groups only because they are excluded from the medical knowledge and health resources available to society as a whole. However, this does not seem to be the case for middle-aged white Americans, something that has been puzzling demographers for some time. A recent report finds increased mortality among poor and poorly educated white Americans in the age group of 45-54. The study found that this particular group had the most deaths from suicides, alcohol and drug poisoning—mortality so large, in fact, that it affected the mortality statistic for the whole middle-aged white Americans cohort. In contrast, the mortality rate of middle-aged blacks and Hispanics continued to decline [11]. This tells us that it is not inequity in health resources, but another reason, such as inequality in income and opportunity, that is primarily responsible for the high mortality in poor, middle-aged white Americans. Another interesting study calculated seasonal mortality, which is the difference between observed mortality for the winter months compared to expected mortality, among various countries. In fact, seasonal mortality was higher in southern European countries where winters are warmer. The reason given in the study was that income inequality and poverty in these countries was more important than the favorable climate [12].

So the question is two-pronged: Is bad health the cause of inequality or is economic and social inequality responsible for bad health? The question is important, because the solution depends on the answer. If bad health or specific health problems appear randomly, subject mainly to biological causes, catastrophic insurance should be a reasonable and perhaps adequate way of dealing with it. If, however, bad health is the result of income inequality, the solution to the problem belongs not to health policy but to social and economic policy. It is, therefore, a matter for an inspired health minister to discover and an attentive and responsible government to solve, probably through effective health insurance.

If, on the other hand, bad health is the consequence of unhealthy behavior, ignorance, or aversion to preventive measures, due to economic and social factors that set a person or a group apart from mainstream society, and make health-promoting behavior a luxury, the problem is one for the society as a whole to handle. If this is the case, the solution lies not in the health sector, but in society itself. In other words, this is a problem that requires the whole of society to recognize that health is at least as valuable and worthy of protection as property or wealth. I am not sure that the US Constitution makes this distinction as clear as it is in most European countries.

There are wide disparities in the accessibility and quality of health care in the United States. Since 2003, the Agency for Healthcare Research and Quality (AHRQ) has been releasing the National Healthcare Disparities Report. The report documents disparities among racial, ethnic, income, and other demographic groups, and highlights priority areas requiring action [13]. Partial answers for the problem exist, but not a comprehensive solution integral to the American health system. Federally Qualified Health Centers (FQHCs), which are eligible for certain types of public reimbursement, provide comprehensive primary and preventive care regardless of their patients' ability to pay. Initially created to provide health care to underserved and vulnerable populations, FQHCs largely provide safety-net services to the uninsured. Also, Medicaid and the Children's Health Insurance Program (CHIP) provide public health insurance coverage for certain low-income populations. Finally, the ACA contains a number of provisions aimed at reducing disparities, including providing subsidies for low-income Americans to purchase insurance in the exchanges, improving parity for mental health care and substance abuse services, and providing additional funding to community health centers located in underserved communities. Additionally, a multitude of public initiatives and policies at the local, state, and federal levels target disparities, as do a wide range of private initiatives.

References

[1]   Whitehead M. The concepts and principles of equity and health. *International Journal of Health Services*. 1992; 22(3):429–45. (First published with the same title from: Copenhagen: World Health Organisation Regional Office for Europe, 1990 (EUR/ICP/RPD 414)).

[2]   Davis K, Ballreich J. Equitable access to care — how the United States ranks internationally. *New England Journal of Medicine*. 2014; 371(17):1567–70.

[3]   Schoen C, Osborn R, Squires D, Doty MM. Access, affordability, and insurance complexity are often worse in the United States compared to ten other countries. *Health Affairs*. 2013; 32(12):2205–15.

[4]   Van Doorslaer E, Wagstaff A, Rutten F, editors. *Equity in the finance and delivery of health care: An international perspective*. Oxford: Oxford University Press; 1992 Dec 17. ISBN: 9780192622914.

[5]   Frieden TR. The future of public health. *New England Journal of Medicine*. 2015; 373(18): 1748-1754.

[6]   Dworkin R. What is equality? Part 1: Equality of welfare. *Philosophy & Public Affairs*. 1981; 185-246.

[7]   OECD. Society at a glance OECD SOCIAL INDICATORS. Paris: OECD Publishing; 2005.

[8]   Wilkinson RG. *Socioeconomic determinants of health: Health inequalities: Relative or absolute material standards?* BMJ. 1997; 314(7080):591.

[9]   World Health Organization [webpage on the Internet]. Commission on Social Determinants of Health FINAL REPORT: *Closing the gap in a generation: Health equity through action and the social determinants of health*; 2008 [cited 11th July 2016]. Available from: http://apps.who.int/iris/bitstream/10665/43943/1/9789241563703_eng.pdf

[10]   Black D, Morris J, Smith C, Townsend P. *Inequalities in Health: Report of a Research Working Group/The Black Report 1980*. [UK]: Socialist Health Association; 1980 Aug 30.

[11]   Kolata G. Death rates rising for middle-aged white Americans, study finds. [USA]: *The New York Times* [newspaper on the Internet]. 4th Nov 2013 [cited: 7th June 2016]. Available from: http://www.nytimes.com/2015/11/03/health/death-rates-rising-for-middle-aged-white-americans-study-finds.html?_r=0

[12]   Healy JD. Excess winter mortality in Europe: a cross country analysis identifying key risk factors. *Journal of Epidemiology and Community Health*. 2003; 57(10): 784-789.

[13]   Agency for Healthcare Research and Quality. [USA]: US HHS: Agency for Healthcare Research and Quality. National healthcare quality & disparities reports; 2015 Jun 18 [cited: 7th June 2016]. Available from: http://www.ahrq.gov/research/findings/nhqrdr/index.html

A-5: THE HEALTH SYSTEM IS NOT SUSTAINABLE

Does America spend too much for health? How much is really "too much"? One way to answer these questions is to compare the US with countries of similar economic, political, and social characteristics. We then see that America spends almost twice as much as other countries in terms of its GDP, but, for some, this is not too much. The next thing to ask is, What do they get in return for their spending? We have already shown that US dollars buy less health care and produce worse health outcomes and a shorter lifespan than in other rich countries. True, some Americans, especially the wealthy and the old, enjoy life expectancy and quality of life comparable or superior to Canadians and Europeans. The question, then, is why does America condemn part of its young working class to lousy health care at a huge cost?

Even if the answer is that the high cost of the American health system, for whatever reason, is acceptable, another question arises, Who pays the cost and how do those who cannot pay get what they need? We then remember Ted Kennedy and the poignant article he wrote, shortly before his death, on the *huge cost of the health care I could afford to receive.* In this he reflects on the stories of people that "had to go without" for less complicated ailments than his cancer. The conclusion for many is that the American health system is so unfair that it is no longer politically viable. Finally, regardless of politics, the question arises, Do Americans know that their health system may also not be economically viable because of its extremely high cost?

The Sustainability of the Health System

One of the main characteristics of a health system, crucial for the well-being of society, is its sustainability [1]. This, in turn, means that its financing should be consistent with the health of the economy. Appropriately, the 2010 reform was called the Affordable Care Act. Nobody knows what will be left of the ACA when it completes its course through the courts. It is our contention, however, that the next important attempt at health reform should look at "affordability" in terms of the national economy. And this is not consistent with expenditure at 20% of GDP and rising, especially when a substantial part is financed by employment contributions.

The ILO[1] defines affordability as an essential feature of a health system, using four criteria [2]:

1. Lack of financial barriers such as high user fees.

2. Level of insurance contributions set in relation to the household's ability to pay.

3. No risk of catastrophic health expenditure that would exceed 40 percent of household income net of subsistence expenditure.

4. No risk of impoverishment due to ill health.

The ILO criteria are a "yardstick" of health-care coverage based on ensuring that ill health

---

1 The International Labor Organization (ILO) was founded in 1919 to pursue a vision based on the premise that universal, lasting peace can be established only if it is based on social justice. The ILO became the first specialized agency of the UN in 1946, with headquarters in Geneva. Its main aims are to promote rights at work, encourage decent employment opportunities, enhance social protection, and strengthen dialogue on work-related issues.

does not lead to catastrophic loss of income or impoverishment. To meet this objective, costs must be pooled and financed through pre-payment mechanisms in order to reduce out-of-pocket payments at the point of service. Affordability, therefore, is partly tied to national health insurance, the subject of Part D. The most significant defect of the new legislation, however, is that it does not change the way health care is organized, produced, and delivered. It therefore misses the fact that a broad reform of health care itself could, and should, save money. Only broad health reform, hopefully by the next administration, will address the notion that health care is not made up of "marketable" goods and services just like others. We deal with this in Chapter C-1, but we must now see what the ACA seems to be achieving so far, where the problem lies, and how to fix it.

Table A5-1 below shows the yearly National Health Expenditure (NHE) Projections of the Actuary Office of the Centers for Medicare & Medicaid Coverage. The data cover the years after the implementation of the ACA, and to some extent they provide a bird's-eye view of NHE for the next ten years. The most "telling" is that NHE is projected by the government to be close to one-fifth of total GDP. What is even more interesting is that public financing participation is projected to decrease slightly. The ACA may indeed make health care more "affordable," but higher public expenditure will probably increase the total cost of health care, making the system not sustainable for long. Given the main reasons for rising health expenditure, improving equity in financing alone cannot lead to a sustainable health system. Although a matter of national importance, politicians do not seem to recognize the problem of sustainability as such.

Table A5-1. Basic Figures in National Health Expenditure (NHE) Projected Growth.[2]

Estimated Variable	2012-2022	2013-2023	2014-2024
Average growth rate in National Health Expenditure (NHE)	5.8	5.7	5.8
Rate of increase in excess of GDP growth (10-year period)	1.0	1.1	1.1
Projected percent of health to GDP (end of 10-year period)	19.9	19.3	19.6
Federal, state, and local government spending (percent, end of period)	49	49	47
Percent growth of NHE (first year of period)	4.5	3.6	5.5

Sources: National Health Expenditure Projections, the Actuary Office of the Centers for Medicare & Medicaid Coverage.

It is interesting that in 2012 Standard & Poor's, a major credit rating agency, announced that in its national credit ratings it would also take into account the *financial sustainability* of a nation's health-care system.[3] The US government, therefore, must take a closer look at health expenditure, a crucial component of the deficit and the national debt. America must think beyond traditional institutional processes to a broader concept of a health system, controlling health expenditure in addition to revamping its financing mechanism and the equity in health insurance coverage as with the ACA. Besides being equitable, health financing must also become sustainable.

Escalating costs are of major concern to the insurance industry as well. In order to study the

---

2 Data were summarized from National Health Expenditure Projections, the Actuary Office of the Centers for Medicare & Medicaid Coverage for the years 2012-2022, 2013-2023, and 2014-2024.
3 Press release, 31 January 2012.

extent and the causes of the increase in health costs, insurance companies established the Health Care Cost Institute (HCCI) in 2011. The purpose was to study health-care spending drawing on health-care costs and utilization data for Americans covered by private insurance [3]. In its mission statement we read:

> *"The United States has a profound problem with health care spending. Rising health care costs are stifling economic growth, consuming increasing portions of the nation's gross domestic product, and putting added burdens on businesses, the public sector, individuals, and families. In spite of heightened concerns about the harmful impacts of US health care spending, information about what is driving spending is incomplete."* [4]

The cost of the American health system is already unsustainable, but, not surprisingly, the industry publication does not recognize health insurance as the culprit. In 2013, the HCCI reported that *"spending per privately insured person grew by 3.9% in 2013, as falling utilization offset rising prices."* Use of health care services continued to fall in 2014, while prices for all categories of services continued to rise [5]. What concerns the industry, however, is not that less health care can be consumed, but that price increases threaten its profitability.

Health System Financing and its Viability

At the world's most famous gathering of global economic power, the World Economic Forum (or "Davos meeting"), in 2013, among the main proposals was a New Social Contract.[4] It provided that *"governments are responsible for driving health system efficiency and for regulating organizations and individuals to pursue healthy living."* It is not surprising that the major economic gathering in the world would call for health system efficiency. It is disappointing, however, that it drops the ball when it calls for "healthy living" as a remedy to inefficiency.[5] Instead, it presented a study[6] titled *"Sustainable Health Systems: Visions, Strategies, Critical Uncertainties and Scenarios"* [6]. The study presented results from five countries, each chosen for a separate but special reason. Four European countries—Germany, Netherlands, Spain, and England—with distinct differences in health-care financing systems, and China for its size and rapidly rising wealth, and also because its developing health system incorporates features from each one of the other four countries.[7]

There are perhaps no two countries with greater cultural, institutional, philosophical and ethical similarities than the US and Britain.[8] They share language, religious, cultural, and historical roots, and they succeeded each other as world leaders. The prefix "New" in many US cities and states with British names refers to common heritage. More important, they share economic philosophies, and are home to London and New York—financial centers of capitalism for more than two centuries. Adam Smith the father of American capitalism was born in Scotland. And

---

4   A rather audacious attempt to emulate *The Social Contact* by Jean-Jacques Rousseau in 1776.

5   Equally well it could say that "it is better to be rich and beautiful than poor and ugly."

6   Conducted by McKinsey & Company.

7   It is interesting that the Davos meeting did not include the US in the study, perhaps because it would be "embarrassing" to a major economic power. A highly political gathering, the Davos meeting certainly did not wish to be unpleasant to a super power.

8   One might add Canada, Australia, and New Zealand for much the same reasons. The U.S would still be an "outlier."

yet, when it comes to the protection of one's health, allegedly "the most important thing in life," the two societies serve two entirely different "gods." In Britain, the tax-financed National Health Service (NHS) is the most venerable social institution, even more than the Royal Family.[9] On the contrary, in America it is the individual's ability to pay for health insurance that is equally revered. In America, social health insurance, or "one-payer" as it is called, is considered socialist or the work of the devil. When it comes to health, the UK and America are no closer than Mars is to Earth.

A variety of systems are used to pay for health care, perhaps as many as OECD countries. Each has different implications for the stakeholders, patients, taxpayers, employers, government, hospitals, doctors, pharmaceutical companies and other providers in public or private health service. One thing is certain: health care goods and services cost money to produce and disburse to the users. The two questions for which no two countries have the same answer are: (1) How much should health services cost? and (2) Who should bear the cost? The answers given reflect the political, economic, and social conditions prevailing historically. Given the size of the health sector, it is not surprising that the debate on health financing often tests the strength of institutions, political parties, and even societal values.

The first question on the cost seems fairly easy to answer. Health goods and services, as far as production is concerned, are not very different than the other items which enter our daily lives and our consumption pattern. In that sense, production cost depends on wage levels and the prices of materials used. They also depend on technology and the quantities produced. Primarily, the cost of health care depends on whether it is produced for profit or not. The second question, on the bearer of the cost, is more intriguing. It involves ethical and philosophical positions which often result in intractable political problems. The political battle over the Obama health reform tops the list, but reforms in other countries have also proved politically important, in a positive or negative way, for the parties and politicians proposing and implementing them.

Financing Health Care in Times of Crisis

The implications of the two systems of financing on business and the economy have been made painfully obvious as the economic crisis has developed. In Britain, increased expenditures, according to the Conservative government, were to be financed by an increase in the tax rate for high earners.[10] At that time, criticism centered around the alleged implications the increased tax rate would have on starting a new business. The fallacy of this argument was elegantly made by Alexander Nash, a Londoner, in a letter to *The Economist* [7].

> *"No one in a start-up business is worried about the high marginal tax rate you pay in Britain, after $240,000 a year. A friend recently described the reasons why she could not afford to set up her new business in the low-tax US, the main one being that she could not afford the crippling health-insurance bills that are part of a normal employee package there. This raises the intriguing possibility that health care costs are a barrier to entry for foreign businesses in the American market."*

---

9 In the opening ceremony of the 2012 London Olympics, the part featuring the NHS and the Sick Children's Hospital took more time than the spot featuring the Queen.

10 The rate proposed was 50% on incomes exceeding $246,000 (estimated to affect 300,000 people).

i "The Talisman Tax," *The Economist*, Aug. 6, 2011.

A similar, but timid, plan in the US nearly shut down the government and brought about a global financial crisis when President Obama aired plans to repeal the Bush administration tax relief for the "super rich."

Yet, somebody must pay for the ever-increasing cost of health care. The sources of financing in European countries in 2008 are shown in Table A5-2 below. Government and employers account for 75.3% of the burden of financing health care in European Union countries. On the other hand, in America, government and employers account for only 65%. Households, through social and private insurance or out-of-pocket payment (OOP) expenditure, foot the rest of the bill. In either case the health-care system relies on the real economy, a fact which makes it important to see what happens in a time of economic retraction.

Table A5-2. Decomposition of Health Expenditure by Source of Revenue.

	Europe (2008)	US (2012)
General government (federal, state, and local)	38.2	44
Employers (social or private insurance)	37.1	21
Households (social contributions and private insurance)	20.4	28
Out-of-pocket expenditure	4.3	7

Sources: Eurostat and Office of the Actuary, US Medicare and Medicaid.

At this time, we should perhaps mention one of the main arguments put forth by Bernie Sanders when he was running for the Democratic Presidential Nomination. Defending his program, which was estimated to cost $1.38 trillion a year, he argues that:

> *"there would be a large and growing surplus that is not indicated here because of the income tax revenues that will rise with faster economic growth when the burden of health insurance premiums is removed from employment, and when workers are freed of "job lock" associated with employment-provided health insurance leading to increased entrepreneurial activity and better match of workers to employment" [8].*

Financial and Economic Crises

The question "What really is an economic crisis?" has received answers of dubious intellectual honesty. First of all, let us not forget that we started by talking about a "financial crisis." There is a tremendous difference between the two, but reading the everyday economic journals one would hardly know the difference. For the average Joe and Jane, the financial crisis of 2007-2008 and the economic crisis of 2011 are two different worlds. In the first, they had to pay higher interest rates or payments for their new home. In the second, they may have had to lose their home, if either or both lost their job. In the crisis of 2007-8 the cost of their health insurance went up. In 2011, they may have been forced to go without insurance.

The financial crisis which started in the US in 2007 developed into an economic crisis for the whole world in 2011. *The Economist* of August 6, 2011 wondered whether this was the "Time for a double dip?" recession in the US. What happened is that the AAA US debt was downgraded on August 5, 2011, for the first time in its history, by Standard & Poor's, one of the three rating agencies, causing a shiver in financial institutions and central banks all over the world.[11] During the summer of 2011, the decline of stock markets by 20% in the third week of August and the decline in the price of government bonds reduced the amount of "air" income in the ledgers of the financial institutions and many private accounts. Frankly, I don't know how many working class people were concerned by the alarming news in the 2011 financial press that $6-9 trillion were lost in the financial crisis and the stock market crash. The major concern of most politicians and citizens was, instead, the rapid rise of unemployment to 15-20% in certain European countries and the looming recession in major countries such as the US and China.

The financial crisis, therefore, concerns mainly the holders of capital, and, especially, the rich and the super rich. The economic crisis, on the other hand, concerns those who have stakes in what we call the "real economy." For them, economic phenomena and magnitudes such as inflation, recession, unemployment, interest rates, income tax, and VAT have a meaning that affects their everyday life. The cost of health care is one of the most important such magnitudes. In America, when your job is threatened, the last thing you can tolerate is the threat of losing health insurance coverage for you and your family. On the other hand, the economic crisis in Europe, where health insurance is not tied so much to employment but is mostly financed by tax revenue, leaves the average citizen almost unharmed, at least in the medium run.

One debate concerning the health care overhaul of Obamacare is whether it helps or hurts the competiveness of US business. Neeraj Sood at the University of Southern California says the law could increase the number of US jobs by 250,000 to 400,000 per year and significantly reduce health spending for businesses. Harvard's Jennifer Baron argues healthcare reform should not only be framed as a means of cost-cutting, but also as a way to improve worker productivity by improving individuals' health. But Bob Graboyes of the National Federation of Independent Business, an opponent of the law, says it is "laden with disincentives for businesses to grow, to innovate, and to hire" and should be repealed. The American Enterprise Institute's Thomas Miller says the law should be "repealed and replaced" not to boost business competitiveness but to improve the value of healthcare [9].

We Need a Health System for the Future, Not Only for Now

Population aging will have a profound impact on the sustainability of health care systems. ENEPRI,[12] a European Institute, analyses the effects of ageing populations on public finances [10]. More specifically, it focuses on the implications of population ageing for acute health care,

---

11   One should not dismiss allegations that Standard & Poor's is the financial arm of the Republican Party, the political one being the Tea Party. The debacle of American political leadership of both parties over the debt limit legislation exposed the Administration's "soft underbelly," something the Tea Party, dragging the whole Republican Party along, would not fail to exploit. It is perhaps not insignificant, if true as alleged, that Harold McGraw III, President and CEO of McGraw Hill, the mother company of S&P, had not contributed one cent to President Obama's campaign and that he had never contributed to the Democratic Party—despite a tradition according to which major American companies contribute equally to both parties. On August 23, 2011 we read in *The Telegraph* August 23, 2011 that Standard & Poor's president, Deven Sharma, will step down at the end of the year. The reasons cited were his handling of the US debt downgrading, but also the investigations into his AAA ratings given to Lehman Brothers days before it went "belly up."

12   ENEPRI European Network of Economic Policy Research Institutes.

long-term care, and public pension expenditures for 15 EU countries. It pays particular attention to three novel insights:

1. A large proportion of health-care spending relates to time to mortality rather than to age;

2. Life expectancy may increase much faster than current demographic projections suggest;

3. Average health status may continue to improve in the future.

The analysis adopts a generational accounting model that incorporates health-care costs during the last years of life, decomposed into an acute health-care component and a long-term care component. The projections show that gains in life expectancy increase age-related expenditure, while improved health has the opposite effect. Combined, these trends reduce health-care costs and increase pension expenditures. Their joint effect upon public finances is rather modest, however. Hence, the assessment of public finances in most EU-15 countries does not change. If a more rapid increase in life expectancy combines with an improvement in health, current fiscal and social security institutions in Europe will be sustainable. Unfortunately, as we will see below, the same cannot be said for the American health system.

References

[1] Liaropoulos L, Goranitis I. Health care financing and the sustainability of health systems. *International Journal for Equity in Health*. 2015; 14(1).

[2] ILO. *World Social Security Report 2010/11-Providing coverage in times of crisis and beyond*. Gevena, Switzerland: ILO Publications; 2010.

[3] Health Care Cost Institute. 2016 Available from: http://www.healthcostinstitute.org/ [cited: 7th June 2016].

[4] Health Care Cost Institute. About the health care cost institute. Available from: http://www.health-costinstitute.org/about [cited: 7th June 2016].

[5] Health Care Cost Institute. 2013 HCCUR 12 17 14. Washington, DC, USA: Health Care Cost Institute; 2014.

[6] WEF Sustainable Health Systems report 2013. Gevena, Switzerland: World Economic Forum; 2013.

[7] Nash A. A health tax. *The Economist* [magazine on the Internet]. 13 August 2011 [cited: 7th June 2016]. Available from: http://down02.putclub.com/virtual/backup/update/Download/kaoyan/The_Economist_20110813.pdf

[8] Merica D, Bradner E, Luhby T. Hours before debate, Sanders releases Medicare-for-all plan. CNN [website on the Internet]. 18 Jan 2016 [cited 7 Jun 2016]. Available from: http://edition.cnn.com/2016/01/17/politics/bernie-sanders-medicare-plan

[9] Sood N, Baron J, Miller T, Graboyes R, Johnson T. Does healthcare reform help US Business? Council on Foreign Relations. [USA]: Council on Foreign Relations. 8th Dec 2009 [cited: 7th June 2016]. Available from: http://www.cfr.org/united-states/does-healthcare-reform-help-us-business/p24060

[10] Westerhout E, Pellikaan F. Can we afford to live longer in better health? ENEPRI Research Report No. 10. Netherlands: European Network of Economic Policy Research Institutes/Central Planbureau; 2005.

A-6: THE HEALTH SYSTEM HURTS THE ECONOMY

The United States spends an estimated $3 trillion annually on healthcare—more than any other industrialized country. According to OECD data, the United States spends two-and-a-half times more than the OECD average, and yet ranks with Turkey and Mexico as the only OECD countries without universal health coverage [1]. Some analysts say an increasing number of US businesses are less competitive globally because of ballooning healthcare costs [2]. The healthcare reform law signed by President Barack Obama on March 23, 2010 includes measures aimed at making health care less expensive and more accessible, including upgrades to government-run Medicare and Medicaid. Still, reforming health care has proved politically divisive, especially over the option to expand social medicine, as well as new mandates on employers and individuals. Whether, however, these reforms will reduce the health-care cost burden on US industry and the economy remains under debate.

The US Competitive Disadvantage

The United States in 2014 spent 19% of GDP for health, more than any other developed nation. The nonpartisan Congressional Budget Office (CBO) estimated as far back as 2008 that number would rise to 25% by 2025 without changes to federal law [3]. Some economists say these ballooning dollar figures place a heavy burden on companies doing business in the United States and can put them at a substantial competitive disadvantage in the international marketplace [4]. Employer-funded coverage is the structural mainstay of the US health insurance system. A November 2008 report said access to employer-sponsored health insurance had been on the decline among low-income workers, and health premiums for workers had risen 114 percent in the last decade [5]. Small businesses are less likely than large employers to be able to provide health insurance as a benefit. At 7.7%, health care is the most expensive benefit paid by US employers, according to the US Chamber of Commerce (See Chapter D-1, Table D1-1).

Some economists say these ballooning dollar figures place a heavy burden on companies doing business in the United States and can put them at a competitive disadvantage in the international marketplace. For large multinational corporations, footing health-care costs presents an enormous expense. General Motors (GM), for instance, covers more than 1.1 million employees and former employees, and the company says it spends roughly $5 billion on health-care expenses annually. GM says health-care costs add between $1,500 and $2,000 to the sticker price of every automobile it makes. Health benefits for unionized auto workers became a central issue derailing the 2008 congressional push to provide a financial bailout to GM and its ailing Detroit rival, Chrysler. Still, other experts debate the degree to which health care actually affects US industries. *"Health benefits are largely substitutes for other forms of labor compensation,"* says American Enterprise Institute Fellow Thomas Miller in a Council of Foreign Relations roundup. *"Hence US firms have performed well [in the past], despite rising levels of healthcare costs, because high levels of productivity and a favorable investment climate were (and remain) much more important factors in determining competitiveness"* [6].

Health care is one of several factors—entrenched union contracts being another—that make doing business in the United States expensive. In fact, it is difficult to say which hurts more. Economists disagree on the number of US jobs that have been lost due to the transfer of business operations across national boundaries to friendlier operating environments. A RAND Corporation study published in the *Health Services Research Journal* in June 2009 found that industries with the highest level of employer-sponsored health care (such as manufacturing, telecommunications, education, and finance) showed the slowest amounts of growth between 1987 and 2005 compared to industries with the smallest level of employer-provided insurance in the United States. American companies were also at a disadvantage compared to their industry competitors in Canada, where insurance is provided by the state. *US News and World Report* blogger Rick Newman uses some of the RAND data to project the decrease in industry growth and potential job losses for fifteen sectors should healthcare costs rise to 20 percent of US GDP [7].

Some analysts say the health-care situation affects the ability of startup companies to find the best workers, therefore impeding US innovation. "In the cradle of American innovation, workers are making career choices based on co-payments, preexisting conditions, and other minutiae of health insurance," writes David Leonhardt in *The New York Times*. "They are not necessarily making decisions based on what would be best for their careers and, in turn, for the American economy" [8].

The Impact of Obamacare on Business and the Economy

Obamacare largely focuses on decreasing the number of the uninsured. Original projections mentioned a reduction by about 60 percent, but it is less clear how much these reforms would affect the US economy. Overall, the new law would produce close to $1 trillion in new government spending. Although the CBO found that the final law would reduce the federal deficit by as much $138 billion by 2019 [9], the Centers for Medicare and Medicaid Services, a US government agency, also found that the legislation would do little to stem the rise in health-care expenditures, which are expected to increase to more than 20 percent of GDP in the next decade.

The University of Southern California's Neeraj Sood states in the 2011 Council of Foreign Relations Roundup that the law provides a number of incentives to improve costs. "*First, reform establishes health insurance exchanges that foster greater competition among insurers by making it easier for individuals and small businesses to shop for insurance,*" he writes. "*Second, it imposes an excise tax on generous health insurance plans, one of the primary drivers of rising healthcare costs. Finally, it calls for comparative effectiveness research and innovative reimbursement and delivery schemes to improve efficiency in health care. This new knowledge can provide a powerful impetus for cost-cutting, which will help make US businesses more competitive globally.*" In the same roundup, however, a spokesman for the National Federation of Independent Business disagreed that the law was a good thing. "*The effects will hit small business especially hard, and small business is the country's engine of job growth and source of much of the economy's innovation… The healthcare law is laden with disincentives for businesses to grow, to innovate, and to hire. Businesses will experience higher financial and administrative costs, and both effects will diminish American productivity,*" writes Robert Graboyes [2].

The Triple Tax on Business

Many company officials say a wasteful public-private system is pushing costs much higher than they should be. Jeffrey Rideout, a medical doctor and former head of the Internet Business Solutions Group at Cisco Systems' Healthcare Practice, says the amount businesses pay for employee insurance is just one element of their total health-care costs. Rideout says businesses incur a "triple tax." First, they pay for insurance programs through health benefits. Second, businesses indirectly subsidize Medicare and Medicaid, the federally supported programs for primarily poor and elderly Americans. Businesses pay higher insurance premiums to make up for the fact that Medicare and Medicaid reimbursements often do not match the total costs hospitals incur treating these patients—a "hidden tax." Third, Rideout says, businesses also subsidize the strain on the system wrought by the cost of treating America's uninsured, again through higher insurance premiums [10].

It is unclear to what extent these concerns will be answered under the ACA. The law expands access to Medicaid and the Children's Health Insurance Program (CHIP). It also creates a new health exchange program that would allow small businesses and workers without employer-provided health insurance to purchase subsidized private insurance. In total, the plan is expected to cover more than thirty million people, but roughly another twenty million are expected to remain uninsured (one-third of whom are expected to be undocumented workers). One of the numerous ways lawmakers hope to control costs is through reforms to Medicare, particularly by lowering payments to private insurers participating in "Medicare Advantage" and some health service providers. Whether such measures will simply transfer higher costs to private plans, as some critics suggest, remains up for debate [11]. A 2010 annual survey released in March 2011 by the National Business Group on Health, a coalition of large employers, found that more than two-thirds of large employers surveyed expected their health costs to increase as an impact of reform, and more than a quarter were considering reducing benefits to employees to control costs internally [12].

The Need to Improve the Value of Health Care

Health-care experts agree that the people with the most control over what drugs get prescribed and what procedures get done have little incentive to lower these costs. Indeed, to the extent that they get paid by procedure, their incentives are often quite the opposite. Likewise, patients often feel little need to control the costs of their own medical care if it is covered by insurance. The system bears the brunt of the excess, and employers make up the difference in the rates they pay. Some experts say companies should do more than focus their attention strictly on the direct costs of providing health care and look at the benefits of reducing poor health. Some health analysts argue there are "spin-off" benefits to supporting healthy employees, such as productivity, intellectual capacity, and reduced absenteeism. Reviews have been mixed on whether the costly US health system leads to health outcomes as good as developed countries with lower health costs. Obamacare contains some measures that would monitor the quality of health outcomes of the insured, but these clearly are not the real target of the new legislation, which mainly focuses on health care financing and affordability, leaving all else pretty much the same.

I would like to close this Part A with the introductory paragraph from a recent OECD Report titled "Fiscal Sustainability of Health Systems: Bridging Health and Finance Perspectives" [13]. It is interesting that it was written by an organization representing wealthy countries which, on average, spend half as much as the US but provide better health to their citizens.

"The health systems we enjoy today, and expected medical advances in the future, will be difficult to finance from public resources without major reforms. Public health spending in OECD countries has grown rapidly over most of the last half century. These spending

increases have contributed to important progress in population health: for example, life expectancy at birth has increased, rising on average by ten years since 1970. The challenge now is to sustain and enhance these achievements in a context of tight fiscal constraints in many countries combined with upward pressure on health spending from factors such as new technological advances and demographic changes. Finding policies that can make health spending more sustainable without compromising important achievements in access and quality requires effective co-operation between health and finance ministries. Sound governance and co-ordination mechanisms are therefore essential to ensure effective policy choices."

From all the points discussed above and in Chapter A-5, on the viability of the American health-care system, one thing is apparent. The dependence on private health insurance and the health market are the main threats that the ACA and, in fact, the American economy face. Private health insurance is the main cause of the escalating health cost which threatens the viability of the system. The only way to contain costs to business, individuals, and the government budget is to change the way money flows through the system. And this can be nothing else but some form of national health insurance based on taxes as the foundation of the health financing scheme. We will address this in Chapter D. Before this, however, we must make an assessment of the ACA in Chapter B and discuss the political and moral underpinnings of American health care in Chapter C.

References

[1]   Johnson T. Lessons in universal health insurance models. Council on Foreign Relations. [USA]: Council on Foreign Relations. 27th Jul 2012 [cited: 7th June 2016]. Available from: http://www.cfr.org/health-policy-and-initiatives/lessons-universal-health-insurance-models/p19871.

[2]   Sood N, Baron J, Miller T, Graboyes R, Johnson T. Does healthcare reform help US Business? Council on Foreign Relations. [USA]: Council on Foreign Relations. 8th Dec 2009 [cited: 7th June 2016]. Available from: http://www.cfr.org/united-states/does-healthcare-reform-help-us-business/p24060

[3]   Congressional Budget Office. Budget Options, Volume 1: Health Care. USA: The Congress of the United States/Congressional Budget Office; 2008.

[4]   Goodell S, Ginsburg P. *High and rising health care costs. Demystifying US Health Care Spending.* Robert Wood Johnson Foundation. [USA]: RWJF. 1st Oct 2008 [cited: 7th June 2016]. Available from: http://www.rwjf.org/en/library/research/2008/10/high-and-rising-health-care-costs.html

[5]   Ginsburg P. Research Synthesis Report No. 16: *High and rising health care costs. Demystifying US Health Care Spending.* USA: Global Printing Inc.; 2011.

[6]   Nichols L, Van de Water PN, Baron JF, Muggah A, Miller T, Ginsburg PB, Austin A. Squaring healthcare with the economy. Council on Foreign Relations. [USA]: Council on Foreign Relations. 8th Dec 2009 [cited: 7th June 2016]. Available from: http://www.cfr.org/health-policy-and-initiatives/squaring-healthcare-economy/p20909

[7]   Newman R. Industries Hurt Most by Soaring Health Costs. *US News & World Report* [publication on the Internet]. 4th Aug 2009 [cited: 7th June 2016]. Available from: http://money.usnews.com/money/blogs/flowchart/2009/08/04/industries-hurt-most-by-soaring-health-costs

[8]   Leonhardt D. If health reform fails, America's innovation gap will grow. *The New York Times* [newspaper on the Internet]. 30 th Dec 2014 [cited: 7th June 2016]. Available from: http://www. nytimes.com/2009/12/16/business/economy/16leonhardt.html?_r=1

[9]   Congressional Budget Office. H.R. 4872, Reconciliation Act of 2010-Distribution among types of providers of savings from the changes to updates in section 1105 of reconciliation legislation and section 3401. USA: The Congress of the United States/Congressional Budget Office; 18 th Mar 2010.

[10]   Teslik LH. Backgrounder: Healthcare Costs and US Competitiveness. *The New York Times* [newspaper on the Internet]. 14 th May 2007 [cited: 7th June 2016]. Available from: http://www.nytimes. com/cfr/world/slot1_20070514.html?pagewanted=print

[11]   Greene J. Ignagni: Lack of cost containment fatal flaw in health reform bills. *Crain's Detroit Business* [news publication on the Internet]. 3rd Dec 2009 [cited: 7th June 2016]. Available from: http:// www.crainsdetroit.com/article/20091203/FREE/912039980/ignagni-lack-of-cost-containment-fatal-flaw-in-health-reform-bills

[12]   Hilzenrath DS. Employers plan to shift more health-care costs to workers, survey reports. *The Washington Post* [newspaper on the Internet]. 12th Mar 2010 [cited: 7th June 2016]. Available from: http://www.washingtonpost.com/wp-dyn/content/article/2010/03/11/AR2010031100740.html

[13]   OECD. Joint network of health and budget officials on the fiscal sustainability of health systems. OECD Better Policies for Better Lives. [FRANCE]: OECD. 2016 [cited: 7th June 2016]. Available from: http://www.oecd.org/gov/budgeting/sbonetworkonhealthexpenditures.htm

PART B

OBAMACARE CANNOT CURE IT ALL

INTRODUCTION

THE ACA, A TIMID ATTEMPT THWARTED BY POLITICS

"The Affordable Care Act (ACA) was enacted in 2010 as the signature domestic achievement of the Obama presidency. It was intended to contain costs and achieve near-universal access to affordable health care of improved quality. Now, five years later, it is time to assess its track record. . . . Based on the evidence, one has to conclude that containment of health care costs is nowhere in sight, that more than 37 million Americans will still be uninsured when the ACA is fully implemented in 2019, that many more millions will be underinsured, and that profiteering will still dominate the culture of U.S. health care. More fundamental reform will be needed." [1]

President Obama himself called the day the ACA was signed *"the best day of my presidency."* Still, the excerpt above is an excellent assessment of the impact of the ACA by mid-2014, only four years after a hesitant intervention in health financing. The complete effects of the ACA will take more time to track down. At this time, however, scattered evidence points to a timid and incomplete improvement of a failed health insurance situation, but not a movement towards a better health system. When I read the excellent article by John P. Geyman, cited above, I thought I was reading a bird's-eye view of this book, and it probably reinforced my decision to write it.

Health-care financing is, of course, a major issue in the way health-care systems everywhere function. Whether through tax-funded social security, statutory social insurance with employer and employee contributions, or private—voluntary or mandated—insurance, the implications of health-care payments throughout the health system are immense. In every case, system financing affects the welfare of society with large implications for everybody's well-being. This huge sector, close to a fifth of the economy in the US, with millions of people, and the whole economy directly and indirectly affected, is inevitably influenced by ideology, politics, and economic interests covering the whole of society.[2]

The ACA is a major extension of public health insurance financing. Before we proceed, therefore, we should distinguish between two concepts, often used interchangeably but not correctly. The concepts of "security" and "insurance" and their corollaries, social security and social insurance, refer to the way the cost of health benefits are defrayed to the user. Social security, as the term implies, is something offered free of charge to the user, and is covered by government through taxation. Social insurance, on the contrary, is covered—at least partly—by contributions paid by the beneficiary and/or the employer, usually as an employment tax. In this sense,

---

1 Excerpt from John P. Geyman, "A Five-Year Assessment of the Affordable Care Act: Market Forces Still Trump the Common Good in U.S. Health Care," the *International Journal of Health Services*, 2015.
2 In Chapter D-1 we discuss the issues involved and the many forms health financing takes throughout the world.

Medicare belongs mostly to the category of social insurance.[3] Medicaid, on the other hand, is part of social security, since, as a federal or state program, it is covered through government revenue.[4] Both are government programs, parts of the long and hesitant trek of building a "caring society" in America.

This has not been an easy journey, and it took great presidents to lead the way. More than a century ago, in 1912, Theodore Roosevelt first made national health insurance part of his campaign as a Progressive. He failed, and Harry Truman followed in 1948, again unsuccessfully. Two solid programs for parts of the population were finally enacted in 1965 as Medicare and Medicaid by President Johnson as part of his "Great Society" vision. The idea of national health insurance, however, was always shut down as a point of discussion by conservative interests, including the insurance lobby and other private stakeholders in the American market-based health system, such as the American Medical Association (AMA).

In 1937, Justice Owen Roberts saved the Roosevelt New Deal from being overturned in the Supreme Court. It was another Roberts, Chief Justice John Roberts, who 78 years later saved the Affordable Care Act (ACA) in June 2015, and ended the debate on the legality of "Obamacare." And just as the earlier Roberts' decision, the recent *King v. Burwell* may go down in history as the moment Obamacare's long-term survival was guaranteed, opening the road to national health insurance.[5] The long way to this day started when the health care bill (H.R. 3590) was passed by the House of Representatives on November 7, 2009. It then passed the Senate, with amendments, on December 24, 2009. On March 21, 2010, the House passed the Senate bill, with these changes, with a final vote of 219-212. The bill passed to the Senate, which voted 56-43 in favor of the changes. On March 25 the bill returned to the House, as the "Health Care and Education Reconciliation Act of 2010," where it received a final vote of 220-207.

The reader must understand the ACA as simply a timid first attempt in the long trek towards a successful health system which would provide universal access to a comprehensive package of services, mostly free at the point of use. This must be the aim of a progressive society worthy of America's wealth and stature in the world. Although the basic facts on health insurance in the US before the ACA and at the "real starting point" in 2015 are not well known, it is important to list the most germane to this book. These facts on health insurance coverage must always be kept in mind in order to form a sound opinion on the problematic situation concerning health insurance, as a step towards a successful health system.

- The United States is the only wealthy nation without universal health insurance or universal health care coverage. *Source: Institute of Medicine of the National Academy of Sciences.*

- Of the 83.7% of people with health insurance in 2010, coverage was:
  - Employment based (55.3%),
  - Direct purchase (9.8%),
  - Government funded (Medicare, Medicaid, and military) (31%).
  Source: US Census Bureau.

- The primary reason given for lack of health insurance coverage in 2005 was:

---

3 Since Part A is paid for by contributions paid through a person's working life and Part B-Medical Insurance is paid by monthly premiums by the beneficiary.

4 https://www.medicare.gov/Pubs/pdf/11306.pdf

5 http://www.newyorker.com/news/daily-comment/why-obamacares-future-is-secure

- o Cost (more than 50%),
- o Lost job or a change in employment (24%),
- o Medicaid benefits stopped (10%),
- o Ineligibility for family insurance coverage due to age or leaving school (8%).

Source: National Center for Health Statistics.

- More than 40 million adults stated that they needed but did not receive one or more of these health services (medical care, prescription medicines, mental health care, dental care, or eyeglasses) in 2005 because they could not afford it. *Source: National Center for Health Statistics.*

- Medicaid, which accounted for 15.9% of health-care coverage in 2010, is a health insurance program jointly funded by the federal and state governments to provide health care for qualifying low-income individuals. *Source: US Census Bureau.*

- Medicare, a federally funded health security program that covers most individuals 65 years of age and over and disabled persons, accounted for 14.5% of health care coverage in 2010. *Source: US Census Bureau.*

- Since the Children's Health Insurance Program (CHIP) was created in 1997, the percentage of children ages 0-17 with health insurance has increased from 86% to 93%. *Source: National Center for Health Statistics: December 2011.*

- As a result of the provision in the ACA that allows them to remain on their parent's insurance plans until age 26, 2.5 million young adults have gained health insurance. *Source: National Center for Health Statistics: December 2011.*

The picture described above is of a health system that fails to provide affordable health care worthy of the nation's economic strength and world stature. It is interesting to examine if and how the situation started to improve after the first hesitant steps in the implementation of the ACA. That insurance coverage increased is already evident, as we will see later. What is important, however, is to see whether the ACA promises to work in the direction of a more affordable, effective, efficient, equitable, and sustainable health system. We will, therefore, follow the structure of Part A—analyzing each of the five main characteristics of health system looking for a "silver lining" in the debate which has clouded the ACA so far.

B-1: IS THE ACA A STEP FOR A SUCCESSFUL HEALTH SYSTEM?

In Europe, as in other countries, there has been a long debate about whether health care should be a public or a private responsibility. In most of the developed world, the issue was resolved decades ago, mostly after WWII, with the public sector assuming a major part of the burden. In some countries this took the form of national health insurance. The exact public-private mix was resolved either with mandatory private insurance, as in the Netherlands, or supplementary and complementary insurance in many other countries, like France and Germany. In fewer countries, with the UK and the Scandinavian countries foremost, the step was bolder by instituting national health systems. The State assumed the full burden of public financing as well as a large part of health-care delivery, with the private sector both in health insurance and in the delivery of care limited to a supplementary or complementary role.

In America, the question was only partly answered in 1965 with Medicare and Medicaid. It was timidly asked again ten years ago, again partially, concerning financing. The day when the ACA became law was the day when this question was partly answered. The Affordable Care Act, or Obamacare,[1] was signed into law on March 23, 2010. Some provisions went into effect by the end of that year and some over the following three years. By popular perception, the act "kicked in" on October 1, 2013, when enrollment for individual insurance plans via the federal and state exchanges opened nationwide. The *Los Angeles Times* celebrated the one-year anniversary of the ACA on Oct 2, 2014 [1], stating:

> *"For all intents and purposes, then, Wednesday was Obamcare's first birthday. How's it doing? The inescapable answer is: very well, thank you. This will disappoint the legions of politicians and pundits, chiefly Republicans and conservatives, who became heavily invested in the act's failure--so heavily that where they couldn't point to tangible evidence of failure, which was most of the time, they resorted to distortion, outright fabrication and obstructionist legal strategies. Yes, the federal enrollment website, HealthCare.Gov, was a botch at the beginning. It has since been fixed, and federal enrollments ended up outpacing even the original, pre-botch, expectations."*

The best description of the ACA, its conception, stated purposes, method and timeline for its implementation is perhaps in the *Yale Journal of Medicine and Law,* January 3, 2012 [2]. The opening paragraph describes the purpose of the ACA as:

> *". . . [The ACA] reforms private and public health insurance policies in an effort to broaden healthcare coverage in the United States. Together with the Health Care and Education Reconciliation Act of 2010, the law's major provisions include an expansion in health insurance options and Medicaid coverage, the creation of health insurance exchanges, and the implementation of an individual mandate that taxes groups that do not purchase health insurance."*

This is the logic and purpose behind the Affordable Care Act. Its passage, with the still scant

---

1 A term used in a derogatory way, mostly by its opponents.

evidence at hand, does not seem to have improved the situation in the rest of the health-care system by much. This was not, after all, its expressed intention, and the task at hand is, indeed, formidable. It will be enough of a revolution in health financing, for the "political taste" of America, if the ACA merely survives the 2016 presidential election. Unhappily for Americans, however, the job is much bigger than the ACA. It is the revamping of the whole health system, including the production and delivery of health care, to make it more efficient, effective, and equitable. Primarily, the system must become sustainable in the long run, since spending three trillion dollars in 2018 simply will not do. In other words, the ACA must be redefined to imply a "system affordable by the national economy," not just by individuals.

How difficult will this task be? In 2015 the Commonwealth Fund published its comparison of health systems in the US between 2007 and 2014. We quote [3]:

> "The mixed performance of states' health systems over the five years preceding implemen-
> tation of the Affordable Care Act's major reforms sends a clear message that states and the
> nation are still a long way from becoming places where everyone has access to high-qual-
> ity, affordable care and an equal opportunity for a long and healthy life. In tracking 42
> measures of health care access, quality, costs, and outcomes between 2007 and 2012 for
> the 50 states and the District of Columbia, The Commonwealth Fund's Scorecard on State
> Health System Performance, 2014, finds that, on a significant majority of measures, the
> story is mostly one of stagnation or decline. In most parts of the country, performance
> worsened on nearly as many measures as it improved."

It is rather early for an assessment, but there are indications that the Affordable Care Act is working, at least to some extent, in extending health insurance coverage [4]. In the next three chapters we will discuss the progress in terms of its early and probable future effects on the key aspects of a successful health system analyzed in Part A. According to John P. Geyman, an advocate of the single-payer system mentioned in the introduction, efficiency, effectiveness, equity, and sustainability should be the main goals, which, however, the ACA does yet not seem to achieve, or even address [5].

We believe that the ACA should pave the way for national health insurance, the cornerstone of a successful health system. Before we proceed, we should stress the main defect of the ACA, namely its dependence on private health insurance. We deal with this point in detail in Part D, but we should mention here as a negative sign that the stocks of insurance companies surged when the *King vs. Burwell* decision was handed down in 2015 [6]. Not only did the future of Obamacare seem certain then, but the future of the insurance industry did as well. This is also the reason why Obamacare, to some, seems to actually support large industrial concerns such as private health insurance [7]. Unfortunately, this is not good for the health of Americans or the US economy, as we will show in what follows. It is interesting, therefore, to examine the progress towards the stated goals of the ACA.

Data released at the end of February 2016 from the CDC's National Health Interview Survey show that since the Affordable Care Act was passed in 2010, the number of uninsured Ameri-cans fell by nearly 20 million from January–September 2015 [8]. While rates of both private and public health insurance coverage were on the rise, the percentage of people ages 18 to 65 with a private health plan had climbed to 70 percent, the highest level since 2005 [9]. The report also adds to the widening body of evidence that this new coverage is helping to protect Americans from health care costs. The percentage of people who reported that they *"had failed to obtain needed medical care because of cost"* in the last year dropped from 6.9% in 2010 to 4.6% in 2015, even below the 2004 figures. (Figure B1-1).

Figure B1-1. Decline in the Rate of People Reporting They Had Failed to Obtain Needed Medical Care Because of Cost in the Past Twelve Months, 2004-2015.

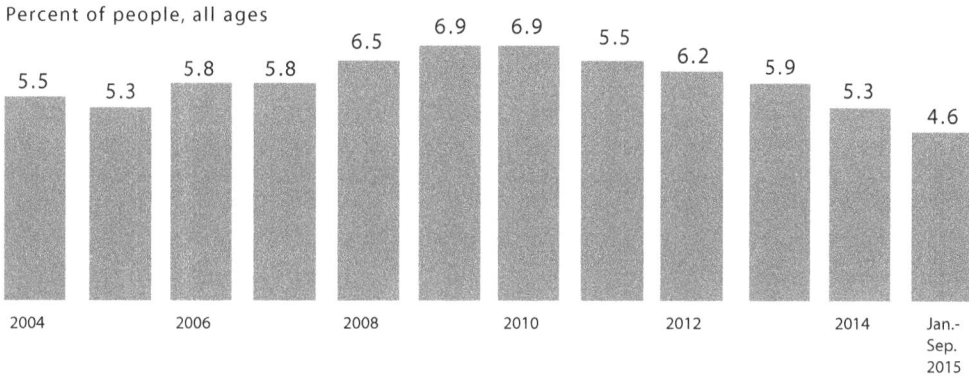

Percent of people, all ages

Year	Value
2004	5.5
	5.3
2006	5.8
	5.8
2008	6.5
	6.9
2010	6.9
	5.5
2012	6.2
	5.9
2014	5.3
Jan.-Sep. 2015	4.6

Note: Crude percent (95% confidence interval).
Source: CDC/NCHS, National Health Interview Survey, 2004-September 2015. Family Core Component.

Other recent federal and private surveys are showing similar trends. A December 9, 2015 Commonwealth Fund analysis of the Federal Behavioral Risk Factor Surveillance System (BRFSS) survey found that cost-related delays in getting needed care had fallen in 21 states between 2013 and 2014 [10]. Another, more recent (January 5, 2016), multiyear survey of low-income people in the South found larger declines in two states that had expanded their Medicaid programs, compared with one that had not, in the share of people who reported they had skipped a medication because of cost [11]. And the latest (January 15, 2015) Commonwealth Fund Biennial Health Insurance Survey found similar downward trends in reports of cost-related problems with getting needed care [12].

The new health insurance exchanges are the core of the Affordable Care Act's insurance reforms, but insurance markets beyond the exchanges also are affected by the reforms. In its June 2016 issue brief, the Commonwealth Fund compares the markets for individual coverage on and off of the exchanges, using insurers' most recent projections for ACA-compliant policies. In 2016, insurers expect that less than one-fifth of ACA-compliant coverage will be sold outside of the exchanges. Insurers who sell mostly through exchanges devote a greater portion of their premium dollars to medical care than do insurers selling only off the exchanges, because exchange insurers project lower administrative costs and lower profit margins. Premium increases on exchange plans are less than those for off-exchange plans, in large part because exchange enrollment is projected to shift to closed-network plans. Finally, initial concerns that insurers might seek to segregate higher-risk subscribers on the exchanges have not been realized [13].

The June 2015 Supreme Court decision on the legality of the ACA will probably prove the first step in the direction of National Health Insurance (NHI). By deciding that "*the intent of Congress was that any citizen of the United States, assuming they met the income criteria, should be eligible for health insurance subsidies,*" *King v. Burwell* brought NHI and the single- payer a lot closer. Much more needs to be done, however, before the answer is full and correct. The conclusion so far is that the ACA is achieving its primary goal to provide more Americans with needed private health insurance. Being a step towards a "better" health system does not seem to have been among the intents, much less the results, of the ACA so far. We will discuss this in the remainder of Part B, because we believe this should be the aim of the comprehensive health-care reform needed in America.

References

[1]   Hiltzik M. Obamacare at one year: A birthday assessment. *Los Angeles Times* [newspaper on the Internet]. 2nd October 2014 [cited: 7th June 2016]. Available from: http://www.latimes.com/business/hiltzik/la-fi-mh-obamacare-at-one-year-20141001-column.html

[2]   Yale Journal of Medicine & Law [webpage on the Internet]. New Haven: Yale University [cited: 7th June 2016]. Available from: http://www.yalemedlaw.com/the-affordable-care-act-and-the-great-recession/

[3]   Radley DC, Mccarthy D, Lippa JA, Hayes SL, Schoen C. Aiming higher. Results from a scorecard on state health system performance [monograph on the Internet]. Washington: The Commonwealth Fund 2014 [cited: 7th June 2016]. Available from: http://www.commonwealthfund.org/~/media/files/publications/fund-report/2014/apr/1743_radley_aiming_higher_2014_state_scorecard_corrected_62314.pdf

[4]   U.S. Department of Health & Human Services [webpage on the Internet]. The affordable care act is working. 24th June 2015 [cited: 7th June 2016]. Available from: http://www.hhs.gov/healthcare/facts-and-features/fact-sheets/aca-is-working/index.html#PAGE_2

[5]   Geyman J, Ed. *How Obamacare is unsustainable: Why we need a single-payer solution for all Americans.* Washington: Copernicus Healthcare 2015.

[6]   The Supreme Court of the United States [webpage on the Internet]. SUPREME COURT OF THE UNITED STATES Syllabus: KING ET AL. v. BURWELL, SECRETARY OF HEALTH AND HUMAN SERVICES, ET AL. USA: The Supreme Court; 2014 [cited: 17th June 2016]. Available from: https://www.supremecourt.gov/opinions/14pdf/14-114_qol1.pdf

[7]   Waitzkin H, Hellander I. The Neoliberal Model Comes Home to Roost in the United States—If We Let It. *Monthly Review* [publication on the Internet]. 1st May 2016 [cited: 7th June 2016]. Available from: http://monthlyreview.org/2016/05/01/obamacare/

[8]   U.S. Department of Health & Human Services [homepage on the Internet]. 20 million people have gained health insurance coverage because of the Affordable Care Act, new estimates show. Washington: U.S. Department of Health & Human Services; 2016 [cited: 17th June 2016]. Available from: http://www.hhs.gov/about/news/2016/03/03/20-million-people-have-gained-health-insurance-coverage-because-affordable-care-act-new-estimates

[9]   Collins SR, Blumenthal D. New federal survey shows gains in private health coverage and fewer cost-related problems getting care. The Commonwealth Fund [webpage on the Internet]. 24th February 2016 [cited: 7th June 2016]. Available from: http://www.commonwealthfund.org/publications/blog/2016/feb/new-federal-survey-shows-gains-in-private-health-coverage?omnicid=EALERT996743&mid

[10]   The Changing Landscape of Health Care Coverage and Access: Comparing States' Progress in the ACA's First Year. The Commonwealth Fund [webpage on the Internet]. c2015 [cited: 17th June 2016]. Available from: http://www.commonwealthfund.org/publications/issue-briefs/2015/dec/changing-landscape

[11]   Both the 'Private Option' and Traditional Medicaid Expansions Improved Access to Care for Low-Income Adults. The Commonwealth Fund [webpage on the Internet] c2015 [cited: 17th June 2016]. Available from: http://www.commonwealthfund.org/publications/in-the-literature/2016/jan/medicaid-expansions-improved-access-low-income

[12]   The Rise in Health Care Coverage and Affordability Since Health Reform Took Effect: Findings from the Commonwealth Fund Biennial Health Insurance Survey, 2014. The Commonwealth

Fund [webpage on the Internet]. 15th January 2015 [cited: 17th June 2016]. Available from: http://www.commonwealthfund.org/publications/issue-briefs/2015/jan/biennial-health-insurance-survey

[13]   McCue MJ, Hall MA. Promoting value for consumers: comparing individual health insurance markets inside and outside the ACA's exchanges [monograph on the Internet]. Washington: The Commonwealth Fund 2016 [cited: 7th June 2016]. Available from: http://www.commonwealthfund.org/~/media/files/publications/issue-brief/2016/jun/1876_mccue_aca_exchanges_promoting_value_indiv_market_rb_v2.pdf

B-2: NO PROGRESS TOWARDS THE 3 E's

After concluding that the ACA was modestly successful in increasing insurance coverage, we should look for any improvement in the American health system. Among the "three E's" discussed in Part A as the pillars of a successful health system, only the improvement in equity is a "given," due to improvement in the affordability of insurance coverage. On the contrary, we cannot find any improvement in efficiency and effectiveness among the achievements of the ACA. At the same time, the sustainability of the system is improving as the cost of health care continues to rise, but at a slower pace than predicted. As early as 2014, the Congressional Budget Office (CBO) predicted an increase in some of the largest programs, including a 15 percent increase in spending for Medicaid, partly because of the ACA. At the same time it predicted a significant drop in Medicare spending, a phenomenon observed consistently since 2010 [1].

Some of the recent reductions in Medicare spending are due to differences in estimates about the economy and demographics that affect the program, and some are due to cuts in health-care spending passed by Congress. The Affordable Care Act, in particular, made significant reductions to Medicare's spending on hospitals and private Medicare plans, to help subsidize insurance coverage for low- and middle-income Americans. The Budget Control Act, which Congress passed in 2011, also made some across-the-board cuts to Medicare spending. According to the CBO, "*The reduced estimates are an indication of what's happening in the overall health care system. Even as more people are getting access to health insurance, the costs of caring for individual patients is growing at a super-slow rate. That means that health care, which has eaten into salary gains for years and driven up debt and bankruptcies, may be starting to stabilize as a share of national spending*" [2]. The CBO estimates have been wrong before. The fact of the matter remains that the three-trillion-dollar health expenditure, 20% of GDP, in the next decade can still be seen on the radar. We will see why in the paragraphs that follow.

Finally, before we proceed with the examination of the effect of the ACA on the three E's, we should mention that at least one beneficial effect has been noted in the increase of the number of people voluntarily in part-time employment, especially of those in the age-bracket of 16-35.[1] These are the people most likely with very young children and/or elderly parents who need special care. Even if health care production under the ACA did not gain in efficiency or effectiveness, as we will see below, health insurance through the ACA, as a social equalizer, certainly did. The fact that health insurance became available to this group through the government subsidy allowed them to reduce their working hours without loss of coverage. This amounts to a net gain for social welfare which must not be overlooked.

Efficiency Gains: No Cause for Celebration

Since the passage of the ACA in 2010, there seem to be some efficiency gains, at least in Medicare. According to the CBO, many of the recent reductions in Medicare payments come from changes in behavior among doctors, nurses, hospitals, and patients. Medicare

---

1 According to the Bureau of Labor and Statistics data.

beneficiaries are using fewer high-cost health-care services than in the past—taking fewer brand-name drugs, for example, or spending less time in the hospital. The CBO's economists call these changes "technical changes," and they seem to dominate the downward revisions since 2010, after the passage of the first legislation on the ACA. Medicare, however, is not even half the story in health expenditure. The ACA, as we already mentioned, was a boon to the private health insurance industry. There is really no reason to expect the American health system to become more efficient simply because more people will be covered by insurance. In fact, *ceteris paribus*, we should expect even higher health expenditure, something already shown in the figures given by the Medicare and Medicaid Actuary Office. It is a well established fact that sooner rather than later, certainly by 2020, we will be looking at 20% of GDP for health care. The new president will have to give a different and much more difficult political battle—against the drug and insurance industries and the medical profession. If Obama thought he had a rough journey in health, Hillary Clinton will probably envy him.

Effectiveness: Only Time Will Tell

In an effective health system, relevant indices such as morbidity, mortality, life expectancy, absenteeism due to illness, medical outcomes, safety, and many others show improvement over time. A system is cost-effective when such improvements are achieved at small or no increase of total cost to society. The American health system is, historically, an underachiever on both fronts. Looking at the data, this is an understatement. Nothing is more effective in health than the prevention of epidemics. Perhaps the least understood failure is in the areas of public health and the prevention of disease. America's National Academy of Medicine suggests that just $4.5 billion a year devoted to preparing for pandemics would make the world a lot safer [3]. Although America is not "the world," it is close to it when it comes to developing drugs and vaccines. After all, a pandemic is exactly what the term implies, a threat for everybody in the world.

The fact that almost 20 million people obtained health insurance between 2010 and 2015 implies improved access to all health services, including preventive ones. This, in turn, makes the health system not only more effective in dealing with disease, but also with preventing it [4]. It is still early to tell whether and when this will appear in the health statistics. However, even for people who gained insurance under the ACA and the tens of millions who already had coverage, substantial barriers to timely access to affordable medical care remain. Two features of exchange-based coverage—high cost sharing and narrow provider networks—can limit access and are increasingly common in employer-sponsored plans as well. The average deductible in 2015 was just under $3,000 for silver-level exchange plans and $5,200 for bronze-level plans. Deductibles reduce costs to insurers by discouraging the use of low-value care, but they may also drive patients to skimp on necessary care. Responsible insurance designs could reduce financial barriers for high-value care while maintaining cost sharing for remaining services. Fortunately, the ACA takes a step in this direction by requiring evidence-based preventive services to be covered without cost sharing. Sensible plan design would similarly encourage ongoing management for chronic conditions such as diabetes, heart disease, and hypertension, without patients first having to exhaust several thousand dollars in out-of-pocket spending. This is a task the private insurance industry should face up to as long as it remains the main "player" in health insurance.

Narrow provider networks are another area that demand a nuanced policy. This phenomenon of limited access to providers derives from competition among plans to keep premiums down. Though patients generally dislike restrictions on where they can obtain care, narrow networks could conceivably reduce spending without harming quality. This approach can be taken too far, however, and reports that some plans are entirely excluding certain specialties from their networks indicate that greater oversight is needed [5]. Similar concerns exist in Medicaid, in which the costs of higher provider reimbursements must be weighed against enhanced access for beneficiaries.

Equity: Modest Improvement in Insurance Coverage and Access to Care

In Chapter A-4 we defined equity as the equal opportunity of access to health services. In that sense, the increase in the number of people covered by some sort of health insurance is a step in the right direction. In 2010, when the ACA became the law of the land, the Census Report stated that the number of Americans without health insurance increased by 900,000 from 49.9 million in the previous year. The number of uninsured as a percentage of the population remained the same, at 16.3%. Those covered by employer-based health insurance continued to decline in 2010 to about 55%, down from 65% in 2000. Government-provided coverage (Medicare, Medicaid, and armed forces) continued to rise slightly to 31%.

In 2009, when the debate about the ACA was heating up, the question was whether coverage for low-income people should be through Medicaid expansion or subsidies to purchase insurance through an exchange. At the time, pundits estimated insurance through Medicaid expansion to be 26-30% less costly in terms of total medical expenditures than covering the uninsured through private health insurance [6]. Equally important, Medicaid was considered more affordable from a low-income consumer's perspective. The amount that each newly insured adult would have to pay out-of-pocket for copayments or deductibles would average seven times as high with private insurance.[2] Medicaid and the Children's Health Insurance Program (CHIP) were similarly more affordable for children. In principle, it was thought that health insurance exchanges might try to limit out-of-pocket expenses by capping cost sharing for low-income members to some percentage of income, but, as various researchers conclude, experience indicates that "such caps are almost impossible to administer and confuse both patients and providers." On top of this, the administrative cost of Medicaid was estimated "at about half those of typical private insurance" [7].

The initial goal of the ACA was to extend health insurance coverage to 32 million of the more than 50 million uninsured, half of them through Medicaid expansion, by 2019. According to the September 2015 Census survey, in 2014—the first full year of coverage expansion—the uninsured rate fell to 10.4 percent, or 33 million people, from about 41.8 million people the previous year [8]. As of September 2014, about 7.3 million more Americans were enrolled in private coverage through the Affordable Care Act marketplaces and more than 80 percent qualified for federal subsidies to help with the cost of their monthly premiums [9]. In March 2015, the Obama administration said that the ACA had extended coverage to 16.4 million people who had been previously uninsured, including 2.3 million young adults who were able to remain on their parent's insurance until age 26. At the end of March, about 10.2 million people were covered under individual private health plans; another 12.2 million people gained health insurance through Medicaid and its related children's program [10].

---

2 Estimated at $771 per year with private insurance in 2005, compared with $109 under Medicaid.

By 2015, the scientific literature on Obamacare was proliferating [11]. The main conclusion was that health reform is still unfinished, with barriers to coverage and access remaining to a considerable extent. The reasons are lack of adequate information on the benefits of the ACA, the "Medicaid Gap,"[3] and political impediments in mostly Republican-led states [12]. Finally, many people are still on the hook for deductibles that can top $5,000 for individuals and $10,000 for families. According to insurers, this is the trade-off for keeping premiums for the marketplace plans relatively low. The result is that some people reported in 2014 that they hesitated to use their new insurance because of the high out-of-pocket costs [13]. It is this part of the population that still needs to be taken care of for the ACA to be a success in promoting equity in the system.

Is, then, the ACA a Step in the Right Direction?

This is what I would describe as *a modest success,* or *good for starters,* but hardly a breakthrough in the search for a better health system. The reduction in the number of people who go without medical care is only one, albeit major, criterion by which we can judge the contribution of the ACA to the goal of an affordable, efficient, effective, and sustainable health system. Until the people themselves realize that health insurance and access to health care is a universal right and not a privilege for those who can afford it, those who profit from the health market or entertain their political and ideological prejudices will continue to make America "a failed state" when it comes to health care. The continuing rise in the cost of health care is still a fight between the common good and market forces [11]. The main obstacle in this fight is political, as the lack of competition in the health market, which fosters inefficiency, is the product of political "arrangements." The issues of efficiency and cost are important enough to warrant further examination in the next chapter.

References

[1]   Congressional Budget Office Panel of Economic Advisers. An update to the budget and economic outlook: 2014 to 2024. Washington: Congressional Budget Office 2014 [cited: 7th June 2016]. Available from: http://cbo.gov/sites/default/files/cbofiles/attachments/45653-OutlookUpdate_2014_Aug.pdf?version=meter+at+1&module=meter-Links&pgtype=article&contentId=&mediaId=&referrer=&priority=true&action=click&contentCollection=meter-links-click

[2]   Sanger-Katz M, Quealy K. Medicare: Not such a budget-buster anymore. *The New York Times* [newspaper on the Internet]. 27th August 2014 [cited: 7th June 2016]. Available from: http://www.nytimes.com/2014/08/28/upshot/medicare-not-such-a-budget-buster-anymore.html?action=click&contentCollection=The%20Upshot&region=Footer&module=WhatsNext&version=WhatsNext&contentID=WhatsNext&moduleDetail=undefined&pgtype=Multimedia&_r=1

[3]   *The Economist* [publication on the Internet]. An ounce of prevention. 19th March 2016 [cited: 7th June 2016]. Available from: http://www.economist.com/news/leaders/21695036-crises-infectious-diseases-are-becoming-more-common-world-should-be-better-prepared

[4]   Sommers BD, Gunja MZ, Finegold K, Musco T. Changes in self-reported insurance coverage, access to care, and health under the Affordable Care Act. *Journal of the American Medical Association*

3   It is in Republican-led states that 3-4 million people are caught up in a partisan tug-of-war—those who are too poor to qualify for "exchange subsidies" but also too rich for states' Medicaid eligibility. This is the apotheosis of partisan shenanigans "on the backs" of citizens.

(*JAMA*) 2015; 314(4):366-74.

[5]   Dorner SC, Jacobs DB, Sommers BD. Adequacy of outpatient specialty care access in marketplace plans under the Affordable Care Act. *JAMA* 2015; 314(16):1749-50.

[6]   Ku L. Expanding coverage for low-income Americans: Medicaid or health insurance exchanges? *Health Affairs* Blog [magazine on the Internet]. 23rd June 2009 [cited: 7th June 2016]. Available from: http://healthaffairs.org/blog/2009/06/23/expanding-coverage-for-low-income-americans-medicaid-of-health-insurance-exchanges/

[7]   Ku L, Broaddus M. Public and private health insurance: Stacking up the costs. *Health Affairs* 2008; 27(4):w318-27.

[8]   Smith J, Medalia C, Eds. Health insurance coverage in the United States: 2014 [monograph on the Internet]. Washington: U.S. Government Printing Office 2015 [cited: 7th June 2016]. Available from: http://www.census.gov/content/dam/Census/library/publications/2015/demo/p60-253.pdf

[9]   Pear R. Health care act still covers 7.3 Million. *The New York Times* [newspaper on the Internet]. 18th September 2014 [cited: 7th June 2016]. Available from: http://www.nytimes.com/2014/09/19/us/over-seven-million-still-have-coverage-under-health-act.html?_r=0

[10]   Mittelman M. Obamacare helped pull uninsured rate down to 10.4% in 2014. Bloomberg [homepage on the Internet]. 16th September 2015 [cited: 7th June 2016]. Available from: http://www.bloomberg.com/news/articles/2015-09-16/obamacare-helped-pull-u-s-uninsured-rate-down-to-10-3-in-2014

[11]   Geyman JP. A Five-Year assessment of the affordable care act: Market forces still trump the common good in U.S. health care. *International Journal of Health Services* 2015; 45(2):209-25.

[12]   Sommers BD. Health care reform's unfinished work — remaining barriers to coverage and access. *New England Journal of Medicine* 2015; 373(25):2395-7.

[13]   Goodnough A, Pear R. Unable to meet the deductible or the doctor. *The New York Times* [newspaper on the Internet]. 17th October 2014 [cited: 7th June 2016]. Available from: http://www.nytimes.com/2014/10/18/us/unable-to-meet-the-deductible-or-the-doctor.html?emc=edit_th_20141018&nl=todaysheadlines&nlid=12129446&_r=2

B-3: HEALTH COST CONTAINMENT? NOT VERY LIKELY

With total health expenditure almost double what other developed countries spend, the cost of care can hardly be a matter of indifference to Americans. Assuming the architects of the ACA were also concerned, the way they went about achieving lower costs of care was naïve, to say the least. It was, supposedly, based on competition among insurers in a market-based system. Worse, the hopes were on competition in the new "health insurance exchanges" to contain costs for patients. This is like "putting the wolf to guard the sheep."[4] Health care in America is perhaps the industry least suitable to competition. It is a largely for-profit, relatively deregulated market, with little transparency of prices and perverse incentives among providers to maximize revenue. Studies show that health providers have enough market power to set their own prices and dictate the terms of their arrangements with insurers, and that there is insufficient competition among local health care systems [1].

For a possible early impact of Obamacare on total health expenditure, we have the OECD figures for health-care expenditure, as a percent of GDP, before and after the passage of the ACA (Figure B3-1). Although considerably higher throughout the whole period, health expenditure rose much faster after 2000, throughout the Bush years. Between 2010 and 2013, total health expenditure as a percent of GDP in the US remained the same. The figures for 2013, the last available for OECD countries at the time of writing, show stabilization in the share of GDP going to health care, compared to what happened in the 2000-2010 period.

Figure B3-1. Health Expenditure as a Percent of GDP—OECD, US, EU, 1990-2013.

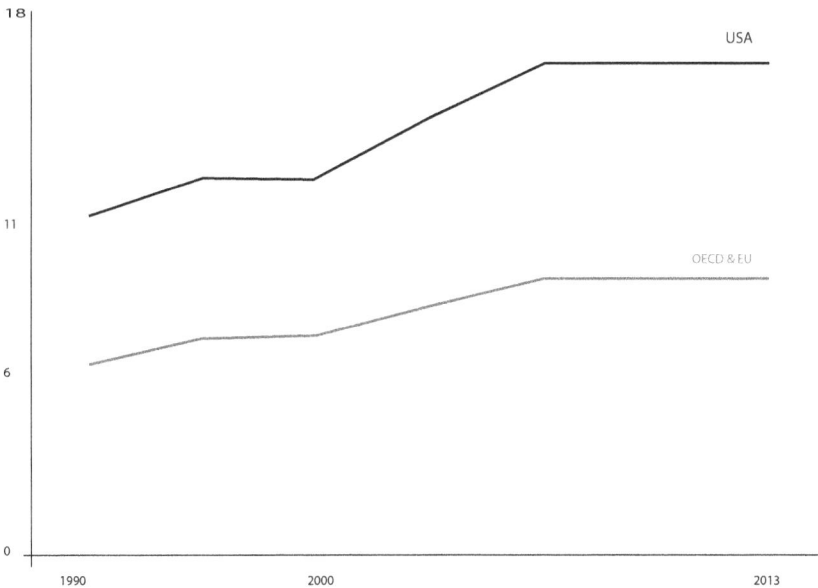

Source: OECD Health Data, 1990-2013.

---

4   A popular expression in Greece.

The main purpose of the ACA was to increase the number of Americans who could afford health insurance. However, whether a family can afford health care is one thing and whether the nation can afford to spend a fifth of its total income on health care alone is another, completely different, story. The most reliable data on the projected fiscal effects of the ACA are the series on total health expenditure each year and a decade later (for example, 2013 and 2023, 2014 and 2024, etc.) published by the Office of the Actuary, Centers for Medicare and Medicaid Services, titled "National Health Expenditure Projections." An examination of the numbers after the passage of the ACA shows that it may have steadied national health expenditure (NHE) until 2014, but it will not do so in the future. The situation until 2023, for example, will bring total NHE just shy of one fifth of GDP, as shown in Figure B3-2.

Figure B3-2. Projected Growth of National Health Expenditure as a Percent of GDP.

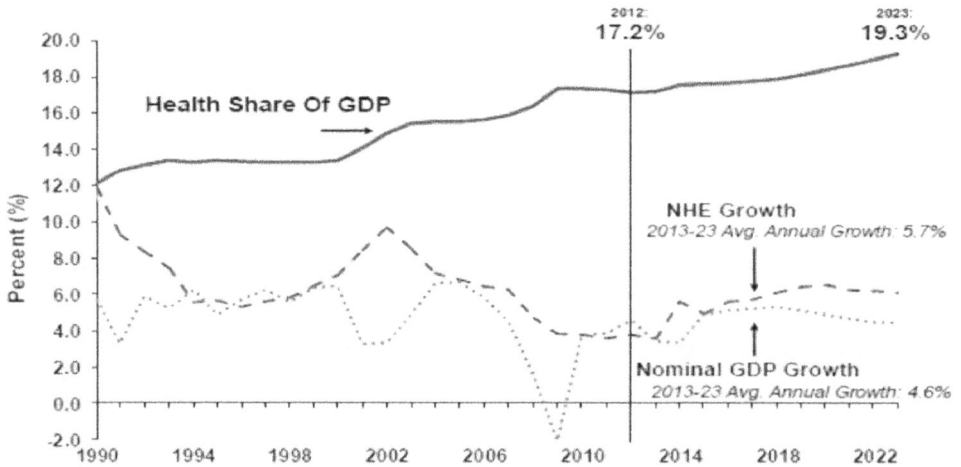

Source: Adopted from the Centers for Medicare and Medicaid Services (CMS) Office of the Actuary, Various Years.

The picture on total health expenditure after the ACA will not be without repercussions for public and private health expenditure. There are already indications that the effect of the ACA will not be total cost containment in the longer run, despite the expressed interest in the law. Health spending is projected to grow 1.1 percent faster than the Gross Domestic Product (GDP) per year over this period. As a result, the health share of GDP is expected to rise from 17.4% in 2013 to 19.6% by 2024 [2]. The main cost drivers are expected to be the net costs of health insurance and government administrative costs [2]. Given the characteristics of the US medical "market," one might actually expect this.

Affordability and the ACA's Potential Impact on Cost

The average American family of four in 2013 spent a big share of its income (20.7%) on health care, second only to what it spent on child care (25.4%) and more than for housing (18.7%) [3]. As the prices of the various health care components continue to increase, the cost of health insurance, inadvertently, increases as well. It is not surprising, therefore, that an Associated Press poll in 2014 found that 25% of insured Americans feel insecure about their ability to pay regardless of whether their insurance is employer-provided or through the insurance exchange [4]. The issue, therefore, in this chapter, and throughout this book, is more the cost of health care itself, rather than the way health insurance is paid for.

Initially, the conventional wisdom was that the ACA by itself might very well exert an upwards influence on the total cost of health care. Findings in the beginning of 2014 suggested that people signing up for personal health insurance through the ACA tend to be older and potentially less healthy [5]. There were fears that this demographic shift may weaken the law's economic underpinnings and cause premiums to rise in the future. Here we must remind the reader that the cost of administration involved in personal health insurance is anything but negligible. The evidence is that Medicare operates with 3% overhead, non-profit insurance with 16% overhead, and private (for-profit) insurance with 26% overhead [6]. Trying to fix the "insurance gap" through private insurance, therefore, is not the most efficient way. Besides, if enlargement of the pool of insured people is needed, the largest pool, which is easily available and requires no advertising or other "gimmicks" for signing up customers, is the total population of the country. Neither the NHS in Britain nor the Canadian health system needs to spend a single pound or Canadian dollar to entice Britons or Canadians to sign up to national health insurance in Britain or Canada. Their birth certificate is more than enough.

The initial surge of older and sicker people seeking health insurance to take advantage of the lower actual cost should have been expected. Also, the fact that the law finally removed obstacles to insurance because of the enrollee's medical history or pre-existing conditions were a strong incentive for a surge of previously "unprofitable" customers. As a result, the White House and health policy experts insisted that insurers should try to sign up younger people to balance the risks. At that time, the 18-34 age group accounted for only 24%. There are indications that the proportion of younger people with personal health insurance has increased. But, there are also indications that average insurance premiums for sought-after 23-year-olds rose most dramatically, with men in that age group seeing an average 78.2% price increase before factoring in government subsidies, and women experiencing a rise of 44.9% in their premiums [7]. This is definitely no proof that competition works in the private insurance market, despite the often-cited claims.

What Do the Data Tell Us?

The concern of the US government should not, after all, have been whether the premiums charged by personal health insurance would rise. Instead, it should concentrate on the actual cost of producing the necessary health services. The government should be concerned with the real problem in the American health system, namely its huge cost and its impact on other national priorities, instead of being complacent with the success of the ACA—which, in any case, is only an attempt to increase insurance coverage. In order to give the reader a good perspective on the officially expected effects on the cost structure and the potential economic impact of the ACA on health-care costs, there is nothing better than to look at the data from the CMS, Office of the Actuary for the 2014-2024 period in greater detail.[5]

For 2014-24, health spending is projected to grow at an average rate of 5.8 percent per year (4.9 percent on a per capita basis). Health spending is projected to grow 1.1 percent faster than

---

5   CMS. National Health Expenditure Projections 2014-2024 Forecast Summary Major Findings for National Health Expenditures: 2014-2024. This was the latest report at the time of writing. We copy in full (text is italicized).

the Gross Domestic Product (GDP) per year over this period. As a result, the health share of GDP is expected to rise from 17.4 percent in 2013 to 19.6 percent by 2024. Given the ACA's coverage expansions and premium subsidies together with population aging, federal, state, and local governments are projected to finance 47 percent of national health spending by 2024 (from 43 percent in 2013). Although projected health spending growth is faster than in the recent past due to the combined effects of the ACA's major coverage expansions, stronger expected economic growth, and population aging, it is still slower than the growth experienced over the last three decades prior to the recent recession.

After six years of growth below 5 percent, national health spending is projected to have grown 5.5 percent in 2014. Faster health spending is due mainly to ACA health insurance coverage expansions and rapid growth in prescription drug spending. Factors moderating health spending include the effects of continued increases in cost sharing requirements in private health insurance plans and near historic low rates of medical inflation. The insured rate is projected to have increased to 89 percent in 2014 (from 86 percent in 2013) as 8.4 million are projected to have gained coverage. After 2014, national health spending is projected to grow 5.3 percent in 2015 and peak at 6.3 percent in 2020. Over this time, medical inflation rates are anticipated to return to levels closer to the decade prior to the recession. Medicare spending growth is expected to accelerate after 2015 due to expected increases in use of medical goods and services by aging beneficiaries and continued baby-boomer enrollment. Finally, expected improvements in the economy contribute to faster projected growth in private health insurance spending, particularly after 2018.

Major Findings by Payer

Medicare

Medicare spending is projected to have grown by 5.3 percent in 2014, to $616.8 billion, partially due to increased prescription drug spending from recently available hepatitis C treatments. Medicare spending is projected to decelerate in 2015 to 4.7 percent from increased rebates for pharmaceutical drugs and reductions in physician incentive payments. For 2016 through 2024, projected Medicare spending growth is expected to rebound to 7.3 percent per year due to increased enrollment by the baby boomers, greater utilization of care, and higher payment rates driven by improved economic conditions, which increase growth in the cost of input goods and services used to treat Medicare patients. These drivers of growth will be partially offset by slow growth in payment updates due to provisions in the Affordable Care Act.

Medicaid

Total Medicaid spending is projected to have grown 12.0 percent in 2014 due to increased enrollment of 7.6 million beneficiaries. Primarily driving the increase in enrollment are states that chose to expand coverage to adults up to 138 percent of the federal poverty level. The newly insured for Medicaid are expected to have required less medical care than the currently insured, thereby decreasing per beneficiary Medicaid spending from 3.8 percent in 2013 to a projected -0.8 percent in 2014. For 2015 to 2024, Medicaid spending growth is projected to be 5.9 percent per year on average, reflecting more gradual growth in enrollment as well as increased spending per beneficiary due to aging of the population.

Private Health Insurance (PHI)

PHI premiums are projected to have grown 6.1 percent and to have reached $1.0 trillion in 2014 due to higher projected per enrollee spending and increased enrollment through Marketplace plans. PHI spending growth is expected to remain somewhat elevated at 6.4 percent in 2015, primarily due to additional enrollment in health insurance plans.

For 2016 through 2024, PHI spending growth is projected to moderate to 5.4 percent per year due to the proliferation of employers providing high deductible health plans as their only insurance option, narrow network designs for health plans, and the excise tax on high-cost employer-based insurance plans starting in 2018.

Out-of-Pocket (OOP)

OOP spending is projected to have decelerated due to the Affordable Care Act's coverage expansions to 1.3 percent in 2014 ($343.8 billion). While OOP spending growth is projected to accelerate after 2014, reaching a peak of 5.7 percent in 2021, the out-of-pocket share of health spending is projected to fall from 11.6 percent in 2013 to 10.0 percent by 2024.

Major Findings by Sector

Hospital

Total hospital spending grew by 4.4 percent in 2014 (to $978.3 billion), which is similar to the 2013 growth rate of 4.3 percent. Increased enrollment from the ACA coverage expansions is projected to have differentially impacted spending among payers including decreasing out-of-pocket hospital spending by 7.2 percent, but increasing Medicaid hospital spending and private health insurance hospital spending by 8.9 percent and 6.3 percent, respectively, in 2014. In 2015, hospital spending is projected to increase 5.4 percent due primarily to the continued effects of the ACA insurance expansions. For 2016 through 2024, continued population aging and the impacts of improved economic conditions are expected to result in projected average annual growth of 6.1 percent.

Physician and Clinical Services

Growth in spending on physician and clinical services is projected to have accelerated in 2014 to 4.8 percent ($615.0 billion), after growth of 3.8 percent in 2013. Despite the effects of the coverage expansions, growth in physician and clinical services spending, in particular, is expected to have been restrained by the proliferation of high-deductible health plans. Growth in prices for physician and clinical services is expected to remain near historically low rates through the early part of the projection. Several factors contribute to modest expectations of price growth for these services, including increases in cost sharing in private health insurance plans which are expected to ease demand pressure on price and cost growth, PHI plans, slower growth in Medicaid payments due to the expirations of the temporary increase to primary care providers in 2015, and Medicare physician payment updates legislated to remain under 1.0 percent per year through 2019.

Prescription Drugs

Prescription drug spending is projected to have grown 12.6 percent in 2014 to $305.1 billion. Driving growth were new specialty drugs designed to treat conditions such as hepatitis C coupled with increased prescription drug use among people who were newly insured and those who moved to more generous insurance plans as a result of the premium and cost-sharing subsidies offered by the Affordable Care Act. Prescription drug spending growth is projected to average 6.3 percent annual growth from 2015 through 2024 due to improving economic conditions, changes in benefit management designed to encourage better drug adherence for people with chronic health conditions, and anticipated changing clinical guidelines designed to encourage drug therapies at earlier stages of treatment.

Major Findings by Sponsor

Health care spending sponsored (or financed) by federal, state, and local governments is projected to have grown 8.1 percent to nearly $1.4 trillion in 2014. Reflecting growth trends in PHI and OOP spending, outlays by businesses, households, and other private sources are projected to have risen by 3.5 percent in 2014, and to have reached $1.7 trillion. The government-sponsored share of health spending is projected to increase and account for 47 percent of national health expenditures by 2024, largely driven by Medicaid coverage expansions, marketplace plan premium cost-sharing subsidies, and increased use and intensity in medical services for the Medicare program as the baby boomers begin to require more care.

The conclusion from the analysis of the data and the projections of the CMS 2014-2024 for the cost of health care in America and the future burden is not encouraging. The 20% of GDP total health expenditure milestone seems to be very near, and the whole country should actually already be "up-in-arms" to face it. The complacency with which all interested parties—the government, the industry, and the public—seem to approach health care costs in America is astounding. I believe that this is a good reason to ask what this means for the actual sustainability of the health system itself, the subject of the next chapter.

References

[14]   Nichols LM, Ginsburg PB, Berenson RA, Christianson J, Hurley RE. Are market forces strong enough to deliver efficient health care systems? Confidence is waning. *Health Affairs* 2004; 23(2):8-21.

[15]   Cuckler GA, Sisko AM, Keehan SP, et al. National health expenditure projections, 2012-22: Slow growth until coverage expands and economy improves. *Health Affairs* 2013; 32(10):1820-31.

[16]   Gould E, Cooke T, Kimball W. *What families need to get by. EPI's 2015 family budget calculator* [monograph on the Internet]. Washington: Economic Policy Institute 2015 [cited: 7th June 2016]. Available from: http://www.epi.org/files/2015/epi-family-budget-calculator-2015.pdf

[17]   Alonso-Zaldivar R, Junius D. *AP-GfK Poll: Obama's health care fails to gain support; Americans expect fixes, not repeal.* **The Associated Press [webpage on the Internet].** 28th March 2016 [cited 7th June 2016]. Available from: http://ap-gfkpoll.com/featured/our-lastest-story

[18]   Shear MD, Pear R. Older pool of health care enrollees stirs fears on costs. *The New York Times* [newspaper on the Internet]. 13th January 2014 [cited: 7th June 2016]. Available from: http://www.nytimes.com/2014/01/14/us/health-care-plans-attracting-more-older-less-healthy-people.html?_r=1&mtrref=undefined&gwh=AA036A559CC13AE278E9918442221A29&gwt=pay

[19]   HealthPAC Online [webpage on the Internet]. Health Care Statistics in the United States: Health Insurance. c2001-2016 [cited: 7th June 2016]. Available from: http://www.healthpaconline.net/health-care-statistics-in-the-united-states.htm

[20]   Richardson V. Obamacare premiums soar as much as 78% to help cover 'essential health benefits'. *Washington Times* [newspaper on the Internet]. 28th October 2014 [cited: 7th June 2016]. Available from: http://www.washingtontimes.com/news/2014/oct/28/obamacare-sends-health-premiums-skyrocketing-by-as/

B-4: HEALTH SYSTEM SUSTAINABILITY

LITTLE PROGRESS

As we mentioned in Chapter A-5, health system sustainability is the economic architecture that guarantees that a health system will secure long-run financing and achieve its goals in the foreseeable future. By these standards, and before the ACA, the American health system was not considered sustainable, mostly because it was too expensive and unaffordable to many. It is expensive not because it offers more services than in other countries, but because some factors of production are overpaid, because of induced demand for expensive services, and because the health system is functioning in an unregulated for-profit market. If anything, the ACA by itself, by increasing the purchasing power of those previously without insurance, will eventually increase the total cost of health care in America, and therefore make it less sustainable.

However, it is important to point out here that, looked at together with tax reform and the source of financing health care, the ACA may eventually prove to be a step towards improving system sustainability. For example, the fact that in 2013 President Obama took away the G. W. Bush Tax Relief to the top 1% income bracket, increasing their tax payments by 4%, and, especially, the increase in the tax paid by the top 0.1% of taxpayers by 6.5% made the health system not only more equitable but also more sustainable. Despite partisan claims to the contrary, Obamacare effectively did not cost a penny to 99% of American taxpayers. In fact, making the tax system fairer to all leaves significant margin for the expansion of the ACA, perhaps all the way to universal health coverage (UHC) and national health insurance (NHI). In other words, the effect of the ACA on sustainability will be the result of two by-products of the ACA working in opposite directions. Before we can conclude the possible or probable effect, it is useful to agree on the known cost of the ACA, and then estimate possible counterbalancing developments included in the provisions of the law.

What Will Obamacare Actually Cost?

The cost of Obamacare in 2015 was estimated by the government to be $1.207 trillion dollars by 2025 [1]. This includes the cost of Obamacare's major insurance-related provisions, but does not take into account all of the cost curbing measures in the law [2]. Due to insurance related provisions, six **in ten Americans can get covered for $100 or less on the Health Insurance Marketplace**, with the average plan costing just $82 after Premium Tax Credits in 2014. In more detail, the facts on the net cost of the ACA are as follows [3]:

- As of March 2015, the net cost of ObamaCare is projected to be $1.207 trillion over the 2016–2025 period. This is down from $1.35 trillion estimated in January 2015, which itself represented a 7% reduction from April 2014.

- The net cost includes coverage provisions like: Marketplace subsidies, the expansion of Medicaid and CHIP, and employer tax credits.

- The net cost also includes revenue provisions like: penalty payments, the excise tax, and other taxes.

- The net cost, however, does not include other reforms, which continue to contribute to a downward trend in healthcare costs, including many Medicare related reforms. Medicare spending is calculated separately in the budget projections, but Medicare reform comprises a bulk of the Affordable Care Act itself.

- In 2015, due in part to the ACA, health-care spending grew at the slowest rate on record (since 1960). Meanwhile, health-care price inflation is at its lowest rate in 50 years.

From the information above, one may conclude that the ACA itself will not have a substantial effect on health-care costs. This does not mean, however, that the other forces at work will not keep pushing costs towards the 20% of GDP estimate of the CMS Office of the Actuary.

Health System Financing

The new discoveries in medicine and medical technology have brought new realities in health care. The fact that people live so much longer means that they need more money for health care at a later age [4]. Older people have property and savings and pay taxes, but they don't pay employment contributions. This means that as the percentage of older people in the population gets larger, it makes sense to rely on tax proceeds from all sources rather than on employment contributions. This is a point we have also raised elsewhere, but it is worth saying more about its theoretical underpinnings.

Whenever Ben Bernanke was asked to comment on the reasons for the slower response to the crisis in Europe, he always blamed the lack of sufficient funding of an expansionary policy. It is in fact true that the quantitative easing by the European Central Bank came more than two years after Ben Bernanke essentially "saved" the US economy. However, as an article in Reuters pointed out, the reason for the persistent unemployment in Europe may lie more in rigidities in the labor market and especially in the high taxation of labor in the form of contributions to social security systems in Europe [5]. It is perhaps one of the most important, although indirect, indictments of social insurance in countries where it is financed mainly by labor contributions.[1]

What Ben Bernanke didn't mention, perhaps because bankers do not "stoop" to low and "mundane" issues, is that the US is not doing much better than Europe in terms of health-care financing. He undoubtedly knows that among the central issues concerning the health of the economy is the competitiveness of American industry. The next thing to take into account, then, would be the central issue concerning the sustainability of the health system, in terms of the competitiveness of the economy. The extremely high cost of health care covered by private insurance—the cost of which is borne to a large extent by both employers and employees—certainly does not favor competitiveness, especially in manufacturing.

Warren Buffett, on the other hand, who is much more knowledgeable on the nitty-gritty of business, went so far as to call the US health system "the tapeworm, essentially, of the American economy" [6]. I am sure he is one of the first who should look at tax-financed health insurance as a "gift" to American industry and the economy in general. The main key for this should be the potential of substantial gains in productivity when employer-based insurance is substituted by government financing [7]. As we see in Table D1-1 in Chapter D-1, employer-provided health insurance in the US in 2015 amounted to 7.7% of total labor costs to industry. It is probably

---

1 We remind the reader that by "labor contributions" we mean by both employers and employees.

because of this that the CMS Office of the Actuary projects that health insurance spending by businesses will decrease from 21% of total health expenditure in 2012 to 19% in 2023. This is a true gain in the sustainability of the health system due to the ACA.

Neither Ben Bernanke nor Warren Buffett, however, had the intellectual or moral courage to hit the nail on the head. Nor did they bother to look for a cure for the American economy in a sector responsible for 20% of the national GDP. As we will see in Chapter C-2, simply infusing some good-old competition in the health market, along with reasonable ethical concern for real tax progressivity would work miracles for the economy as well. Simply revamping the patent protection regime in the drug industry, for example, would lower national drug expenditure, and of course federal government expenditure by $3.4 trillion in the period 2011-2020. At the same time, eliminating the Bush tax cut for the super wealthy, mentioned above, will have cost only $680 billion in the same period [8].

Health System Costs Revealed

Before the ACA Reform, there was the phenomenon called "uncompensated care," meaning that physician and hospital services were often not compensated due to the financial inability of the patient. A recent article estimated that there was a *"marked increase in Medicaid encounters, and a small decrease in private payer encounters. For example, there was an increase in payment per physician encounter in the outpatient setting. This means that ACA increased provider incomes for care they otherwise produced but not reimbursed for. The conclusion, scanty as it is so far, points not to a decrease of the cost of care in the US, but to an increase in public expenditure. Between 2013 and 2014, uncompensated hospital care was estimated to have dropped by $7.4 billion. A majority, or $5 billion, of this decrease in uncompensated care was realized by hospitals in the 28 states which extended Medicaid under the ACA"* [9].

This increase in compensated care is obviously an increase in total recorded health expenditure, but not an increase in the actual health system cost. Uncompensated care, before the ACA, was a real cost for the hospitals which produced it but was not "counted" in health expenditure. It represented either lost revenue or losses which are not recorded in National Health Accounts. It is anybody's guess, but I suspect that this hidden cost somehow showed up in inflated prices and, eventually, in higher insurance costs and premiums. This cost, however, was compensated for in 2014, as patients obtained insurance through the ACA. The hidden costs to the private sector were thus "revealed" as public cost of care. In the sense that true costs of care are actually revealed, this is another side-benefit from the ACA, and, indeed, for all Americans with private insurance.

Conclusion

The main benefit of the ACA, so far, seems to be in an area which was not among the expressed targets of the health reform. This is not surprising, since the issue of health system sustainability has actually not been raised so far. The assumption always was that "all is well with health care in America, so long as I can afford the insurance." The main lesson to be learned, however, is that if you want to live in a just and thriving society, health care must be available to all. For this to happen, the total cost of health care must be affordable by the society, something that seems increasingly unlikely with things the way they are now, ACA or not.

References

[1]   Congressional Budget Office Panel of Economic Advisers. Updated budget projections: 2015 to 2025. Washington: Congressional Budget Office 2015 [cited: 7th June 2016]. Available from: https://www.cbo.gov/sites/default/files/cbofiles/attachments/49973-Updated_Budget_Projections.pdf

[2]   Obamacare Facts [website on the Internet]. *How Does ObamaCare Control Costs?* [cited: 7th June 2016]. Available from: http://obamacarefacts.com/obamacare-control-costs/

[3]   Obamacare Facts [website on the Internet]. *What is the Health Insurance Marketplace?* [cited: 7th June 2016]. Available from: http://obamacarefacts.com/insurance-exchange/health-insurance-marketplace/

[4]   Bland J. The health care crisis: The financing fight obscures more fundamental issues. *The Huffington Post* [website on the Internet]. 23rd January 2014 [cited: 7th June 2016]. Available from: http://www.huffingtonpost.com/jeffrey-bland/health-care-crisis_b_4038066.html

[5]   Habas E. *Productivity is a nonsense measure.* Reuters, republished in *Kathimerini*, July 24, 2015.

[6]   Lazarus D. Warren Buffett calls healthcare the 'tapeworm' of US economy. *Los Angeles Times* [newspaper on the Internet]. 13th July 2012 [cited: 7th June 2016]. Available from: http://articles.latimes.com/2012/jul/13/business/la-fi-mo-buffett-tapeworm-20120713.

[7]   Squires D, Blumenthal D. Could the affordable care act make the US More competitive abroad? The CommonWealth Fund [homepage on the Internet]. 6th August 2015 [cited: 7th June 2016]. Available from: http://www.commonwealthfund.org/publications/blog/2015/aug/could-the-affordable-care-act-make-the-us-more-competitive-abroad

[8]   Baker D. *The End of Loser Liberalism: Making Markets Progressive.* Washington: Center for Economic and Policy Research, 2011.

[9]   Office of the Assistant Secretary for Planning and Evaluation. Insurance Expansion, Hospital Uncompensated Care, and the Affordable Care Act [monograph on the Internet]. US Department of Health & Human Services. 23rd March 2015 [cited: 7th June 2016]. Available from: https://aspe.hhs.gov/sites/default/files/pdf/139226/ib_UncompensatedCare.pdf

PART C

POLITICS AND MORALS
IN US HEALTH CARE

INTRODUCTION

POLITICS AND MORALS:
STRANGE BEDFELLOWS IN AMERICA

The central conservative view is that it is culture, not politics, that determines the success of a society. The central liberal truth is that politics can change a culture and save it from itself.

—*Daniel Patrick Moynihan[1]*

The international attitudes towards health care mentioned in Chapter A-3 have become part of the societal value system over countless generations. In this sense, they must represent a true account of what is really important in a society. And yet, it is often said that, as individuals, we realize how precious health is only when we lose it. It is very common to see people indulge in dangerous activities, or adopt lifestyles they know are harmful to their health. Health care lies in the nexus between politics and morality. Rudyard Kipling thought of East and West when writing "*and never the twain shall meet,*" but he might as well have been thinking of health care in the US. In most countries, the health system was born, shaped, and developed out of a sense of *a moral obligation* in the face of the need for health care. On the contrary, in the United States, the health system is structured according to what *the market dictates*. The health care "industry" is a market with revenue and profit centers. Precisely for that reason, it has grown to a fifth of the whole economy, the largest employer, and a major force in local, state, and federal government—and, of course, politics.

The main problem behind health-care reform in the US has been the issue of government involvement in the sense that the legislation made the purchase of health insurance mandatory. We copy from an article in *The Economist* on August 20, 2011, under the title "Health reform under attack: Doubtful prognosis" [1]. We copy it here, almost in full, because it clearly reflects the political and legal fight for health in the US as it evolves on an ethical position. It refers to the time back when the simple extension of government-funded health insurance, what would be a modest move by all accounts in the rest of the world, almost shut the government down. It is an account of how far politics have moved from morality. The article states:

> "*Uncertainty continues to plague health reform. Minutes after Barack Obama signed his health bill into law, 13 states filed a lawsuit aiming to overturn it. Others soon clamored to join in. When Georgia's attorney-general was reluctant, local Republicans demanded*

---

1 Caption used by Lawrence E. Harrison in his book *The Central Liberal Truth*, (2006).

that he should be impeached. In the end 26 states challenged the law. On August 12th they were vindicated, at least for now. A federal appeals court in Atlanta ruled that the law's requirement that everyone must buy insurance is unconstitutional. In the battle to overturn health reform, this has been the Republican's biggest victory yet. Still, the health law remains a reminder of just how long it will be before the law's fate is settled.

"Since Democrats passed the reforms in March 2010, they have faced a multi-fronted attack. Some threats have been serious, other less so. Many states have been slow to create health exchanges, where people will buy their insurance. Some governors have refused money from Washington. Least important are the votes by Republican congressmen. They have passed big measures, such as Repealing the Job-Killing Health Care Law Act, and small ones, such as barring money for preventive health care. None of these is designed to pass the Democrat-controlled Senate. All are designed for next year's campaign flyers.

"The real fight, any Republican would admit, has been in the courts. The many suits filed share a central argument: the individual "mandate" is an unconstitutional expansion of Congress's power to regulate interstate commerce. By failing to buy insurance, an individual is merely inactive. Regulate inactivity, the suits claim, and there will be no limit to congressional meddling. Perhaps people will be made to buy gym memberships.

"The court in Atlanta agreed: "This economic mandate represents a wholly novel and potentially unbounded assertion of congressional authority," the judges wrote in a two-to-one decision of a lower court which wanted to throw the whole thing out. But the individual mandate is one of the reform's main tenets. After the decision, Republicans triumphantly heralded its imminent doom.

"They may wait for some time. The decision was the most notable to date, thanks to the suit's long list of plaintiffs. But in June an appeals court in Ohio ruled in favor of the mandate. Decisions are pending in two other appeals courts, in Virginia and in Washington, D.C. The battle seems sure to move to the Supreme Court, but it is unclear when."

It finally happened in June 2015 when the Affordable Care Act won the battle in the Supreme Court. In order to solve the healthcare problem, however, America will need more than Obamacare, something like a new social and economic paradigm in health. If the mandate to buy health insurance seems to be coercive and unconstitutional, there is nothing in the American Constitution that bars the government from offering universal health coverage and national health insurance. After all, as Protagoras told us in the 5th century BC in Athens, "*the law of the land is a political decision.*" And it must be a decision for the American political system to look at health in a way where the law protects people's health not the health industry's profits.

The health system must be seen as a source of pride not a cause of panic. In a properly functioning health system, a person's or a family's life or career may be ruined by serious illness, but not because health services are unavailable or unaffordable. This implies the need for a "paradigm shift," which would limit illness to its natural dimension as a threat to wellbeing or even to life, but not as financial hardship or even ruin. Changing the national paradigm in health is a huge undertaking involving radical change in the prevention of illness, access and delivery of health services, as well as the financing mechanism. Before, however, the US even gets to this, other, more fundamental, changes are required in the way society as a whole looks at health care. And with this change, morality and politics in America must reexamine their relationship with each other. As we will analyze further in Part E, a lesson or two from Europe and from history in the last 50-60 years would be useful. According to Tony Judt, a British historian who has lived and taught both in Europe and in the US,[2] the Europeans have rightly understood the demise of communism as a suicidal implosion, not to appear again. The Americans, instead, seem to think that communism was "defeated" by American policy and might. As a result, they often seem to be still fighting a war of the past when mistakenly and, I believe, hypocritically, they label as "communist ploy" anything designed to increase social justice.

References

[1]   The Economist [magazine on the Internet]. Doubtful prognosis. Uncertainty continues to plague health reform. 20th August 2011 [cited: 7th June 2016]. Available from: http://www.economist.com/node/21526390

2   We refer to Judt again more extensively in Chapter E-1.

C-1: POLITICS CAN HARM YOUR HEALTH

Before the 5th century BC in ancient Greece, the answer to the question whether justice was based on the law of the land or on nature, was that justice had a divine origin. It was Protagoras in the 5th century BC who first said that "values and rules" are based on the political decisions of Man and not on the "will of God."

The major problem arising at the nexus of politics and health care is that the right ideology is used to serve the wrong political ends. The main characteristic of American political ideology is the recognition that "all men are created equal." Starting fifty years ago, in the 60s, a movement to ensure equal rights to all has created a society which guarantees equal rights, regardless of gender, race, religion, and sexual orientation. Unfortunately, this did not, until a few years ago, guarantee the right to health care to those that could not afford health insurance. This outright discrimination was due to a deeply rooted disconnect between economic status and some notion of civic virtue. Somehow, the American ethic seems to connect low income or poverty with sin.[1] Such notions abound in many Evangelical [1] and other ultra-conservative groups which have stopped many states from expanding Medicaid to include the ACA [2].

It is clear that the Republican Party and especially its ultra-conservative component, the Tea Party, are the staunchest opponents of the ACA. The ideological reason is the "mandate," namely the fact that employers and individuals are required to obtain health insurance, and only in the case that they cannot, the government assistance steps in [3]. A rather complicated program, by European standards, it nevertheless has already helped millions of Americans obtain health coverage. It is remarkable, but the Republican candidates in the 2016 presidential election seem willing to forego this "political clientele," and they try to balance this loss with their supposed adherence to the venerable concept of "freedom from government intrusion."

In October of 2015, *The New York Times* reported that 158 families had already provided nearly half of the early money for efforts to capture the White House [4]. The article opines:

> *"In marshaling their financial resources chiefly behind Republican candidates, the donors are also serving as a kind of financial check on demographic forces that have been nudging the electorate toward support for the Democratic Party and its economic policies. Two-thirds of Americans support higher taxes on those earning $1 million or more a year, according to a June New York Times/CBS News poll, while six in 10 favor more government intervention to reduce the gap between the rich and the poor. According to the Pew Research Center, nearly seven in 10 favor preserving Social Security and Medicare benefits as they are. Seven in ten voters say the economy is in bad shape, but other <u>surveys</u> have consistently shown that they want more wealth redistribution, not less."*

In other words, the majority of Americans seem to agree with the basic political direction in which health-care reform should move. Even more telling is an analysis of the aftermath of the

---

1 See for example: http://www.randygage.com/is-poverty-a-sin/

2014 congressional election which finds that "while 47 percent of voters say Obamacare went too far, even more either say that it was just right or didn't go far enough" [5]. While Americans seem to agree on the basic principles on which universal health care (UHC) and national health insurance (NHI) in other countries are based, for some reason, the political process in the US proves unable to let public opinion be really heard. This is the precise definition of a "dysfunctional democracy," as described by British historian Timothy Garton Ash. He writes in October 2015 in the *Guardian*, a British newspaper: *"The 2016 US elections will almost certainly be the most expensive in recent history"* [6]. Total campaign expenditure will probably exceed the estimated $7 billion splurged on the 2012 presidential and congressional contests. "The sums involved," says *The Economist,* "dwarf those in any other mature democracy" [7].

In fact, there is evidence from the 2014 gubernatorial races that the Affordable Care Act was already one of the major issues and fault lines [8]. The Republican victory in the 2014 election—the first since the main provisions of the ACA, including the Medicaid expansion, took effect—was telling. Of the 71 gubernatorial candidates, 56, or 80%, discussed health care focusing on the ACA. Of the Republicans who did so, 90% referred to it as Obamacare, while no winning Democrat used this term. Among the winning governors, only 3 of 12 Democrats or Independents spoke favorably for the ACA, while the majority of the 24 Republican governors (62%) opposed it. Their top reason for this was that "it is a failure" (53%), that it represented "government overreach into States" (47%), that it "raised premiums" (47%) and that it caused plan cancellations [8]. The arguments used in the political debate showed that there is still much work to be done to win over the "hearts and minds" of the electorate.

The next big political battle, in 2016, may be fought to a considerable extent on health care, if for no other reason but that the health-care industry is among those that can fork out enough dollars to help elect a president of their choice.[2] The choice between the ACA as conceived now and full-fledged national health insurance funded by tax dollars might be the main issue. The main reason for this will be that the ACA has failed to contain US health expenditure which will become impossible for the economy to support. ACA or no, the US health "system," as we showed in Chapter A-5, is simply not sustainable. And, to make matters worse, if health expenditure continues to rise faster than GDP, there may be negative repercussions in other public and private expenditure.

An extreme example of politics and, indeed, of political obsession, with health care was the "messing around" of the G.W. Bush administration with the Veterans Health Administration (VHA) and the Medicare Advantage program. The quality of care offered at US Department of Veterans Affairs (VA) hospitals and physicians' long-lasting relationships with the veterans and the good record-keeping, management, and preventive medicine practiced, especially during the Clinton administration, kept many veterans away from the private hospital sector. This was not ideologically palatable to the Bush administration, and was seen by Conservatives as "a Trojan horse, setting up another large healthcare program and taking more business from the private sector" [9].

Such ideological tampering with good policy was also attempted back in the 1990s. The intent was to channel Medicare recipients to private Health Maintenance Organizations (HMOs). The 2003 Medicare Advantage program by the Bush administration was a type of Medi-

---

2 Among the 158 major donors mentioned in *The New York Times* article, 17 are in the health-care industry.

care health plan offered by a private company that contracts with M*edicare* to provide citizens with all the Part A and Part B *benefits.*[3] It proved a failed attempt based on the bogus idea that HMOs, through the "magic" of the marketplace and private-sector efficiency, would provide better care at a lower cost. The Medicare Advantage program to subsidize HMOs ended up costing 11 percent more than the traditional Medicare program and "scoring" mortality rates 40 percent higher than those of elderly veterans covered by the VA [9].

The health sector has proven a fertile ground for political maneuvering. While the real purpose is to encourage further income redistribution to the top, the fight against the ACA is disguised as a fight to preserve the free market. In fact, the free market was never in real danger. Instead, it was used by Conservatives to produce ever-increasing income inequality and concentration of wealth [10]. Political interfering in health is made possible precisely because health care is run like any other industry or economic activity. The view that health care is just another market is a very strong indication that political opposition to anything that smacks of government interfering will always have a huge hurdle to overcome. This is nowhere seen more clearly than in the biggest single market, that of drugs and pharmaceuticals and, especially, in the way patents result in private profits. It is not surprising, therefore, that the pharmaceutical and insurance industries are among the biggest contributors come election time. The amazing thing is that the people most vocal in opposition of Obamacare as government interference are precisely the ones who have benefited the most by government interference in patents and copyrights.

Economic Inequality as Major Political Issue

Inequity in health is beginning to appear as an issue in mainstream America. When Nicholas Kristof, ten years ago, gave President Bush a "shopping list" of the ten things that could save his presidency, the ninth suggestion was to "*address our disgraceful inequities in health care*" [11]. A question increasingly asked in the US is "have we become too selfish and cynical? Or is America, despite being shaken by terror and distressed by the unending conflict in Iraq, ready to roll up its sleeves and renew its commitment to some of the goals and themes that once formed the basis of the American dream?" [12]. In a speech for the National Press Club in June 2006, John Edwards answers [13]:

> "*It is wrong to have 37 million Americans living in poverty, separated from the opportunities of this country by their income, their housing, their access to education, jobs, and health care, just as it was wrong that we once lived in a country legally separated by race.*"

One of the reasons so many working Americans remain trapped in poverty is that work often does not pay enough. In his remarks to the National Press Club, in 2006, former senator John Edwards said, "a single mother with two kids working full time for the minimum wage was $2,700 below the poverty line." The minimum wage as a partisan issue was nowhere more apparent than in the recent Republican primary campaign for the presidency, where Donald Trump uttered the incredible "Wages are too high" [14]. The recent increase in the minimum wage is a step in the right direction, but one should not forget that it had been frozen for almost a decade, and that wages and salaries as a share of national income have been losing ground to profits and interest income for the last few years. In the beginning of 2007, a change of paradigm was

---

3 I presume the American reader is familiar with these.

already seen as necessary to extricate the US from a morass aptly summarized by Bob Herbert, in *The New York Times*, right after the president's State of the Union Address [15].

> *"The State of the Union speech was boilerplate at a time when much of the country, with good reason, is boiling mad. The United States, the most powerful nation in the history of the world, seems paralyzed. It can't extricate itself from the war in Iraq, can't rebuild the lost city of New Orleans, can't provide health care for all of its citizens, can't come up with a sane energy policy in the era of global warming, and can't even develop a thriving public school system."*

At the end of 2015, ten years later, all these are still evident to a large extent. The war and New Orleans have been replaced by other serious problems, but the US health-care system is still the most privatized and problematic in the developed world. It is not far behind other developed countries in the share of public expenditure in total health expenditure, it is just that total health expenditure is twice that of other countries that make it unsustainable. Somebody is "making a killing" out of health in America, but also threatens to kill Americans and the American economy as well.

A health system has two main areas in which the predominance of the private for-profit element over the public character gives it a distinctly unique character. The first is the way the health system deals with the demand for health care. The main elements which determine demand are the payer and the way prices are determined. When the payer is the individual, the demand for health care is determined by his, hers, or the family's "budget constraints." This works in two ways, either directly through private payments for medical goods and services, or through health insurance. In the case of a private insurer, the individual has an incentive to seek lower premiums, knowing this may affect the quantity and quality of care he receives. If the payer is the government, the "moral hazard" danger is obvious, but it is the role of the government to deal with it through utillization control and other measures.

The second area is the supply side, namely the way medical goods and services are produced and distributed through the health system. The Clinton health reform attempt in the mid-1990s and the US experience since then suggest a clear lesson for the next US president. Public confidence in a major reform proposal must first be won, and congressional support must then be garnered, even if the election is a landslide. For example, insisting on universal health coverage as a precondition for any change may undercut the ability to enact other policies needed to improve the health system. Excessive regulation and price controls are likely to exacerbate underlying problems. The next president should take full advantage of market incentives to promote a high-value health system [16]. This, to a large extent, involves finding a balance between competition and regulation.

Two starkly different visions of health system reform have long been debated without resolution. One would have individuals (rather than employers or government) make their own decisions in a market of competing health plans and providers. The opposite approach is a publicly financed single-payer system, with major decision-making responsibilities shifted to the government. The Clinton reform tried to split the difference between the two models, promoting greater consumer involvement in a more tightly controlled health system. Despite its trappings of consumer choice and competition among health plans, President Clinton's "managed competition" was far from competitive. The efficiencies that could be gained through well-functioning competitive markets would have been lost under the weight of regulation. The core concepts and objectives of the Clinton reform continue to shape the thinking of Democrats on health policy. Two closely related provisions are particularly relevant: mandating insurance to achieve universal coverage, and controlling prices and premiums to restrain health costs. Such direct and seemingly simple policies to address specific health system problems are unlikely to work as they are intended to.

Universal coverage was one of the rallying cries of 1993, and dominated the Democratic side of the 2008 presidential race. Most of the Democratic contenders, however, supported a mandate on individuals to buy insurance, to avoid small-business opposition to an employer mandate faced by President Clinton [17]. Their proposals were grounded in the current employment-based insurance system that is familiar to almost everyone, instead of creating an entirely new way for people to buy coverage. Despite these strategic refinements, the next president (Democrat or Republican) may find that making universal coverage the prerequisite will frustrate other necessary and fundamental reforms.

A mandate to purchase health insurance does not make it more attractive to young people and others who are uninsured; it simply compels them to buy insurance and promotes scofflaw behavior. Similar mandates have had limited success in promoting automobile insurance. According to the Insurance Research Council, all but three states require that drivers carry liability coverage for property damage and bodily injury. Despite the relatively low cost of such mandated insurance, 14.6% of drivers did not have automobile coverage in 2004. That is nearly identical to the Census Bureau's estimate that 14.9% of the population did not have health insurance in that year. Eighteen states (including the District of Columbia) had uninsured motorist rates of 15% or higher. Fully a quarter of all California drivers had no automobile coverage.

An individual health insurance mandate is likely to be less effective in ensuring coverage than the automobile insurance mandate because health insurance is much more expensive and because the mandate is difficult to enforce. Massachusetts, which requires its citizens to purchase health insurance, has exempted from the mandate about 60,000 low- and moderate-income residents—almost 20 percent of the uninsured—because they could not afford the premiums and were not eligible for subsidies. Enrollment in Commonwealth Care is higher than expected, but that success would not have been possible without generous subsidies that threaten to create a $147 million state budget deficit. Money, not the mandate, is the stronger driving force behind the Massachusetts reform.

The health care safety net, which offers at least emergency treatment to anyone needing it, regardless of whether they have health insurance, also undercuts the effectiveness of a mandate. It would be difficult to prevent people from delaying their purchase of health insurance until they were "caught" by an illness requiring immediate treatment. Such delaying tactics make sense to the person who is least likely to gain from paying insurance premiums: the young, healthy person with relatively low earnings who places a low value on the financial security that health insurance affords.

One of the objectives of an insurance mandate is to eliminate this "free rider" problem and bring more paying customers into the insurance system. However, other provisions of the Clinton proposal worked against this objective. Insurers were required to issue insurance to all applicants ("guaranteed issue") and had to charge the same premiums to everyone ("community rating"). This potentially lethal combination of requirements on private insurers would reward those who delayed buying health insurance until they needed treatment. Those people would not be excluded from coverage even if they had developed a serious and expensive health condition, and they would pay the same premiums as everyone else, even though they did not previously pay for insurance. Financial penalties might be imposed to reduce the adverse selection, but enforcement would be difficult for those with low incomes who do not qualify for a subsidy.

Democrats and Republicans endorse the principle that responsible citizens should be expected to protect themselves against potentially staggering health care costs by purchasing health insurance. Perhaps a mandate is the only way to create a new social consensus, but this approach generates a host of thorny issues. What would be included in the minimum benefit package? Could people choose different benefit packages that better reflected their individual health needs and willingness to face financial risks? Would insurers and health plans be permitted flexibility to experiment with alternative benefit designs? Who ultimately decides what to buy—the consumer or the government? And when it comes to the issue of financing the minimum health plan, obviously out of general tax, our readers, but most importantly, the government, should learn a thing or two about the "tricks" required to become "filthy rich" in America [18].

References

[1]   *The Economist* [magazine on the Internet]. The religious left: The least of these. 27th February 2016 [cited: 7th June 2016]. Available from: http://www.economist.com/news/united-states/21693555-politics-american-christians-more-nuanced-sometimes-assumed-not-al

[2]   Scotti S, Waugh L, Garcia A. Affordable Care Act Medicaid Expansion. National Conference of State Legislatures [homepage on the Internet]. 17th May 2016 [cited: 7th June 2016]. Available from: http://www.ncsl.org/research/health/affordable-care-act-expansion.aspx

[3]   ObamaCare Facts [website on the Internet]. ObamaCare Employer Mandate; 2016 [cited: 7th June 2016]. Available from: http://obamacarefacts.com/obamacare-employer-mandate/

[4]   Confessore N, Cohen S, Yourish K. The Families Funding the 2016 Presidential Election. *The New York Times* [newspaper on the Internet]. 10th October 2015 [cited: 7th June 2016]. Available from: http://www.nytimes.com/interactive/2015/10/11/us/politics/2016-presidential-election-super-pac-donors.html?_r=1

[5]   Goldberg M. People Voted for Republicans Last Night—That Doesn't Mean They Like Them. *The Nation* [webpage on the Internet]. 5th November 2014 [cited: 7th June 2016]. Available from: https://www.thenation.com/article/people-voted-republicans-last-night-doesnt-mean-they-them/

[6]   Ash TG. The billion-dollar question – when will the US repair its damaged democracy? *Guardian* [newspaper on the Internet]. 1st October 2015 [cited: 7th June 2016]. Available from: http://www.theguardian.com/commentisfree/2015/oct/01/us-presidential-election-america-damaged-democracy-campaign-spending

[7]   *The Economist* [magazine on the Internet]. Why American elections cost so much. 9th February 2014 [cited: 7th June 2016]. Available from: http://www.economist.com/blogs/economist-explains/2014/02/economist-explains-4

[8]   Scott KW, Blendon RJ, Sommers BD. The 2014 governors' races and health care: A campaign web site analysis. INQUIRY: *The Journal of Health Care Organization, Provision, and Financing*. May 2015, 5;52.

[9]   Krugman P. Health Policy Malpractice. *The New York Times* [newspaper on the Internet]. 4th September 2006 [cited: 7th June 2016]. Available from: http://www.nytimes.com/2006/09/04/opinion/04krugman.html

[10]   Baker D. *The End of Loser Liberalism: Making Markets Progressive.* United States: Center for Economic and Policy Research 2011.

[11]   Kristof N. Ten Suggestions for Rescuing the Bush Legacy. *The New York Times* [newspaper on the Internet]. 31st December 2006 [cited: 7th June 2016]. Available from: http://query.nytimes.com/gst/fullpage.html?res=950DE3DD1630F932A05751C1A9609C8B63

[12]   Herbert B. America in 2026. *The New York Times* [newspaper on the Internet]. 22nd June 2006 [cited: 7th June 2016]. Available from: http://www.nytimes.com/2006/06/22/opinion/22Herbert.html

[13]   Edwards J. [transcript]. The fight against poverty. The National Press Club 2006. Available from: http://www.press.org/sites/default/files/062206_edwards.pdf [cited: 7th June 2016].

[14]   Levine G. The fight against 15: Republicans in debate oppose minimum wage hike. *AlJazeera America* [newspaper on the Internet]. 11th November 2015 [cited: 7th June 2016]. Available from: http://america.aljazeera.com/articles/2015/11/11/the-fight-against-15-republicans-in-debate-oppose-hike-in-minimum-wage.html

[15]   Herbert B. Long on Rhetoric, Short on Sorrow. *The New York Times* [newspaper on the Internet]. 25th January 2007 [cited: 7th June 2016]. Available from: http://www.nytimes.com/2007/01/25/opinion/25herbert.html

[16]   Antos J. Lessons From The Clinton Plan: Incremental Market Reform, Not Sweeping Government Control. *Health Affairs* [magazine on the Internet]. 2016 [cited: 7th June 2016]. Available from: http://content.healthaffairs.org/content/27/3/705.full.html#ref-5

[17]   Harrington B. Inside the Secretive World of Tax-Avoidance Experts; *The Atlantic* [magazine on the Internet]. 26th October 2015 [cited: 7th June 2016]. Available from: http://www.theatlantic.com/business/archive/2015/10/elite-wealth-management/410842/

C-2: HEALTH-CARE POLITICS—A DEEPLY PARTISAN ISSUE

"What is happening in this primary is just a distillation of what's been happening inside their party for more than a decade. I mean, the reason that many of their voters are responding is because this is what's been fed through the messages they've been sending for a long time—that you just make flat assertions that don't comport with the facts. That you just deny the evidence of science. That compromise is a betrayal. That the other side isn't simply wrong, or we just disagree, we want to take a different approach, but the other side is destroying the country, or treasonous. I mean, that's—look it up. That's what they've been saying."

—President Barack Obama, 2016

President Obama offered up this analysis of Donald Trump and the broader fight for the Republican presidential nomination in a historic speech on Friday, March 11, 2016 at a Democratic National Committee event at the Austin Music Hall in Texas [1]. At that time Donald Trump was not yet the Republican nominee, and Obama was clearly referring to national politics. It is, however, very useful in analyzing the way opposition against the ACA, national health insurance, or the single payer has been developing, mainly among Republicans, and especially Tea-Partiers. Political opposition has not been based on arguments, evidence, or data supporting the status quo on health care, but they have tried to attach the label of un-Americanism to those supporting an alternative social policy.

It should be expected, but it is unfortunate, that health care in America has been such a deeply partisan issue. Major newspapers and other media with political agendas and distinctly partisan orientation host opinion pieces, news, articles and other stories which pursue distinguishable positions with a clear target. In fact, championing a political agenda often results in open "warfare" using populist slogans as ammunition [2]. Perhaps one of the most vocal opponents of the Affordable Care Act has been the Heritage Foundation, a distinguished Conservative champion. On the Foundation's webpage it states as its identity: *"Founded in 1973, The Heritage Foundation is . . . a think tank . . . [devoted to] the principles of free enterprise, limited government, individual freedom, traditional American values, and a strong national defense."* It hosts what may be the most vocal and sometimes "viral" attack on health reform in the US. In a 15-article Health Care Policy series, addressed to the 112th Congress in 2010 and 2011, it attempted to dismantle the ACA on ethical, political, and economic grounds. It has been doing the same thing ever since, fortunately to no avail.

Partisan politics sometimes also find fertile ground in major judicial decisions. In 2012 the Supreme Court ruled that States may choose not to expand Medicaid, although the federal government put down 100% of the expansion costs for the first three years, to be reduced to 90% by 2020. By November 2015, 26 out of 50 states had decided not to expand Medicaid, leaving 4.8 million people still uninsured in what became known as the "Medicaid Gap" [3]. This is a crucial blow to people already too poor to qualify for federal subsidies, but a "victory" for those opposed to the "socialization" of health care in America [4]. Recent estimates in *The New York Times* put the number of people "stuck" in the Medicaid Gap at three million in 19, mostly Republican, states [5]. Even now, five years after the passage of the Act and after the Supreme Court in 2015 put its stamp on it, Obamacare was still widely used by Republicans and other Libertarians as the "ultimate scare ploy" on every government policy. As far back as January 2014 we read on the Bloomberg website, *'Obamacare for the Internet,' and 4 Other Ways Republicans Tie Everything to the ACA [6]*:

> *"Why Ted Cruz (and every other conservative) tries to link every government program to Obamacare. The "Obamacare of" permutation generated a lot of laughter, but if anything Cruz was late to the field. Five years after passage, conservatives have found that comparing any government program to Obamacare works to immediately brand it as horrible and unworkable. It's a sure bet, like casting Channing Tatum in a summer movie."*

Still, Obamacare is a success and the Democrats rightly seem to stick to their guns. In early 2016, Bernie Sanders openly endorsed the ACA, and, in fact, went much further to endorse UHC [7]. He even provided a rough estimate of the "financials" behind his proposal, where his main claim is that although his plan would increase costs, these would be paid for by a drop in administrative costs.[1] His position on health is accurately reflected in the following:

> *"It has been the goal of Democrats since Franklin D. Roosevelt to create a universal health care system guaranteeing health care to all people. Every other major industrialized nation has done so. . . . The Affordable Care Act was a critically important step towards the goal of universal health care. . . . But as we move forward, we must build upon the success of the ACA to achieve the goal of universal health care. Twenty-nine million Americans today still do not have health insurance and millions more are underinsured and cannot afford the high copayments and deductibles charged by private health insurance companies that put profits before people" [7].*

On the other hand, despite her previous history, Hillary Clinton seems to lag somewhat behind. Although she clearly supported the ACA as a major gain in health policy, she has cast aside Bernie Sanders' plan for single-payer health insurance as *"an idea that will never, ever, come to pass"* [8]. The swipe built on Clinton's repeated rhetoric about Sanders' proposed single-payer, Medicare-for-all health care plan. The plan, she said, *"would provide health coverage to all Americans but would be paid for by raising taxes on most Americans"* [9]. Clinton's position simply did not take into account that health costs in America are already unnecessarily too high, perhaps because she is wary of what she might have to propose as a remedy. After all, most of her contributions came from "big money" as opposed to Sanders' reliance on small contributions.

Sanders replied on January 17, 2016. In an e-mail by Gerald Friedman, Professor of Economics, University of Massachusetts at Amherst, to Warren Gunnels, policy director to Senator Bernie Sanders, titled "United States can afford single payer health care program." Friedman says that *"several financial issues have arisen with respect to Secretary Clinton's attack on the Sanders health program."* He then goes on to provide the necessary calculations which claim that:

> *"The net savings from single payer come from reduced spending on administrative activities, in both private insurers and providers' offices, reduced spending on monopoly prices*

---

1   The plan was estimated to cost $1.38 trillion per year.

for pharmaceuticals and medical devises, and a slowdown in the growth of spending because of controls on administrative costs and drug prices. While these savings come to over $10 trillion in 10 years, they are offset by increased spending because of the extension of coverage to the uninsured and increased utilization with the removal of copayments and deductibles."[2]

Health reform was definitely an issue in the 2016 presidential campaign and not only among Democratic contenders. One would hope for something more than the "simple" plan that Ben Carson, a Republican candidate, introduced in his campaign for the Republican nomination. In his words, he proposed:

"A very disruptive but simple plan to reform the health care system in the United States . . . replace Obamacare, Medicare and Medicaid with an easy-to-understand universal, cradle-to-grave annual cash allowance for health spending" [10].

Ben Carson, among the most renowned physicians in the world, was narrowly leading in some national polls for the GOP presidential nomination until October 2015. By early March 2016, he had withdrawn from the race, pledging support for Donald Trump, although Trump did not exactly embrace Carson's "simple solution" for health care, since he campaigned against the ACA from day one. The Carson plan is a good example of how simple ideas are not suited for an issue as infested with political rhetoric as health care financing in the US. This is because political money in health does not follow the partisan route based on ideology. It is partisan, but it is also perfectly tuned to its immediate and medium-term economic interests [11]. It will support whoever it thinks will be the winner, aiming at influencing whatever decisions it can, but it will never support a policy that changes the rules of the game away from free market politics. It is for that reason that Republican money would not flow to a "loser" candidate. And the "health money" is not necessarily against the ACA, as long as the public purse pays for the inefficient, hence profitable, health sector. The "health money," in other words, would gladly support even UHC as long as coverage was through private health insurance and with no controls on the "health market."

The proposition above will probably be tested soon. The best example of what Ms. Clinton as the Democratic candidate—and perhaps as president—will propose cannot, logically, be very similar to the 1993 Clinton health care plan. Known officially as the Health Security Act, it was a reform package closely associated with then First Lady Hillary Rodham Clinton, chair of the task force devising the plan. President Clinton campaigned heavily on health care in the 1992 presidential election, and the task force was created in January 1993, to come up with a comprehensive plan to provide universal health care for all Americans. This was to be a cornerstone of the administration's first-term agenda, and a major speech was delivered by President Clinton to the US Congress in September 1993. The core element of the proposed plan was an enforced mandate for employers to provide health insurance coverage to all of their employees. The Clinton health plan also required each US citizen and permanent resident alien to become enrolled in a qualified health plan and forbade their disenrollment until covered by another plan. It listed

---

2   See Bernie Sanders's website at https://berniesanders.com/issues/medicare-for-all/.

minimum coverage and maximum annual out-of-pocket expenses for each plan. It proposed the establishment of corporate "regional alliances" of health providers to be subject to a fee-for-service schedule. People below a certain set income level were to pay nothing. The Act listed funding to be sent to the states for the administration of the plan, beginning at $13.5 billion in 1993 and reaching $38.3 billion in 2003.

The first time is always difficult. Opposition to the plan was heavy and almost universal, coming mainly from Conservatives, Libertarians, and the health insurance industry.[3] The latter, in order to rally public support against the plan, produced "Harry and Louise," a highly effective series of television ads, lamenting the bad fortune awaiting all Americans under the Clinton plan. Instead of uniting behind the president's original proposal, Democrats, wary of re-election, offered a number of competing plans of their own. The plan ultimately backfired amid the barrage of fire from the pharmaceutical and health insurance industries and considerably diminished Hillary Clinton's popularity. By September 1994, the final compromise of the Democratic bill was declared dead by Senate Majority Leader George J. Mitchell. President Clinton in 2016 will find it easier, although there is no doubt she will often have to forget the time she was drafted by the Clinton administration to sell her plan to the American people. She will especially have to prove that her new plan, although similar to the first, will not be the same.

Coming back to the present, we should remember that political criticism need not always be on ideology, but must always use common sense. In an article in *The Economist* on Bernie Sanders' economic policy the subtitle read: "*Health-care costs and high taxes would sink the Sanders economic plan*" [12]. The perennial nightmare that "*taxes would soar*" leads the second paragraph. The main "scare point" is a half-truth, "*his most ambitious policy calls for the government, rather than private insurers, to pay health care bills.*" The "dragon" comes next. "*That would cost $14 trillion over a decade, requiring new taxes on most workers worth 8.4% of their incomes.*" For a news magazine like *The Economist*, read all over the world,[4] ignoring the fact that—by their "arithmetic"—the tax-payers would also save what they previously spent on private insurance, seemed like a feat worthy of a North Korea government pamphlet. Shame on *The Economist*.

It is hard to choose a starting point. Cost, however, is not something I would pick when talking about an industry already costing Americans twice as much as, say, the Germans, the Swiss, or the French, and three times as much as the British. America will pay more than $34 trillion over a decade for health care. Sanders wanted to change a system that absorbs a fifth of American GDP and give back half or less of the value in terms of health outcomes and consumer satisfaction than other rich countries. Attacking Bernie Sanders on his health care platform was simply a no-brainer. If one were to be magnanimous, one might even concede discussing the locus of the burden for that huge health bill. According to *The Economist*—and, unfortunately, Hillary Clinton—Bernie Sanders would put it mostly on the government, which means taxes, while now it rests mostly on individuals and employers, in fact, on the wage bill. What Sanders wanted is to move the burden from wages to income, profits, and capital gains. And this is a very good plan.

Given what all the data on income distribution in the last 20 years show, the average working citizen should rejoice at the prospect of a Sanders presidency.[5] Unfortunately, most of the

---

3 Which obviously did not relish the idea of having to bargain with strong employers' organizations, instead of the general public.
4 And by me, for at least 30 years now.
5 Which was not meant to be, but this doesn't mean all his ideas were bad.

attacks on UHC seem to take for granted that America will keep spending one fifth or more of GDP on health. On this premise, the notion that public funds will cover the insurance costs for those who cannot afford them seems like a serious fiscal problem, which will require additional taxation. It is a pity that in today's political debate one does not hear much about this fundamental problem. And this is quite simply that the "free market orientation" of US health care is responsible for the extraordinary medical costs which no insurance system—public or private—can afford. The dragon is not universal health coverage. It is the health care cost inflation caused by an insatiable health care industry which has simply run amok, but exists because it spends a lot on campaign contributions.

Health care and health insurance are probably the most difficult for politicians to deal with. For many, ideology is clearly at loggerheads with reality and indeed the public feeling in general. The situation during the 2016 Primaries in both the Republican and the Democratic races was indicative. On the Republican front the battle against "Obamacare" was a major rallying point which a candidate could overlook only at his peril. The case of the most vocal of them all, Donald Trump, is telling. He had already broken with many Republicans on taxing the rich, threatening trade wars, and keeping Planned Parenthood alive. Nevertheless, he faced criticism for an even bolder act of conservative heresy: embracing the core tenet of the Affordable Care Act.

Mr. Trump, in the beginning of his campaign, offered only bits and pieces of his health agenda, generally a vow to repeal Obamacare and replace it with "something great." In a town-hall meeting hosted by CNN on February 18, 2016, he shared some more expansive views on the subject, and, unlike most Republicans, he did not call for removing the individual mandate that requires Americans to have health insurance. Asked how people with pre-existing medical conditions would purchase insurance if the health law and the mandate were eliminated, Mr. Trump said, "*I like the mandate. So here's where I'm a little bit different.*" He continued, "*I don't want people dying on the streets*" [13]. Less than 24 hours later, Mr. Trump backed away from his remarks, proclaiming himself to be the "fiercest opponent of the health law."

The Affordable Care Act sometimes put Republicans in an awkward position on the campaign trail.[6] While the popularity of the law remained mixed nationally, many Americans had benefited from aspects of the legislation that would be lost if it were repealed. Senator Ted Cruz of Texas faced an uncomfortable silence in Iowa in January 2016 when a supporter of Hillary Clinton explained to him how a relative who was riddled with tumors had not had insurance before the law. While Governor John Kasich of Ohio, like his Republican opponents, wanted to repeal the law, he was also criticized by conservatives for using it to expand Medicaid in his state.

For years, President Obama's health care overhaul, and the individual mandate specifically, have been anathema to Republicans who look at it as a vivid example of government overreach. Without providing many details, Mr. Trump said that he would promote health savings accounts and spur interstate competition among insurance companies to reduce prices. As for patients who could still not afford insurance, Mr. Trump said, "*We're going to take care of them through, maybe, concepts of Medicare,*" suggesting expansion of that government program. Conservatives were taken aback. Senator Ben Sasse, a Republican from Nebraska who opposed Mr. Trump, said in a series of posts on Twitter that the billionaire businessman appeared to embrace most of the health law and wondered "*what kind of Supreme Court justices he would appoint if elected.*"

The legality of the mandate and the government's power to impose fines on people who

---

6   Defending their positions admittedly required leaps in logic and reason.

ignore it was central to the Supreme Court decision that upheld the law in 2012. Many Republicans have called Chief Justice John G. Roberts Jr., a George W. Bush appointee, a "turncoat" for having written that decision. Mr. Trump has been one of the loudest among them. *"Would you nominate a Supreme Court justice who agrees with you that federal government can mandate purchasing specific products?"* Mr. Sasse asked Mr. Trump, again, on Twitter. Rush Limbaugh, the conservative radio host and defender of Mr. Trump in many instances, was also incensed. He actually took issue with Mr. Trump's suggestion that other Republicans are not disturbed by the idea of people *"dying in the street."* The extent to which ideological prejudice can lead to bigotry is enormous. And when applied to health care, it is frightening, to say the least.

The relationship between equity and health is central in this book. The negative relationship between health status and income distribution is well documented in the literature [14]. But the true nature of the relationship is not clear. There are two questions that seem a little like the "chicken and the egg" argument: Is bad health due to unequal income distribution because poverty prevents access to essential services, or is unequal distribution of income a source of bad health in itself and irrespective of the accessibility of services? In other words, is dealing with bad and deteriorating population health outcomes a matter for health policy (i.e. providing access to the poor), or a matter for economic and overall social policy by addressing the much more difficult issues of the distribution of income and the ensuing class and social exclusion problems?

Depending on the answer to the two questions, a different set of policies is required. In both cases, however, a major change in ideology and, hence, of politics will be necessary. Even in the seemingly easier case of changing health care financing, major political decisions are needed, which have never been easy in the US. It is interesting to examine the reasons why the one-payer system, twice submitted to the California legislature since 2007, finally "disappeared" in 2013, ostensibly because it could be replaced by the ACA. As Karen Bernal, Chair of the California Democratic Party's the Progressive Caucus, said then:

> *"The Legislature is focused on the implementation of the Affordable Care Act (ACA, aka "Obamacare") only, and they simply aren't going to deal with single payer this year. Those are the marching orders which, I think, probably come from three directions — the Governor, the legislative leadership, and the White House. It's understood by all that Assembly Member Richard Pan will not let a single payer bill out of the Assembly Health Committee" [15].*

There is something to be said about compromising with the ACA instead of going "all the way" to a single-payer system (SPS). California failed where Vermont succeeded. Maybe it was because in Vermont the governor was supportive, while Governor Swarzenegger was not. Or it may be because of the one fundamental difference between the ACA and SPS. The former works with and benefits the insurance industry, while the latter does not. This is why the president who will legislate universal health insurance, as it already exists in Canada or many European countries, will deserve a place in US history comparable to that of Franklin D. Roosevelt. There is something magical about the number seven in human history, and, perhaps, a seventh attempt at establishing national health insurance in the US will prove successful where the previous six failed. But, even in this case, the disentanglement from the health insurance industry will be a difficult political task.

Unfortunately, the way the American people choose their presidents and most of the personnel available for the job in 2016 do not offer much promise that long-term fundamental

changes will prevail over short-term political calculations. But, of course, this is just specula-
tion at this point. What is important is to see what really is at stake. The main argument in our
book is that globalization will make the position of the working middle class, not to mention
the working poor, much more vulnerable. In a worsening economic environment America's
poor and uninsured will demand solutions that current American ideology cannot provide. It
is important for Americans to realize and understand the dangers ahead, and that health is not
suited for the application of rigid market logic. This is a point with particular importance for the
United States where the market is an especially strong institution which seems to provide the
analytical framework even for aspects of societal organization and personal attitudes such as religion.[7] As we tried to show in this chapter, reliance on the market, although useful on efficiency
grounds, is not an effective principle on which the organization of health care can rely. What is
needed instead, is a philosophy of caring, a government that dares to see things under a different
light, and a healthy dose of ideological DNA change.

References

[1]   Chokshi N. Barack Obama gives his brutal assessment of the rise of Donald Trump. *Independent*
[newspaper on the Internet]. 13th July 2013 [cited: 7th June 2016]. Available from: http://www.
independent.co.uk/news/world/americas/us-elections/barack-obama-donald-trump-rise-repub-
lican-party-us-election-2016-a6928736.html

[2]   Hiltzik M. A Koch op-ed that USA today should have fact-checked -- but didn't. *Los Angeles Times*
[newspaper on the Internet]. 7th August 2014 [cited: 7th June 2016]. Available from: http://www.
latimes.com/business/hiltzik/la-fi-mh-the-koch-oped-20140807-column.html#page=1

[3]   Radnofsky L. Upgraded health site faces test this week. *The Wall Street Journal* [newspaper on the
Internet]. 9th November 2014 [cited: 7th June 2016]. Available from: http://www.wsj.com/articles/
health-care-website-update-seen-reducing-strain-on-system-1415561769

[4]   Quadagno J. Right-Wing Conspiracy? Socialist Plot? The Origins of the Patient Protection and
Affordable Care Act. *Journal of Health Politics, Policy, and Law* 2013; 39(1):35-56.

[5]   Bui Q, Sanger-Katz M. We mapped the uninsured. You'll notice a pattern. *The New York Times*
[newspaper on the Internet]. 30th October 2015 [cited: 7th June 2016]. Available from: http://www.
nytimes.com/interactive/2015/10/31/upshot/who-still-doesnt-have-health-insurance-obamacare.
html?_r=0

[6]   Weigel D. 'Obamacare for the Internet,' and 4 other ways Republicans tie everything to the ACA.
Bloomberg [webpage on the Internet]. 10th November 2014 [cited: 7th June 2016]. Available from:
http://www.bloomberg.com/politics/articles/2014-11-10/obamacare-for-the-internet-and-four-
other-ways-republicans-tie-everything-to-the-aca

[7]   Sanders B. *Medicare for all: Leaving No One Behind*. [cited: 7th June 2016]. Available from: https://
berniesanders.com/issues/medicare-for-all/

[8]   Merica D. Clinton: Sanders' health care plan 'will never, ever come to pass'. CNN [webpage
on the Internet]. 29th January 2016 [cited: 7th June 2016]. Available from: http://edition.cnn.

---

7   A recent analysis in *The Economist* shows the application of market principles in the amazingly rapid
growth of Pentecostalism in the United States ("Christianity Reborn," *The Economist*, December 23, 2006).

com/2016/01/29/politics/hillary-clinton-bernie-sanders-health-care/index.html

[9]   Merica D, Bradner E, Luhby T. Hours before debate, Sanders releases Medicare-for-all plan. CNN [webpage on the Internet]. 18th January 2016 [cited: 7th June 2016]. Available from: http://edition.cnn.com/2016/01/17/politics/bernie-sanders-medicare-plan/

[10]   Harwood J. 10 questions for Ben Carson. CNBC [homepage on the Internet]. 19th May 2015 [cited: 7th June 2016]. Available from: http://www.cnbc.com/2015/05/08/10-questions-for-ben-carson.html

[11]   Hernandez R, Pear R. Health sector puts its money on democrats. *The New York Times* [newspaper on the Internet]. 29th December 2014 [cited: 7th June 2016]. Available from: http://www.nytimes.com/2007/10/29/us/politics/29health.html?_r=0

[12]   *The Economist* [magazine on the Internet]. A vote for what? 13th February 2016 [cited: 7th June 2016]. Available from: http://www.economist.com/news/united-states/21692895-health-care-costs-and-high-taxes-would-sink-sanders-economic-plan-vote-what

[13]   Rappeport A. Donald Trump in triage mode after shocking conservatives with health care comments. *The New York Times* [newspaper on the Internet]. 25th February 2016 [cited: 7th June 2016]. Available from: http://www.nytimes.com/2016/02/20/us/politics/donald-trump-in-triage-mode-after-shocking-conservatives-with-health-care-comments.html?ref=topics

[14]   Deaton A. Health, Income, and Inequality. The National Bureau of Economic Research [webpage on the Internet]. Spring 2003 [cited: 7th June 2016]. Available from: http://www.nber.org/reporter/spring03/health.html

[15]   Gallagher T. California's disappearing health care reform. *Salon* [magazine on the Internet]. 2nd May 2013 [cited: 7th June 2016]. Available from: http://www.salon.com/2013/05/02/what_happened_to_californias_single_payer_health_care_bill_partner/

C-3: THERE IS NO PLACE FOR A "MARKET" IN HEALTH

"Markets are not God-given or natural."

—Jacob Hacker

When Jacob Hacker published his short paper on "The Free-Market Fantasy" [1] in 2014 he offered five propositions on which the market must be based in order for it to act as an efficient producer and distributor of goods and services. All five of them, the first being the caption under the title, are that markets cannot function with no rules, that powerful interests have to be countered, that progressive market reform is needed based on predistribution[1] as a governing idea, and that society needs a new organizational power base. All together, his preconditions for an effective, efficient, and equitable market system will have a hard time passing in American health care.

There are many aspects of health care that make it unsuitable ground for market economics. Obviously, the main postulates of the market on which economic theory depends, such as consumer sovereignty, perfect information, and many others, fail in the case of the health industry.[2] The agency relationship, with the doctor as the agent, and the triangular relationship, patient–provider–insurance carrier, where the incentives to efficiency, quality of care, affordable price, etc. all get distorted, are the order of the day in health economics [2]. However, where the market model really fails is when we consider the essential characteristic that a health system should possess in a developed and democratic society, namely that health care should be available to all, irrespective of income and other social characteristics. As John P. Geyman wrote in his 2015 assessment of the ACA:

> *"The country still needs to confront the challenge that our for-profit health insurance industry, together with enormous bureaucratic waste and widespread investor ownership throughout our market-based system are themselves barriers to health care reform. Here we consider the lessons we can take away from the ACA's first five years and lay out the economic, social/political, and moral arguments for replacing it with single-payer national health insurance" [3].*

And yet, one of the myths in the US is that health costs can be brought under control by running health care more "like a business" and encouraging more competition. Markets can be enormously effective, but not always, and they are never self-governing, despite Adam Smith's venerable notion about the proverbial "invisible hand." In America, health care is already more

---

1 Predistribution, as opposed to redistribution, is an interesting concept mostly advanced by Progressives in the US. It is based on the premise that there is need to change the economy's underlying structure to boost employment and wages.

2 The reader only has to ask simple questions, such as, Do I know better than my doctor? Is my doctor looking after my interests more than those of the drug company or the insurer paying for his vacation? The answers will be another "inconvenient truth" for the future of health care in America. I hope Americans pay more attention to this than to the other inconvenient truth they ignored in 2000, when they elected George W. Bush rather than Al Gore.

commercial and competitive than anywhere else. And yet, perhaps as a result, costs are the highest on earth by far and the quality of care is extremely uneven. The rules of the game in American health inevitably favor some while they "rob" others. Powerful interests develop which have to be countered if the markets are to have a beneficial effect on the distribution of opportunity. It was Adam Smith, after all, who warned almost three centuries ago in the Wealth of Nations that unchecked merchants and manufacturers would act as "an overgrown standing army that would upon many occasions intimidate the legislature repressing wages and rigging policies in their favor."

Such is the "market" that the "father of economics" rightly saw in it an ideal instrument for the production and distribution of goods and services. We should not forget, however, that this was no religious fanaticism, but rather a well-thought-out theory based on rules and assumptions. One of these was the supremacy of the "consumer" who with his "perfect knowledge" will impose competition among producers. The other was the existence of some type of authority like the government, which will ensure competition among producers.[3] It is not clear whether Adam Smith in the 18th century saw health care as belonging to the realm of the market, but the books of A.J. Cronin[4] a century later, leave little doubt that this was the case in 19th century England. Fortunately, many things have changed in Europe since then, but, unhappily, not in America.

In Europe today the "market" is *part* of the picture when it comes to the way economic agents, producers, and consumers "do things." In the US it is *the* picture. The realization that "*money makes the world go round*" was, presumably, a fact of life in 1936 Berlin,[5] but so was Nazism then, and the Welfare State established by Otto von Bismarck fifty years before. Politics and economic issues broadly determine elections in Europe, just as they do in the US. In no way, however, would the Europeans tolerate a health system that explicitly denies one sixth of the population access and the right to health care. No government that reneged on its responsibility to secure access to affordable quality care to all would last long in Europe. In America, it almost seems that the people are ready to reward a party and a president that would "guarantee" to do just that.

The Health Industry as an Economic Endeavor

Powerful economic interests do not exist only in business and finance. They exist in every human endeavor where goods and services are traded in a market. In the US this includes health care, but to an extent unknown in the rest of the world. American health care is a good example of what happens when ideology is applied to fix problems for which it is not suited. There is also good reason to believe that even the reforms suggested recently will prove inadequate because they do not seem to grasp this fundamental problem. The basic flaw in the American health system is the central role the market plays with private insurance as a major player. There are many documented cases where the application of well tested industrial techniques and incentives in other sectors are applied in health with devastating results. The tendency of drug companies to solicit the willing cooperation of physicians is, perhaps, the most obvious, but there are also strong business incentives everywhere from insurers, to profit and non-profit hospitals,

---

3 In his case, this was the "invisible hand" in the market.
4 Scottish novelist and physician born in 1896 in Scotland; author of *The Citadel*, one of the greatest medical novels of all time.
5 Remember the song from *Cabaret*.

and physicians working on a fee-for-service basis, that have profit maximization as their main objective.

In March of 2016 *The Economist* ran a special briefing on business in America [4]. It is useful to pick a few points that highlight the way health care in America operates when viewed as a strictly economic endeavor. One of the first observations is that pharmacies are among the "niche concerns" which operate in an oligopolistic manner, meaning that the four top firms control two-thirds or more of sales. In 893 industries, grouped by sector, health care is listed among the most concentrated, with the top four firms accounting for more than 12% of total revenue. High concentration in an industry is seen as a source of "abnormal profits" according to *The Economist*,[6]

> *"Roughly another quarter of abnormal profits comes from the health-care industry, where a cohort of pharmaceutical and medical equipment firms make aggregate returns on capital of 20-50%. The Industry is riddled by special interests and is governed by patent rules that allow firms temporary monopolies on innovative new drugs and inventions. Much of health care purchasing is ultimately controlled by insurance firms. Four of the largest, Anthem, Cigna, Aetna, and Humana, are planning to merge into two larger firms."*

Speaking of competition in the health industry, *The Economist* also mentions that the Federal Trade Commission (FTC) *"spends a lot of time and energy looking at health care, be it hospital mergers or pay-for-delay deals when pharmaceutical firms try to stop generic competition."* I suspect that mergers in insurance companies will follow. It is interesting that increasing competition was one of the main tools the ACA expressly counted on when the legislation was proposed—probably the greatest conceptual weakness in the ACA, unfortunately strictly for political reasons.

The idea of a private for-profit health sector, on the other hand, is not foreign or even unusual to Europe or elsewhere in the world, as in Canada or Australia. The notion, however, that doctors, hospitals, and other providers would set their goals and charges solely or largely on business principles is not something Europeans would easily agree with. There are huge implications arising from the notion that health care is an industry just like other industries. The only European government that attempted to test this "sacred" ground was Margaret Thatcher's in England, and she probably had this to count among her major failures. Health care is probably the sector where the presence of government control is most justified, even for ardent supporters of a free market, baring extremists of the sort of Donald Trump.

As we will see in greater detail in following chapters, the reason why America spends so much and gets so little in return is political and, in fact, mainly ideological. The absolute faith of Americans in the "market" for solving all problems of distributing goods and services is, sometimes, carried to extremes. The limited appreciation in the US for what we call "public goods" is shown by assigning health care to the realm of the private, profit-seeking sector. It was only 50 years ago that the care of the aged and the very poor was placed within the realm of public interest, a choice with which not few Americans still disagree.[7] However, the very core of the ar-

---

6   As I have done elsewhere, I must point out, again, that *The Economist* is anything but a left-leaning publication.

7   It is not unusual to read or hear statements which challenge the very existence of Medicare and Medicaid.

gument for a market in health care is flawed. Neither the demand nor the supply preconditions for a functional market, in the sense of Adam Smith, exists.

On the demand side, financing health care through private health insurance when health care is produced basically by profit-seeking producers, at prices determined by "the market," is suicidal, sometimes even literally. It means, quite simply, that the private sector can profit from a human need, producing goods and services which the individual cannot predict the need for, avoid, or choose to consume, compared to others. This very basic precondition for the existence of a market, namely the supremacy of the consumer, does not exist in the health-care sector. And health care is not something consumers, given their income, can "chose not to consume" at the price charged.

On the supply side of the market lies another important obstacle that has to do with the concept of profit when applied to the health area. The decision to produce, the production process and technology, and the amount produced are decisions that give very different results when made by profit-seeking or by non-profit enterprises, or by the government. These differences, however, do not leave society or the consumer indifferent. In the hospital sector, for example, the application of economic principles in the case of an oversupply of hospitals would produce different results in Europe than in the US. For the last ten years, in many countries in Europe we observe a tendency to merge hospitals, or convert them to other uses [5]. The process of restructuring is made easier by the existence of public authorities which "paper over" the problems caused by inevitable political considerations [6]. In the US, such agencies do not exist and the decision to close a hospital or merge it with another, simply for economic reasons guided by a market mentality, can be much more painful to the community it serves and to its employees.

It is precisely the commercialization of health care and the effects of business incentives on the provision of care that are responsible for the huge and increasing cost of health in the US. In 2010, Arnold Relman, one of the most respected physicians and health-care advocates, wrote a very important article in *The New York Review of Books*, criticizing the ACA on basically the same grounds that we have developed here, in fact using the term "a disquieting truth" [7]. The main criticism was that the ACA failed to address the main problem with American health care, namely its dependence on the market. It is true that the realization that health is not a field where the market can play freely will not come easily for the American society. This is because the American health system is so much owned by investors and medical care is a commodity traded in the market rather than a right. Again in 2010, Arnold Relman, in a seminal book promoting the need for universal health coverage, warned [8]:

> "The US healthcare system is failing. It is run like a business, increasingly focused on generating income for insurers and providers rather than providing care for patients. It is supported by investors and private markets seeking to grow revenue and resist regulation, thus contributing to higher costs and lessened public accountability. Meanwhile, forty-six million Americans are without insurance."

To remain competitive, many not-for-profit hospitals promote their "bottom line" like their for-profit counterparts, vigorously advertising their facilities and services to the public. No other health care system in the world is as focused on generating income, and in no other country is medical care marketed and advertised as aggressively, as if it were just another commodity. This not only increases costs, but also forces hospitals to concentrate on the delivery of profitable, rather than effective, services. It also, obviously, favors those who can pay over those who need medical care but cannot afford it.[8]

Health Market "Politics" in America

There is another view that considers the market a useful tool even for sectors such as health, as long as they are handled the "right way."[9] In his *The End of Loser Liberalism: Making Markets Progressive*, Dean Baker tries to dispel the myth that Liberals are for the government while Conservatives are with the market. "*This is not true,*" he says. "*Conservatives actually rely on the government all the time, but most importantly in structuring the market in ways that ensure that income will flow upwards.*" This myth, he says "*puts liberals in the position of seeming to want to tax the winners to help the losers*" [9].

Patents and copyrights are an example of how and why conservatives, quietly, support massive intervention by the government. Though we think of them as integral parts of the free market, patents and copyrights are explicit government policies to promote innovation and creative work. They reward inventors, musicians, writers, and other creative workers with government-enforced monopolies for set periods of time. These monopolies allow the holders to charge prices far above the free-market price. For example, in 2011 the US spent close to $300 billion on prescription drugs. In the absence of government-enforced patent monopolies, the same drugs would cost around $30 billion. This implies a transfer to the pharmaceutical industry of $270 billion a year, or about 1.8 percent of GDP—15 times current federal spending on the main government welfare program, Temporary Assistance for Needy Families (TANF) [9]. The higher expenditures are almost entirely a function of patent protection. An interesting calculation was made by Dean Baker using data from the Center for Medicare and Medicaid Services (2011b) and the Department of Treasury, Tax Policy Center (2010). In the period 2011-2020, the potential savings from free-market drugs could be $3.4 billion. This should be compared with the $680 million which the Bush tax cut for the wealthy cost the US budget, the elimination of which became the main goal of progressives [9], much to the consternation of *Forbes*, of course [10].

More importantly, the public also seems increasingly skeptical about the suitability of the market to handle the intricacies of the health-care industry in its entirety. I will draw from the work produced by the Center for Studying Health System Change (HSC). Founded in 1995, the Center worked to fulfill a vision set out by leaders at the Robert Wood Johnson Foundation. That vision was based on the premise that "*rigorous information and analysis built up from the community level could inform national health policy making.*" For almost 20 years, as a subsidiary of *Mathematica Policy Research* [11], HSC pursued that mission conducting policy research and analyses focused on the US health-care system to help policy makers in government and private industry make better decisions.[10] As they very aptly defined it in their mission statement:

> "*The quest for greater efficiency in the delivery of health care services is eternal in a country that spends far more on health care than any other, consistently has growth in spend-*

---

8   As we will see elsewhere, Obamacare also reduced non-paying hospital stays. This should, normally, put many hospitals on the ACA's side.
9   No pun intended.
10   Having established a high bar with respect to producing policy-relevant health services research, HSC ceased operations as an independent organization on December 31, 2013.

ing that outstrips that of income, is unable to provide insurance coverage to at least 15 percent of its population, and ranks poorly among industrialized countries in system-wide measures such as life expectancy and infant mortality. Add to this our quality problems, and it is hard to be complacent about the value US citizens receive for their health care dollars. Inefficiency also puts a very high public-sector price tag on universal coverage, which helps polarize the politics of this issue."

The Community Tracking Study (CTS) [12] has put the functioning of US health-care markets under a microscope for nine years. It has conducted periodic interviews in sixty communities with 60,000 households and 12,000 physicians, and additional surveys of employers and insurers. The CTS zooms in on twelve representative markets with site visits every two years that have produced nearly 2,700 interviews with local health system leaders.[11] An impressive amount of research on "health markets" has been produced and is available at the HSC website. As early as 2004, based on the results of the CTS, an important article in *Health Affairs* draws lessons for policy makers from twelve communities [13]. According to the authors:

". . . we identify the power and limits of general market-based strategies for improving the efficiency of health systems. The vision of market forces driving our system toward efficiency attracted politicians, policy analysts, and practitioners in the 1990s. Today some policy advocates profess even more faith in unfettered market forces. Market participants in the twelve communities in the Community Tracking Study, however, have become doubtful, and our analysis confirms the logic of their pessimism. That makes it difficult to ignore the sober findings. . . . In about 1,000 interviews during the latest round of site visits, CTS investigators found deep skepticism about the ability of market-based reforms to produce urgently needed improvements in the efficiency and quality of the nation's health care system. As much as these predominantly private-sector leaders dread the prospect of deeper interventions by government, few of them seem to be able to imagine other alternatives. Many health care market participants are now willing to consider strong governmental intervention to repair the health system."

The main characteristic of health care is that it is often unpredictable in its incidence, in the severity and duration of the need for health services, and in the cost of producing the care required. This uncertainty has led to the need for "pooling the risk," namely health insurance. In the vast majority of countries around the world this is understood as some sort of "public" health insurance, financed either through employer-employee contributions or through taxes. The common characteristic in both systems is that the insurance part is not-for-profit. Also, in the case of social insurance covered by employment contributions, any deficit at year's end is usually covered by public funds. On the contrary, in America, the almost total reliance on private, for-profit insurance threatens to ruin the economy and the society along with it. Apart from the ethical considerations, which we discuss elsewhere, the main point in this book is that insistence on employer-provided health insurance increases the cost of labor, leaves many without insurance, and leads to loss of competitiveness, unemployment, or both. Developments in the labor market in the last thirty years, a time of large increases in the cost of health care, are very illuminating.

---

11   In a testimony to the study's prestige, the Federal Trade Commission began the first two of its comprehensive hearings on competition in health care with framing presentations by senior CTS staff.

As we have shown in Part A, there is serious evidence that the American health-care system is problematic, to say the least. Experts have been ringing the bell for the last few years, and most of them have been either European researchers or Americans with an eye turned to experience in the rest of the world. Unfortunately, some academics, politicians, and business people in America have been rather nonchalant, confident that the American market-based economic system will redress whatever problems may exist, not only in health but in everything. Most of the time, the "knight in shining armor" is none else than what America trusts more, next only to God.

Competition and the Health Market

Competition is almost a deity to which Americans pay more than lip service. Considered the cornerstone of the economic system, it is based on dictums like "hard work," "getting up by your own bootstraps," "go it alone," and other dictums full of emotional undertones. There were times when such simplicities in popular novels worked as rules, promoting progress and social stability. All of these are clearly relics of a past which will never be again, with champions of the "American way," like Donald Trump, "threatening" to "conquer" the White House. Competition in the US health-care system operates at the wrong level, argue Professors Michael E. Porter of the Harvard Business School and Elizabeth Olmstead Teisberg, of the University of Virginia [14]. Porter and Teisberg think that:

> "Competition is both too broad and too narrow. Too broad because much of the competition now takes place at the level of health plans, networks, hospital groups, physician groups, and clinics, instead of addressing particular medical conditions. Competition is also too narrow because it now takes place at the level of discrete interventions or services, instead of addressing medical conditions over the full cycle of care, including monitoring and prevention, diagnosis, treatment, and the ongoing management of the condition."

The Affordable Care Act tries to improve competition through the creation of a "health insurance exchange" for small businesses and individual buyers, but new competition in the marketplace may be limited. The CBO found that premiums for individual plans on these insurance exchanges would increase by 10 to 13% by 2016. In the same book, investment analyst Julia Coranado argues, "Most people covered by employer-sponsored plans will not see many changes or benefits from increased competition, so there is little expected impact on healthcare inflation, although lower Medicare reimbursements will apply some downward pressure." The conclusion from the above is, again, that health care is not an ideal place for a market and the rules that come with it. However, there is another, perhaps more important, reason why the market and health do not mix well.

What Happened to the Moral Imperative?

The supremacy of the market in allocating health resources, admittedly not a very moral position, is not without dispute in America. It is, however, a stone wall on which many an effort to inject some empathy and build a moral case for health reform often crash. Under the title *What happened to the Moral Case for Health-Care Reform?*, Ezra Klein referred to T.R. Reid's *The Healing of America: A Global Quest for Better, Cheaper, and Fairer Health Care.* He wrote, referring to Reid's book, in the *Washington Post* in 2009, just as the debate over the ACA was getting under way [15]:

> *"It's very, very good. For now, however, I want to point out something he says about the successful efforts in Sweden and Taiwan to overcome the political opposition and rebuild their patchwork health care sectors into national health-care systems: Both countries decided that society has an ethical obligation, as a matter of justice, of fairness, of solidarity, to assure everybody has access to medical care when it's needed. The advocates of reform in both countries clarified and emphasized that moral issue much more than the nuts and bolts of the proposed reform plans. As a result, the national debate was waged around ideals like 'equal treatment for everybody,' 'we're all in this together,' and 'fundamental rights' rather than on the commercial implications for the health care industry."*

Elsewhere, Reid quotes Princeton health economist Uwe Reinhardt saying:

> *"The opponents of universal health insurance cloak their sentiments in actuarial technicalities or in the mellifluous language of the standard economic theory of markets, thereby avoiding a debate on ideology that truly might engage the American public."*

Klein concludes his criticism of the way supporters of the ACA were going about presenting it as mainly an attempt to control the cost of health care. He concludes:

> *"This year, however, it's not just been the opponents of the policy who have relied on the 'mellifluous language of the standard economic theory of markets.' It's been the advocates of reform. Ask yourself what the administration's one-line goal is on health-care reform. Is it 'equal treatment for everybody?' Is it 'if every American is guaranteed a lawyer, why not a doctor?' Is it even 'guaranteed health care for everyone?' No. It's 'bend the curve.' And the problem with 'bending the curve' is that it is a broadly testable proposition. This is, in part, why the Congressional Budget Office's skeptical assessments pose such a threat to health-care reform. If the White House's primary objective was health care for every American, or guaranteed care that you could keep even if you lost your job, or choice of insurance plans for every American, you could spend a bit more on health care and say you were achieving your goal. But if you say that the point of health-care reform is to save money, and then the outfit charged with estimating such things says it won't, that strikes at the heart of the project."*

The economic case for health-care reform requires a *really* radical version of reform such as single-payer, or the Wyden-Bennett Healthy Americans Act.[12] The consensus Democratic health-care plan—the basic approach that the Obama campaign committed itself to and that Democrats in Congress were pushing—was primarily a coverage plan. It had some cost-saving features in the margins, but it was primarily a way of getting to universal coverage. You

---

12 The Healthy Americans Act requires each adult individual to have the opportunity to purchase a Healthy Americans Private Insurance plan (HAPI). It makes individuals who are not enrolled in another specified health plan and who are not opposed to coverage for religious reasons responsible for enrolling themselves and their dependent children in a HAPI plan offered through their state of residence. It also sets forth penalties for failure to enroll. https://www.congress.gov/bill/110th-congress/senate-bill/334

can argue for that plan in primarily moral terms, with some economic arguments around the margins. But the administration was pushing it in primarily economic terms, with some moral arguments around the margins. And now, they seem caught in that dissonance.

There is some evidence that a push towards greater equity was gaining ground in the US as early as in the beginning of the new century. David Ignatius, a leading journalist with the *Washington Post*, wrote right after the November 2006 election [16]:

> *"The Democrats now have the opportunity the Republicans spurned, which is to build a broad coalition in the center and become once again the nation's governing party. But to achieve that, the Democrats must stand for values that connect with those of most Americans. There are three main issues on which the Democrats should plant their flag and try to create a new majority."*

According to the journalist, besides a new energy policy, the two other major policy goals should be: *"reviving the Clinton administration's push for national health care policies that can save costs and improves care,"* and *"a focus on economic justice."* The latter is an issue also advanced by Jim Webb, Virginia Senator, with an article in the *Wall Street Journal*, not exactly a favorite forum for liberal voices. Besides Senator Hillary Clinton, who signed on this agenda, former senator John Edwards, another leading contender for 2008, put his stamp on the same issue through his new Center on Poverty, Work, and Opportunity at the University of North Carolina [17].

The moral imperative behind the Affordable Care Act should, in fact, be that no American should have to do without health insurance coverage, even if they could not afford it. This however, seemed to run against a moral position in the Constitution that the government cannot force an individual to act in a way that the government, which presumably represents the will of society, obliges him to. Politics and morality are two concepts which come to mind when we think of Ronald Reagan's famous dictum from his first Inaugural Address: *". . . government is not the solution to our problem; government is the problem."* It is for this reason that the Affordable Care Act became the "battle of battles" between Republicans and Democrats, not resolved, even after June 2015 [18]. It is our position in this book that the battle must be carried to its "natural field," namely the right to health care through national health insurance for universal health coverage.

It is already more than a decade since the idea appeared, but America is a country where good ideas are not discarded easily. They may have to pass the test of time and measure up to values held sacred by the American people. We believe that a caring society does not go against the grain of American values. Some of these positions were vindicated by the legislation passed by President Obama. As we are already in 2016, it is, finally, time that Americans were convinced that a degree of social solidarity is not a "communist ploy" but a prerequisite for a viable society. And the time to show it is the 2016 presidential election. Unfortunately, at the time of writing the result is still not known.

References

[1]   Hacker J. The Free Market Fantasy. In: *Policy Network. Making Progressive Politics Work*. London: Global Press 2014; pp. 34-36.

[2]   Reinhardt UE. What Is 'Socialized Medicine'?: A Taxonomy of Health Care Systems; *The International New York Times* [newspaper on the Internet]. 8th May 2009 [cited: 7th June 2016]. Available from: http://economix.blogs.nytimes.com/2009/05/08/what-is-socialized-medicine-a-taxonomy-of-health-care-systems/?_r=1#more-11767

[3]   Geyman JP. A Five-Year assessment of the affordable care act: Market forces still trump the common good in US Health care. *International Journal of Health Services*. 2015; 45(2):209–25.

[4]   *The Economist* [magazine on the Internet]. Business in America: The problem with profits. 26th March 2016 [cited: 17th June 2016]. Available from: http://www.economist.com/news/leaders/21695392-big-firms-united-states-have-never-had-it-so-good-time-more-competition-problem-lem

[5]   Fulop N, Protopsaltis G, Hutchings A, et al. *Process and impact of mergers of NHS trusts: multi-centre case study and management cost analysis*. 3rd August 2002; BMJ; 325: 246.

[6]   UK Government Web Archive [homepage on the Internet]. UK: Department of Health; The NHS Plan: a plan for investment, a plan for reform; [cited: 7th June 2016]. Available from: http://webarchive.nationalarchives.gov.uk/+/www.dh.gov.uk/en/publicationsandstatistics/publications/publicationspolicyandguidance/dh_4002960

[7]   Relman A. Health Care: The Disquieting Truth. *The New York Review of Books* [homepage on the Internet]. 30th September 2010 [cited: 7th June 2016]. Available from: http://www.nybooks.com/articles/2010/09/30/health-care-disquieting-truth/

[8]   Relman AS. *A Second Opinion: Rescuing America's Health Care: A Plan for Universal Coverage Serving Patients Over Profit*. United States: Public Affairs 2010.

[9]   Baker D. *The End of Loser Liberalism: Making Markets Progressive*. United States: Center for Economic and Policy Research 2011.

[10]   Ferrara P. Why America Is Going To Miss The Bush Tax Cuts. *Forbes* [magazine on the Internet]. 2012 [cited: 7th June 2016]. Available from: http://www.forbes.com/sites/peterferrara/2012/12/06/why-america-is-going-to-miss-the-bush-tax-cuts/#7097d23a5f38

[11]   Center for Studying Health System Change [homepage on the Internet]. *HSC: A Legacy of Policy-Relevant Research to Inform Decisions* [cited: 7th June 2016]. Available from: http://www.hschange.org/index.cgi?file=Mathematica-Dedication

[12]   Center for Studying Health System Change [homepage on the Internet]. *Design and Methods for the Community Tracking Study* [cited: 7th June 2016]. Available from: http://www.hschange.com/index.cgi?data=01

[13]   Nichols LM, Ginsburg PB, Berenson RA, Christianson J, Hurley RE. Are Market Forces Strong Enough To Deliver Efficient Health Care Systems? Confidence Is Waning. *Health Affairs* [journal on the Internet]. March 2004; [cited: 7th June 2016]. Available from: http://content.healthaffairs.org/content/23/2/8.long

[14]   Porter ME, Teisberg EO. *Redefining Health Care: Creating Positive-Sum Competition to Deliver Value*. Boston, MA: Harvard Business School Press; 2006.

[15]   Klein E. What Happened to the Moral Case for Health-Care Reform? *Washington Post* [newspaper on the Internet]. 27th July 2009 [cited: 7th June 2016]. Available from: http://voices.washingtonpost.

com/ezra-klein/2009/07/what_happened_to_the_moral_cas.html

[16]   Ignatius D. Issues Front and Center. *Washington Post* [newspaper on the Internet]. 17th November 2006 [cited: 7th June 2016]. Available from: http://www.washingtonpost.com/wp-dyn/content/article/2006/11/16/AR2006111601362.html

[17]   UNC School of Law [homepage on the Internet]. N.C. Poverty Research Fund [cited: 7th June 2016]. Available from: http://www.law.unc.edu/centers/poverty/

[18]   Bravin J, Radnofsky L. Supreme Court Upholds Obama's Health-law Subsidies. *The Wall Street Journal* [newspaper on the Internet]. 25th June 2015 [cited: 7th June 2016]. Available from: http://www.wsj.com/articles/supreme-court-upholds-obamas-health-law-subsidies-1434737182

PART D

A Long March to a New Health-Care System

INTRODUCTION

A LONG MARCH TO A NEW HEALTH CARE SYSTEM

"We have a long-standing critical problem in our health care system that is pulling down our economy."

—*Barack Obama, June 2009 [1]*

President Barack Obama made reform in health care one of his top priorities. He, inadvertedly, came up against ideological hurdles such as mandates for insurers, individuals, and employers, the level of government participation, and how to pay for health care. There are so many varieties of solutions to choose from when it comes to paying for health care, producing services, and assuming responsibility for the quality and safety as well as the effectiveness of health service provision that a renowned Harvard University professor came up with as many as fifteen solutions [2]. At the same time there is justified concern among economists and business leaders that mounting health care costs affect not only domestic economic health but also the US's ability to compete globally. The number of health-care pundits who see the single-payer system as a solution is increasing but the jury is still out.

The facts and data listed in Part A of this book paint a strange picture of a health system. The most expensive among the world's developed countries, it leaves many unsatisfied, without quality care when needed, and with Americans' life expectancy worsening [3]. It compromises the competitiveness of industries—even whole sectors—and perhaps the economy as a whole. Worst of all, for the exorbitant price America pays, Americans do not get back what other developed nations get for half the money. For many, save partly the elderly and the poor, the main problem is dependence on private employment-based insurance. And yet, the American public views private health insurance as the best way—if not the only acceptable way—of securing appropriate health care at affordable cost available when needed. The nonchalant dependence on the market to secure efficient governance of health care production and distribution in America is put to rest by mentioning just two facts concerning bankruptcy in the US [4]:

- Nearly two-thirds, or 62%, of all bankruptcy filings in the United States in 2007 were due to illness or medical bills.

- Among the medical bankruptcy filers in 2007, most were well-educated, owned homes, were employed in middle-class occupations, and three-quarters had health insurance.

Ill health is probably the worst calamity that can afflict an individual or a family. It saps our energy, denies us the ability to take part in the normal activities of normal life, prevents us from working or impairs our productivity, and prevents us from achieving our full potential as individuals and members of society. And yet, making certain that societal arrangements contribute to the preservation and/or restoration of good health does not seem to be a matter of major concern to politicians, political and interest groups, or political parties in America. As we argue in this book, denial of universal coverage, for whatever economic, political, ethical, or philosophical reasons, is a serious threat to the health of society.

Lack of health insurance, painful for millions, is not all that ails the American health system. In fact, the system is succeeding for the majority, but in an expensive and inequitable way. Henry Mintzberg, faculty director at McGill University, advises on how to fix it by looking at it in a different way. The main point America needs to realize, he says, is that "to build a genuine system that promotes health and treats illness is by cooperation, not by competition" [5]. He proposes a much more humane look at what medical care really is, other than a business endeavor, as we described it in Chapter C-1.

Inequities grow in American society because of growing income inequality. This is not only shown by the rising income at the top 1% of the income distribution [6], but mainly by the increasing number and share of the population who become poor. Roughly fifteen percent (14.8%) of the population was under the poverty level in 2014, up from 12.7% only a decade before [7]. In 2014, more than 46 million people, up from 37 million in 2004, were unable to afford not only health insurance but even the most rudimentary health care.[1] For ten million more Americans, health care became unaffordable in only ten years. This is probably the most powerful argument for universal health coverage through national health insurance.

If the health-care system is the source of such calamities, one must suggest ways to change it. This involves not only the way Americans pay for it, but also how health care is delivered. This, in turn, implies the need for changes in the medical profession and the role of the doctor in the health system. It also means changing the perception that "the American health system is the best in the world," because the market makes it so. Finally, change in the health system must obey philosophical underpinnings, such as the right to health care. As this book must offer a proposal, we chose universal health coverage through national health insurance. We also propose government involvement and regulation, instead of the market, to promote efficiency and effectiveness in health care.

Most of the elements of a good health system, as we described in the Introduction of Part A, exist in America, which, in fact, excels in many aspects essential to a successful health system. But, as we point out on many occasions, the American health system lacks the basic internal logic which in every system governs its operation so as to achieve its goals. Or, rather, we may say that this logic, being the logic of the market, is not suitable to a health system. The market depends on purchasing power, which is the ability to pay a certain price. It is the inability of the individual to bear the full cost of prevention, detection, and treatment at any time that makes universal public health insurance coverage of some kind an essential element of a health system. Protecting the individual from the economic consequences, it enables him to protect, maintain, and restore good health.

There are many excellent health systems around the world to choose from, but this requires a new social and economic paradigm for health care in America, which we address in this Part D. There are three major characteristics in each health system, which can be pictured in the form of a diagram. Figure D-1 below shows the three dimensions in which all health systems develop in order to satisfy the citizens' health needs, incurring the corresponding costs in the

---

1 This dropped to roughly 30 million in 2015, below the 2004 level, because of the ACA.

process. There are three possible courses of action in terms of coverage: The breadth of coverage, or the proportion of the people covered; the depth of coverage, or the proportion of services covered; and the height of coverage, or the proportion of the cost covered. All economic activity occurs, therefore, by default, inside the big white box in Figure D-1. Complete coverage of all people for all health services and for 100 percent of the cost is what a system like the British offers. The shaded box inside the white box, on the other hand, represents the part of the health care activity which is only in the public domain. The smaller the shaded box, the smaller the public sector involvement. This means the fewer people are covered publicly, the fewer services are covered by public insurance, and the smaller the portion of the cost this public insurance covers. The points in question are, therefore, the breadth of the population covered by public insurance, the depth of the services covered, and the height of the cost covered.

Figure D-1 represents a fictional "average" health system, if one existed. If the box were to describe the British system where the National Health Service (NHS) covers every British citizen, for nearly all of the services, at almost 100% of the cost, the shaded box would cover almost the whole area in all three dimensions, leaving only a small part in the "height" axis, for private health insurance. On the contrary, in the US the shaded box would be drawn closer to the right, as public expenditure on Medicare, Medicaid, etc. barely reaches 40%. If the extent of public involvement were to change in one of the three aspects of health care, as with the ACA, the shaded box would change shape accordingly.

In this book we maintain that the box in the horizontal "breadth" axis should be extended all the way, much more than the ACA did. This means that national health insurance (NHI) and universal health coverage (UHC) should cover all Americans. The "depth" axis, however, would not extend "all the way" since the basic UHC package, a political choice, would cover only "essential" services, leaving room for private complementary health insurance. The "height" axis would also be a political choice, as the extent of NHI would also require supplementary coverage. After all, politics and ethics in America, as we saw in Part C, are such that private responsibility in health will likely remain sacrosanct for the years to come.

Figure D-1. The Essential Characteristics of a Health System.

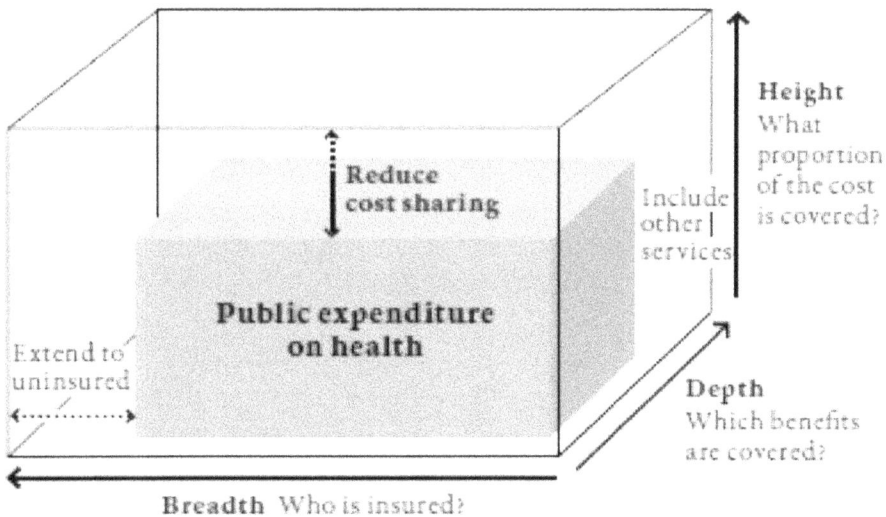

References

[1]   The White House [webpage on the Internet]. Press Conference by the President. Office of the Press Secretary; 2009 [cited: 7th June 2016]. Available from: https://www.whitehouse.gov/the-press-office/press-conference-president-6-23-09

[2]   Reinhardt UE. What Is 'Socialized Medicine'?: A Taxonomy of Health Care Systems; *The International New York Times* [newspaper on the Internet]. 2009 [cited: 7th June 2016]. Available from: http://economix.blogs.nytimes.com/2009/05/08/what-is-socialized-medicine-a-taxonomy-of-health-care-systems/?_r=1#more-11767

[3]   The Economist [magazine on the Internet]. The longevity gap: America's big spending on health care doesn't pay off. 16th November 2015; [cited: 7th June 2016]. Available from: http://www.economist.com/news/21678669-americas-big-spending-health-care-doesnt-pay

[4]   Himmelstein DU, Thorne D, Warren E, Woolhandler S. Medical bankruptcy in the United States, 2007: Results of a national study. *The American Journal of Medicine.* 2009; 122(8):741–6.

[5]   Mintzberg H. To Fix Health Care, Ask the Right Questions. *Harvard Business Review.* 2011. [cited: 7th June 2016]. Available from: https://hbr.org/2011/10/to-fix-health-care-ask-the-right-questions.

[6]   Strachan M. The US Is Even More Unequal Than You Realized; *The Huffington Post* [website on the Internet]. 1st May 2014 [cited: 7th June 2016]. Available from: http://www.huffingtonpost.com/2014/05/01/income-inequality-charts_n_5241586.html

[7]   The United States Census Bureau [webpage on the Internet]. US Department of Commerce: Poverty; 2016 [cited: 7th June 2016]. Available from: https://www.census.gov/topics/income-poverty/poverty.html

D-1: CHOOSING A HEALTH-CARE MODEL

In health care, the days of business as usual are over. Around the world, every health care system is struggling with rising costs and uneven quality despite the hard work of well-intentioned, well-trained clinicians. Health-care leaders and policy makers have tried countless incremental fixes—attacking fraud, reducing errors, enforcing practice guidelines, making patients better "consumers," implementing electronic medical records—but none have had much impact. It's time for a fundamentally new strategy [1].

More than ten years ago, a number of academics noticed the problem of the escalating health care costs. Mostly economists, they looked for "radical" solutions based on economic logic. Michael E. Porter and others, for example, looked for the application of good-old accounting methods. Even before that, in 2006, Michael E. Porter and Elizabeth Olmsted Teisberg wrote an influential book titled *Redefining Health Care: Creating Value-Based Competition on Results*. In promoting the book, Amazon then wrote:

"The US health care system is in crisis. At stake are the quality of care for millions of Americans and the financial well-being of individuals and employers squeezed by sky-rocketing premiums--not to mention the stability of state and federal government budgets. In Redefining Health Care, internationally renowned strategy expert Michael E. Porter and innovation expert Elizabeth Olmsted Teisberg reveal the underlying--and largely overlooked--causes of the problem and provide a powerful prescription for change. The authors argue that participants in the health care system have competed to shift costs, accumulate bargaining power, and restrict services rather than create value for patients. This zero-sum competition takes place at the wrong level--among health plans, networks, and hospitals--rather than where it matters most: in the diagnosis, treatment, and prevention of specific health conditions. Redefining Health Care lays out a breakthrough framework for redefining health care competition based on patient value. With specific recommendations for hospitals, doctors, health plans, employers, and policy makers, this book shows how to move to a positive-sum competition that will unleash stunning improvements in quality and efficiency."

In 2011, Michael Porter, this time with Robert Kaplan, stated that *"the remedy to the cost crisis does not require medical science breakthroughs or new governmental regulation. It simply requires a new way to accurately measure costs and compare them with outcomes."* If only good accounting were enough to fix the fundamental ethical and political problem responsible for the health conundrum in which America finds itself. Porter, Teisberg, and Kaplan's views were only a fragmented and partial look at the health system. Instead of looking at the system holistically, it passes over the predominant funding scheme, mainly through employment-based private insurance, which, in fact, is the reason why the health-care system is no longer sustainable.

When the campaign in the Scotland Referendum of September 19, 2014 was at its peak, both the British government and the Scottish Nationalist Party used the National Health Service (NHS) as the "heavy weapon" in their campaigns.[1] They both extolled its virtues and exorcised the danger, should Scotland secede. The NHS is a venerable institution in all four British nations,[2] not so much for the quality of services it offers,[3] but for the fact that they are free of charge. Tax-financed national health insurance is the strong point in the British (and not only) health system. That it costs half of what Americans spend for health is something one should bear in mind. On the other hand, much is said about the French and the German health systems, a bit more expensive than the British, but also ranked among top world performers— prime examples of social health insurance through mandatory employment contributions, in a varying mix with government financing. The Dutch and the Swiss systems, where private health insurance plays a major role, offer a third way of financing with a more private "bend," but still mandatory insurance.[4]

The interesting part in such comparisons is that all countries mentioned have at one time or the other been declared as the best health system in Europe [2]. At the same time, they all spend much less per head, compared to the US. In fact, they offer the best proof that overall performance is not related to expenditure, but rather to the way the health system is financed and organized in terms of access to and delivery of care. In other words, we are looking for a health system that is effective, which means it attains its health goals, but is also efficient and cost-effective which is to say that it does so at a cost society is willing and, most importantly, able, to pay.

The selection of a health system involves two main choices: the choice of financing scheme and the choice of health service delivery. The choice of a social insurance as a single-payer is really the choice of tax-funded national health insurance (NHI). Social health insurance (SHI), based on mandatory employer-employee (labor) contributions, is the other option. Here the choice is actually the incidence of the burden, which is to say equity, efficiency of resource collection, and sustainability in the future. The choice of delivery mechanism is among private and public providers or between for-profit and non-profit forms of health-care delivery. Perhaps a closer look at European social insurance and social protection mechanisms will be a useful guide.

A Comparison of Social Insurance Systems in Europe

America has a long historical tradition with and cultural roots in Europe. Influenced by European ideological and philosophical trends, the US is also contributing its own ideas to Europe and the world. A comparison of social health insurance in Europe reveals considerable differences, but a general classification into two basic systems is still possible and perhaps useful to America. The Bismarck system is based primarily on social insurance contributions by labor, meaning employers and employees; In the Beveridge system the financing is mainly from taxes. In other words, an optimal Bismarck system leads to no redistribution between various income groups, while Beveridge-type financing redistributes incomes to the extent the taxation system is progressive. There is, however, a trend in Europe today for the two financing systems to converge. The reason is that Bismarck-type systems rely mainly on contributions by labor, the

---

1 The question was whether Scotland should secede from the United Kingdom. The answer was "NO."
2 England, Wales, Scotland, and Northern Ireland.
3 Queuing and waiting times in general are often a matter of criticism.
4 The difference with the US is that the phenomenon of a Dutch or Swiss citizen without health insurance is simply inconceivable.

factor of production losing out in the era of globalization, and it also affects the competitiveness of the economy.

The Bismarck system goes back to Otto von Bismarck who, with the introduction of a statutory health insurance (1883) in Germany, paved the way for a near comprehensive social insurance system. Bismarck's goal was to counter social unrest and socialism and also to weaken the trade unions and church-run labor federations. The Bismarck system is characterized by three points:

- The insured persons are employees or gainfully employed;

- The financing is via contributions, graduated according to income;

- The contributions to be paid are based on wages or salaries.

The Beveridge system is named after William Henry Beveridge, who in 1942 presented a comprehensive report on social policy to the British Parliament. The report contained concrete proposals for the creation of a comprehensive social insurance system which included the integration of existing social insurance types, the creation of a general health service including workplace accident insurance, the introduction of family assistance, the maintenance of a high and stable employment rate as well as protection against mass unemployment. These proposals were the foundation for the postwar British social insurance scheme. The Beveridge system is marked by the following:

- It includes the entire population, not just the gainfully employed;

- It is primarily financed from the state budget;

- It calls for uniform, lump-sum contributions by general tax proceeds.

It is not always clear which country can be assigned to what system, since no country follows either of the two systems in its pure form. Over time, there are also shifts towards the Beveridge or the Bismarck model. This means that a clear system allocation is not always possible. Table D1-1 shows health financing in OECD countries. It is evident that the prevailing source of financing for social protection was social insurance contributions, which accounted for 41.7% of total receipts. Government allocation from tax revenues amounted to 30.6%. In addition, one-fifth of all health expenditure is OOP, although the average is heavily influenced by a few countries such as Mexico, Chile, Korea, and Greece. The most interesting observation is that the US is the only country where private health insurance amounts to almost twice that of either government or social security.

Table D1-1. Expenditure on Health by Source of Financing as a Share (%) of Total Current Health Expenditure, OECD Countries, 2014.

Country	General Government (Government schemes)	Social Security (Compulsory contributory health insurance schemes)	Private out-of-pocket (Household out-of-pocket payment)	Private insurance (Voluntary health care payment schemes)
Austria	31.1	44.7	17.7	6.4
Belgium	11.4	66.2	17.8	4.6
Canada	69.2	1.5	14.3	15.0
Chile	2.3	58.2	32.8	6.7
Czech Republic	11.6	71.9	13.2	3.3
Estonia	9.9	65.6	22.7	1.6
Finland	62.2	13.2	19.1	5.5

Country	General Government (Government schemes)	Social Security (Compulsory contributory health insurance schemes)	Private out-of-pocket (Household out-of-pocket payment)	Private insurance (Voluntary health care payment schemes)
France	4.1	74.5	7.0	14.4
Germany	6.6	78.0	13.0	2.4
Greece	28.4	31.3	35.4	3.7
Hungary	9.4	57.6	28.4	4.6
Iceland	52.1	29.0	17.5	1.5
Ireland	69.0	0.3	15.4	15.3
Italy	75.5	0.3	22.0	2.2
Korea	10.2	46.3	36.8	6.7
Luxembourg	8.5	75.1	10.7	5.7
Mexico	24.5	28.1	40.8	6.6
Netherlands	4.8	75.8	12.3	7.1
Norway	74.2	10.9	14.5	0.4
Poland	9.1	62.4	22.5	6.0
Portugal	64.9	1.3	27.5	6.2
Slovak Republic	4.0	76.2	18.0	1.8
Slovenia	3.4	67.6	13.0	16.0
Spain	65.0	4.8	24.7	5.5
Switzerland	18.6	46.5	26.7	8.1
Turkey	21.3	56.3	17.7	4.7
UK	79.5	0.1	14.8	5.7
United States	26.1	23.1	11.5	39.2
OECD Mean *(28)*	30.6	41.7	20.3	7.4

Source: OECD Health Expenditure and Financing Data, 2016.

Some convergence of the two types of health system in a country comparison over time is apparent in Europe, and one may ask why this convergence occurs. Both systems, initially, had two basic goals. The first was to tackle the problems of poverty and income inequality, to foster social cohesion, and to advance the efficiency of the economy as a whole. This was primarily the function of the taxation system. The second was to improve individual security and alleviate unknown social risks. This was to be achieved by unemployment, health, and old-age insurance.

Since the inception of the Bismarck and the Beveridge systems, the economic and social climate in Europe has changed, and, in fact, greatly improved. This included demographic changes. An increase in life expectancy led to an extension of periods of non-employment and dependency. Moreover, changes in fertility rates have also impacted the financing of the social insurance system. This has been accompanied by a shift in the age structure of the population: the share of people over 65 years old has increased and the share of younger cohorts has declined. This meant a strong increase in the old-age dependency ratio. Figure D1-1 shows this ratio for the year 2000 and the relative increase expected by 2025 and 2050. The combination of an increase in average life expectancies and the decline in the fertility rate will lead to a doubling of the old-age dependency ratio. Whereas in 2000 the ratio between those over 65 and the working-age population was 1 to 4, in 2050 it will be nearly 1 to 2.

Figure D1-1. Old-Age Dependency Ratio, 2000, and Expected Change until 2025 and 2050.

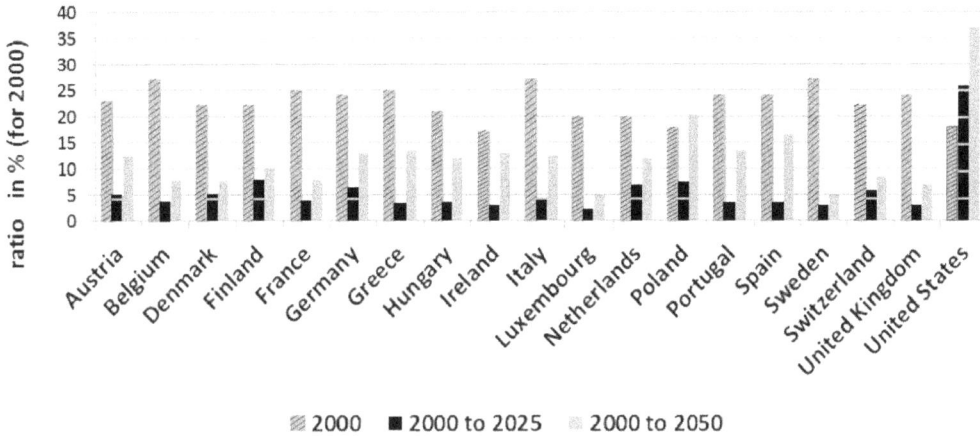

Since the population pyramid has inverted, social insurance contributors must support an increasing number of people who no longer contribute. This is something the Bismarck system did not envision when employment contributions were instituted. But the Beveridge system is also under demographic pressure. In terms of health care, the demographic changes are becoming an increasing burden on tax revenues both quantitatively (more old and illness-prone people) and qualitatively (more expensive medical services and technology). The problem here is that health-care system financing must "compete" for tax allocations with other policy areas. This means that Beveridge-type social insurance systems are also becoming difficult to finance. A pure systemic change in itself is no solution. It is still unclear how far the trend of convergence will go. But one thing is certain: as long as there is a difference in living standards among countries, a full convergence cannot be realistically expected.

In this case, the issue of whether the economy can support a good health system and under what conditions is important. For America, one thing is certain as a lesson from Europe. Apart from building a caring society, a successful country needs a good health system. There are a number of international country listings according to a variety of attributes. We chose the *US News* "Best Countries Rankings" [3], conducted in partnership with brand strategy firm BAV Consulting and the Wharton School of the University of Pennsylvania. The ranking is based on a survey of more than 16,000 people from four regions, asked to associate 60 countries with specific characteristics. Of those, more than 8,000 were "informed elites" (college-educated, middle- or upper-class individuals). More than 4,500 were business leaders, defined as senior leaders in an organization or individuals who own a small business that employ others. The rest belonged to the general public.

Germany tops the list of "Best Countries" with Canada following. The US is fourth, after the UK and before Sweden. This is because America ranks 14th in the category "quality of life" [4]. This sub-ranking is based on an equally weighted average of scores from nine attributes that relate to quality of life in a country: affordable, a good job market, economically stable, family friendly, income equality, politically stable, safe, well-developed public education system and **well-developed public health system.** The "quality of life" sub-ranking score had a 17 percent weight in the overall "Best Countries" ranking.

In the category of quality of life, among the worst US scores are for "a well-developed public health system." It is interesting that the Canadian system has been repeatedly judged as superior to that of the US [5], and that all the countries before and close after the US as "Best Country," except for Canada, were European. Most of the European countries included in the "Best Countries Rankings" have, in fact, at one time or another, been ranked as "Best Health System in Europe" by the Health Consumer Powerhouse (CHP), a specialized international organization [6]. An independent monitor of health care in 35 European countries, the HCP published its 9th edition of the Euro Health Consumer Index (EHCI) on January 26, 2016. Since 2006, this comparison of key values in health-care—taking the patient and the consumer points of view—improved the understanding of European health care, empowered patients, and helped address weaknesses. EHCI, and a wide range of disease-specific studies produced by the Health Consumer Powerhouse Ltd. (HCP), set standards for what could and should be achieved by modern, well-serving health care.[5] It's a pity that it is not possible to "grade" the US health system in a manner comparable to that used by the EHCI.

Health Care and the Economy

As it often happens in the US, the debate before major changes are adopted centers—and rightly so—on the effect on the economy. As early as 2009 John Nichols wrote in *The Nation*:[6]

> "*There is an unhealthy tendency on the part of politicians and journalists to see discussions about economic recovery and health care reform as separate debates. In fact, one of the most important steps on the road to economic recovery – or, more precisely, toward a new, responsible and sustainable prosperity – involves the fundamental reform this country's broken health care system.*"

Since then the literature on a national single-payer style health-care reform system, as for example, by expanding the existing Medicare system to cover all Americans, has proliferated. The debate has gone on for almost ten years, but 2016 was the first year when it entered the central political scene when adopted by Bernie Sanders. Of course, before that it had been embraced by other groups.

According to "Single Payer/Medicare for All: An Economic Stimulus Plan for the Nation," a study released in 2009 by the National Nurses Organizing Committee/California Nurses Association, such a reform would provide a major stimulus for the US economy by creating 2.6 million new jobs and infusing $317 billion in new business and public revenues into the economy. This reform would, according to the study, add $100 billion in wages to the currently sputtering US economy. At that time, it was estimated by the NNOC/CAN that the number of jobs created by a single-payer system, expanding and upgrading Medicare to cover everyone, parallels almost exactly the total job loss in 2008. "*These dramatic new findings document for the first time that a single payer system could not only solve our healthcare crisis, but also substantially contribute to putting America back to work and assisting the economic recovery*," said NNOC/CAN co-president Geri Jenkins, RN. Specifically, expanding Medicare to include the uninsured,

---

5 The Index is freely available on http://www.healthpowerhouse.com/

6 Admittedly, *The Nation* has a distinct political agenda in what it publishes, but then which major magazine doesn't?

and those on Medicaid or employer-sponsored health plans, and expanding coverage for those with limited Medicare, would

- create 2,613,495 new permanent good-paying jobs (slightly exceeding the number of jobs lost in 2008)—jobs that are not easily shipped overseas;

- boost the economy with $317 billion in increased business and public revenues;

- add $100 billion in employee compensation;

- infuse public budgets with $44 billion in new tax revenues;

"If we were to expand our present Medicare system to cover all Americans, the economic stimulus alone would create an immense engine that would help drive our national economy for decades to come," said the study's lead author, Don DeMoro, Director of the Institute for Health and Socio-Economic Policy, the NNOC/CNA research arm.

This was just one example of what could be said for the single-payer system applied in one form or the other by most developed countries in the world. Perhaps adding another economic twist would make the case more convincing.

Health Insurance and Competitiveness

When Wilbur Ross, an American industrialist, was complaining that his foreign competitors had an "unfair advantage," he should have been taken seriously by politicos in Washington. In 2006, Malcolm Gladwell published a very important article in *The New Yorker*. The title was "The Risk Pool: What's behind Ireland's economic miracle—and G.M.'s financial crisis?" [7]. According to Gladwell, when Bethlehem Steel filed for bankruptcy in 2001 it had three billion dollars in unmet health-care obligations and another four billion owed to its pension plan. In 2003, the pension plan was handed over to the federal government's Pension Benefit Guaranty Corporation Plan (PBGC) and the assets were sold to investor Wilbur Ross, a New York-based industrialist. Ross had realized a long time before that industry *"was there for the profits it could make out of the business in which it specialized and not to provide health and pension plans."* He said, *"that means perhaps a fifteen per cent cost disadvantage versus foreigners due to . . . historical accident."*[7]

The article was important and I would like to believe that it played a role in the election of a president with something like Obamacare high on his agenda. This was the first time that the position by the government that the cost of health insurance for working people who could not afford it was to be tested. I don't think ethics played a role in public approval. More important, I think, was the realization on the part of the business community that the costs of health insurance borne to a large extent by them, were no longer sustainable. Many of them were probably business people who voted down the Clinton proposal in 1993.

I think it is time that industry realize that meeting pensions and health care needs the biggest pool possible to share a risk that is common to all, namely old age and illness. The pension question is taken care of by Social Security, financed by contributions and taxes. The health needs of the old are well dealt with by Medicare and those of the poor partially by Medicaid. What is left is the health of the bulk of the population and the *economic health* of their employ-

---

7   Referring to the end-of-the-war period and the '50s when the shortage of workers caused industries to compete for hands and talent by offering pension and health benefits.

ees. To put it simply, the present system penalizes companies for doing what they *ought* to do, which is being profitable for their stockholders, their employees, and the government's tax kitty. The damage inflicted on competitiveness is a "double whammy," among American companies in different sectors and among American firms and their competitors abroad.

Health costs are a function of age, rising at middle age and even more at old age. General Motors (GM), by American standards, in 2006 had an old workforce, much older than Google's, or Audi's in Germany, or China today. In America the cost of private health insurance for an employee aged 35-39 was $3,759 per year, and for someone between 65 and 69, $7.622.[8] This explains two things very well. First, why GM in 2006 had an estimated $62 billion in health-care liabilities. I doubt very much Google had anything to worry about when it let its much younger workers fend for themselves in terms of health insurance. Second, why GM sank under the competition by its foreign rivals, whose governments carried the burden of health-care costs, with state-run health systems and national health insurance.[9] Table D1-2 shows the effect of health insurance on employer costs, with health benefits at 7.7% of employee costs [8]. This is effectively a rough estimate of the competitiveness disadvantage of American industry compared to other countries with government-sponsored health insurance.

Table D1-2. Relative Importance of Employer Costs for Employee Compensation, September 2015.

COMPENSATION COMPONENT	CIVILIAN WORKERS	PRIVATE INDUSTRY	STATE AND LOCAL GOVERNMENT
Wages and salaries	68.6%	69.7%	63.7%
Benefits	31.4%	30.3%	36.3%
Paid leave	7.0%	6.9%	7.3%
Supplemental pay	2.8%	3.3%	0.8%
Insurance	8.9%	8.2%	12.0%
Health benefits	**8.5%**	**7.7%**	**11.6%**
Retirement and savings	5.2%	4.0%	10.4%
Defined benefit	3.2%	1.7%	9.5%
Defined contribution	2.0%	2.2%	0.8%
Legally required	7.6%	7.9%	5.9%

We conclude this chapter by pointing to a system which could serve as a model for both the federal government and the individual American states. Health care in the United Kingdom was organized as a National Health Service originally for the four nations (England, Northern Ireland, Scotland, and Wales). After the devolution of responsibility for organizing health services in 1997, the four nations diverged in the details of how health care was organized. They all, however, maintained their National Health Service which provides universal access to a

---

8   We use the 2006 figures mentioned in the Gladwell article simply to make the point.
9   This is a point many countries with social insurance systems, like France, Germany, and others, should bear in mind, as well.

comprehensive package of services, mostly free at the point of use, financed by tax proceeds. Although the UK spends less on health compared to other European countries, the NHS functions remarkably well, with substantial improvements in major health indicators over the past decades. Although the UK also faces key challenges which it needs to address, these are a trifle compared to the problems in America which the new health system must overcome. The main areas where changes are essential are insurance coverage, the means of financing, and the organization of the health-care market.

References

[1] Porter M, Lee T. The strategy that will fix health care; *Harvard Business Review* [magazine on the Internet]. 1st October 2013 [cited: 7th June 2016]. Available from: https://hbr.org/2013/10/the-strategy-that-will-fix-health-care

[2] Health Consumer Powerhouse [webpage on the Internet]. The Commonwealth Fund; 2014 [cited: 7th June 2016]. Available from: http://www.healthpowerhouse.com/en/news/the-2014-euro-health-consumer-index/

[3] *US News* [webpage on the Internet]. Best Countries: Ranking Global Performance. 2016 [cited: 7th June 2016]. Available from: http://www.usnews.com/news/best-countries

[4] *US News* [webpage on the Internet]. Best Countries: Quality of Life. 2016 [cited: 7th June 2016]. Available from: http://www.usnews.com/news/best-countries/quality-of-life-rankings

[5] Jones DT, Kilgour D. *Uneasy Neighbours: Canada, the USA and the Dynamics of State, Industry and Culture.* United Kingdom: John Wiley & Sons Canada; 2007.

[6] Health Consumer Powerhouse [webpage on the Internet]. Publications; 2016 [cited: 7th June 2016]. Available from: http://www.healthpowerhouse.com/publications/

[7] Gladwell M. The Risk Pool: What's behind Ireland's economic miracle—and G.M.'s financial crisis?; *The New Yorker* [magazine on the Internet]. 28th August 2006 [cited: 7th June 2016]. Available from: http://www.newyorker.com/magazine/2006/08/28/the-risk-pool

[8] Bureau of Labor Statistics. Employer Costs for Employee Compensation--March 2016. USA: US Department of Labor; 2016.

D-2: A NEW LOOK AT HEALTH FINANCING

"Every country against which we compete has universal health care."

—*Willbur Ross, Industrialist*

The US health-care system is a mix of employer-provided insurance, government-provided Medicare and Medicaid, state-provided high-risk pools for the "medically uninsurable," as well as out-of-pocket (OOP) payments by the uninsured, which do not fall into any of these programs. Most Americans, except for those over 65 or the unemployed and poor, get their health insurance through an employer-sponsored program. According to the United States Census Bureau, 60% of Americans are covered through an employer, and only 9% purchase health insurance directly. The US has a joint federal/state system for regulating insurance, with the federal government ceding primary responsibility to the states under the McCarran-Ferguson Act. States regulate the content of health insurance policies and often require coverage of specific types of medical services or health-care providers. State mandates generally do not apply to the health plans offered by large employers, due to the preemption clause of the Employee Retirement Income Security Act.

The US is the prime example of a health system financed to a large extent through private health insurance. In fact, most Americans think this is the only way to obtain health coverage and for this reason the prospect of unemployment is doubly alarming. One way to shake this persisting fallacy is to examine private health insurance (PHI) from an international point of view, since America is not the only country which uses PHI in some form or the other.[1] There are other countries where PHI plays a role in financing health care. In the Netherlands and Switzerland it has a major role, and France and Germany use PHI in a complementary or supplementary way. Only in the US, however, even a major government health insurance program such as the ACA chose the private sector as an "intermediary" for strictly political reasons. If the huge cost of providing care is viewed in a way that even slightly considers efficiency, it is essential that the role of the private health insurance industry as a major player must be re-examined. It is, indeed, difficult for anyone *"to believe that this industry contributes anything that is close in value to what it costs the US health system,"* said an important analysis in the respected *New York Review of Books*, in September 2010, months after the passage of the ACA. The article cited the ACA's *"failure to change our current dependence on private, for profit insurance plans, a young but now dominant industry that scarcely existed a few decades ago"* [1].

Change in the health insurance industry can come through collaboration among private payers and through better organization of the industry. An attempt in this direction is the Health Care Cost Institute, established in 2011 as *"a non-profit, independent, non-partisan research institute dedicated to creating the United States' most comprehensive source of information on health*

---

1   For the interested reader we recommend an OECD study published in 2004, available at: http://www.keepeek.com/Digital-Asset-Management/oecd/social-issues-migration-health/private-health-insurance-in-oecd-countries_9789264007451-en#.V5yjxzWSiPU#page120

care activity and promoting research on the drivers of escalating health care costs" [2]. By agreeing to the creation of the Institute, major health insurers agreed to provide claims data on a regular basis to academic researchers in an effort to "*open a window onto the rising costs of health care.*" Aetna, Humana, Kaiser Permanente, and the UnitedHealth Group decided to supply information on more than five billion medical claims, representing more than $1 trillion in spending. While Medicare makes its data available to researchers, with certain confidentiality restrictions like prohibiting identification of individual doctors, information from private insurers has been largely piecemeal. "*Our perspective is that the nation needs greater transparency about what is driving health care costs,*" said Simon Stevens, an executive vice president for the UnitedHealth Group commenting on the creation of the Institute. Finally, private health insurance must re-examine some of the basic principles on which it is built. For example, one must ask the question, how "smart" has private insurance been? Insurers have long theorized that higher deductibles would force down health-care costs. The idea was that higher deductibles would make patients smarter shoppers. This, however, lately raises a scary possibility: Perhaps higher deductibles don't lead to smarter shoppers but rather, in the long run, to sicker patients, as people avoid or postpone using their high-deductible health insurance [3].

One of the critical differences between Medicare and private health plans is the variation in price that the commercial insurers pay to different hospitals and doctors for the same medical services. While Medicare generally pays a fixed price, with some adjustments for where a hospital or doctor is located and the like, private insurers pay very different rates, depending on the characteristics of the individual market and hospital or doctor. Some researchers also note that the release of Medicare data is often a year or more behind an emerging trend. They say the data should help them to begin to answer fundamental questions about why health care is so expensive and to help determine whether the main culprits are higher prices, high use of services, or some combination of factors. "*At the end of the day,*" said Jonathan Gruber, a health economist at M.I.T., "health care *is the biggest and fastest-growing sector of the economy. We can't know too much.*" [4]

More than transparency, however, what is needed is competition and less concentration—in other words more good-old American capitalism. In a recent, major briefing, *The Economist* addresses the growing lack of competition in the American economy. After concluding that "*profits are too high, America needs a good dose of competition,*" the briefing singles out the health-care industry as an example of a market where concentration leads to "abnormal profits." It separates these abnormal profits into various sectors such as railroads, chemicals, and cable television [5].

In many ways the US failed to accomplish what less developed countries offer their citizens in terms of health care. Although the quality of care in America can be unparalleled at a global level, it is not affordable for many Americans. *The Huffington Post* pondered this, in March 2015, commenting on a major article by Ellen Nolte and C. Martin McKee [6]:

> "*Why is universal health care, which is commonplace around the world, so hard to achieve in the United States? Why are we unable to overcome a market-based system that leads to a hundred thousand unnecessary deaths each year? Corporate interests in maintaining this system are powerful, as is a culture of competition and consumption that sees health as a personal choice rather than a human right. The odds against universal health care advocates are long: What does it take to turn a market commodity into a public good, and dismantle an entire industry along the way?*" [7]

Universal health coverage (UHC), as seen by the WHO and the World Bank, refers to the provision of at least a basic set of health services, publicly financed and broadly accessible without limitations. It is clear that we are not talking about health systems as we know them in the developed world today, but about the availability of basic health services at the time of need. In a study among six low- and middle-income countries,[2] which adopted UHC fairly recently, the authors identify five sociopolitical factors that catalyzed reforms including major health-care legislation [8]. It is interesting to apply these criteria to the "most developed economy and democracy in the world."

1. **Social solidarity**: Health care in the US was never a driver for social development and justice. One would have to look hard to discover such commitment in either of the two political parties.

2. **Economic growth**: The fact that one sector alone "devours" twice as many funds as in any other rich country is a drag on the economy.

3. **Legislative decorum or the maturity of democracy**. The US has long been a functioning democracy, but partisan politics go against the real national interest.

4. **Public disaffection with the governing regime**. This does not apply to the US but the recent Donald Trump "phenomenon" may be pointing in the same direction.

5. **The existence of a transformative leader**. After Franklin D. Roosevelt and Lyndon Johnson, President Obama may prove to be one, as the ACA testifies. Unfortunately, such leaders are not a usual occurrence.

It seems that most of the prerequisites to universal coverage already exist in the US. However, when Obamacare was still being conceived, Paul Krugman, a Nobel Laureate, wrote in an article in *The New York Times* that the danger is that even proposals to establish UHC at the state level, such as the 2007 California proposals by Governor Swarzenegger, risk achieving nothing if not separated from entanglement with the private health insurance industry. Quoting Krugman: *"[The governor] appears to sincerely want universal coverage, but he also wants to keep insurance companies in the loop"* [9].

Universal Health Care: A Basic Package for All

Health spending in America, as a percent of GDP, is nearly double the average for OECD countries, all of which use some form of universal coverage. They have all wrestled with the mix of public and private insurance and could offer valuable lessons. A number of middle-income countries only recently achieved UHC or are moving in that direction.[3] In 2015 the World Health Organization put out a policy brief titled "Funding Universal Health Coverage." As with all WHO publications, the focus is on countries at earlier stages of development, but the message is clear for all. Raising revenues for UHC involves five strategic issues for policy makers (BOX 1) [10].

---

2 Chile, Mexico, China, Thailand, Turkey, and Indonesia.

3 It is interesting that even a conservative newspaper, such as *The Economist,* writes favorably about UHC in Latin America. See "A Time to Heal" in the February 13, 2016 issue of the same magazine.

BOX 1: Funding **Universal Health Coverage**

- From the perspective of revenue-raising policy, moving towards a predominant reliance on public funding for health services is the priority for governments in order to progress towards UHC. Public funds are compulsory and pre-paid (i.e. taxes) whereas voluntary payments are considered private.

- Of primary concern is the overall level of public funding for the health sector; new earmarked revenues for health may bring additional resources, but may be offset by reducing discretionary budget allocations resulting in little if any increase in total public funding available to extend coverage.

- Dialogue between Ministries of Health and Ministries of Finance centers on the priority given to the health sector in government budget allocations. Evidence of improved and more efficient spending on health services is important to make the case for greater investment in the health system.

- Several estimates have been made regarding the level of public funding required for UHC. No formula exists, although evidence shows that when countries rely predominantly on private sources, many households forgo care or face serious financial problems. Ongoing analysis suggests, however, that even at low levels of public spending, countries can make significant steps towards UHC.

- In conjunction with developing policy on revenue raising, policy makers need to think about how public funds are pooled and used to purchase health services; it is the combination of reforms which drives improvements in health system performance.

The approach of the WHO to raising revenue for health is guided by UHC and overall health system objectives. Revenue raising has a direct impact on financial protection and on the fairness or progressiveness of health-service funding. The WHO's perspective is guided by evidence that progress towards these two indicators, both central to UHC, requires health systems to be funded predominantly by public sources, meaning that insurance should be compulsory and pre-paid. Typically, in "public sources" the WHO includes a range of direct and indirect taxes incorporating, in many countries, mandatory payroll contributions to a health insurance scheme. In low- and middle-income countries, however, such schemes rely heavily on budget revenues. While private financing plays a role in all health systems, either through out-of-pocket payments (OOP) or through private health insurance (PHI), the evidence is clear that where the role of private financing is large, it typically has a harmful impact on progress towards UHC. Private payments are a particularly regressive way to fund health services and, broadly speaking, when public sources comprise less than 80% of the total, many patients either forgo needed care or face severe financial difficulties.

National Health Insurance for a Basic Package of Care

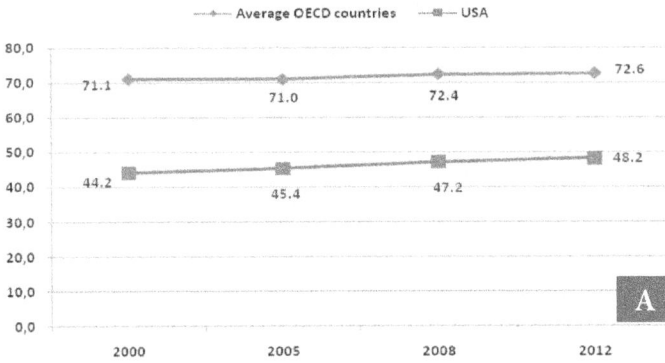

Figure D2-1. General Government Health Expenditure 2000-2012, US and Other OECD Countries, % of GDP (A) and % General Government in Total Health Expenditure (B).

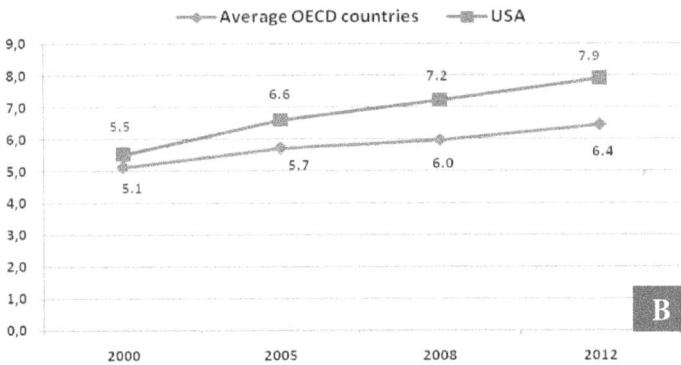

National health insurance (NHI) is probably the talisman[4] of the "good liberal" in America.[5] The academic press is rife with arguments which point to the advantages and ethical arguments which make it necessary as a solution to the American health-care problem. Here it is presented it in a light that Americans can more easily accept, the "imperative" of sound fiscal policy. In Figure D2-1 we see that the general government (GG) in the US already spends a higher percent of GDP on health than the average OECD country (Part A).[6] If we look at it as a percent of total health expenditure (THE), however, the contribution of the government in the US, although slowly rising, is about two-thirds of what it is in the 33 OECD countries. This can have various "readings" pertinent to our discussion here.

First, if the general government in the US were to assume a greater role in financing, for the reasons of equity, fairness, and all the other reasons we have discussed, without solving the problem of the almost three trillion dollars spent on health today, it would probably bankrupt the country. In fiscal year 2015 the federal deficit was $438 billion or 2.5% of GDP. In 2016 the federal government, in its latest budget, estimated the deficit at $616 billion, or 3.3% of GDP [11]. If the general government were to increase public funding of health care from 48% of total health expenditure to the average OECD level of 73.5% (Figure D1-1, Part B), the national debt, from $19 trillion in February 2016 [12], would "go through the roof." With total health expenditure projected at $3 trillion in 2016, increasing public participation by 25.5% of total health expenditure would add $765 billion to the national debt. No political party would advocate this course.

---

4   A talisman is an object believed to contain certain magical or sacramental properties which would provide good luck for the possessor or possibly offer protection from evil or harm.
5   Such as Bernie Sanders in the 2016 Democratic presidential primary.
6   According to the OECD methodology, "general government" includes federal, state, and local government.

Second, let us assume that government and other institutions manage, in some way, to reform the insurance, delivery, management, and organizational issues which plague the American health system, as discussed mostly in Parts A and C, in such a way as to reduce general government health expenditure from 7.9% of GDP to 6.4% of GDP, which is the average of the OECD countries (Part A of Figure D2-1). This would mean, of course, that federal, state, and local governments could maintain present levels of coverage and service quality while spending 1.5% of GDP, or $272 billion, less. Looking at this another way, it would mean that the current level of government participation should more than suffice to make the US a haven of social justice, quality, and excellence in health care at a global level.

There is also a third way to look at health expenditure. A reduction in total health expenditure by 2.5 percentage points of GDP, from, say, 19.6% of GDP projected for 2016, according to 2016 GDP projection figures [13], to the 17.1% spent in 2013, would mean savings of $454 billion. I find it difficult to imagine a good reason why governments or political parties cannot "sell" this idea. And if they cannot, they must either explain why $454 billion more were needed in 2016 for the same job as in 2013, or show, in a convincing manner, the health gain as value-for-money.

A New Financing System for a New Health System

Anyway we look at it, a new health system will be needed to avert bankruptcy or avoid useless expenditure in an inefficient, ineffective, and unfair health system. We maintain that this new system must be outcomes-based, less market-incentivized, with universal coverage, and based on national health insurance financed mostly though taxation on all sorts of income. We should also stress that UHC and NHI refer to a **basic package of essential care** for all, with private insurance in a supplementary or complementary role. There are compelling arguments which we discuss in what follows.

As mentioned earlier, the WHO brief argues in favor of public financing of UHC [10]. The main argument centers on the effectiveness of public financing compared to voluntary private payments and, as with all WHO publications, it addresses WHO member-countries at all levels of development. It centers on the importance of public funding for UHC, as private financing will always be inadequate for public health and essential health-care provision for all. It centers on matters of equity and of the adequacy of funds for UHC but not for financing the entire health system. Our argument in this book is addressed mainly to developed countries and especially to the US.

The Equity and Sustainability Arguments

Thanks mostly to Tomas Piketty [14], it is, by now, well documented that income and wealth inequality has been constantly increasing, while the labor share of the GDP decreases. In the two decades of globalization, as shown in Figure D2-2, the labor share of GDP in the US declined steadily and sharply, while that of corporate after-tax profits increased equally sharply, though not as steadily. This clearly shows that the labor share is in constant decline, and can no longer shoulder the increasing cost of health care, either as personal insurance expenditure or as payroll deductions. There is also the equity argument. Finally, there is a new and perhaps more important reason to change our view on employee contributions.

Figure D2-2. The Effect of Globalization on Corporate Profits and the Labor Share.

Source: Federal Reserve Bank of St. Louis, Economic Research

As a new study has just pointed out, three out of the world's ten largest employers are already replacing workers with robots [15]. If for no other reason, this should be an extreme but convincing argument that relying mainly on labor contributions rather than on capital, through the taxation of corporate profits and wealth, is a counterproductive, inequitable, and insufficient way to finance a health-care system. It is precisely for this reason that we propose NHI financing through the taxation of income from all sources, including wealth and property. In Figure D2-2, above, we can see in a graphic form the most compelling argument for changing the role of taxation and its incidence in health insurance coverage and the need for another look at health-care financing. We will say more on this at the end of this chapter.

The Argument for a Wealth Tax

If personal incomes do not suffice to finance UHC, an alternative source must be found. During the last ten years it has become evident that the personal wealth of the top 1% continued to rise while the personal wealth of the bottom 99% stagnated or dropped. A wealth tax would, therefore, be a suitable source of government revenue for financing the extra cost of UHC [16]. Looking at Figure D2-3 below, we see that globalization has favored high incomes. Especially after 2000, the entire gain in times of economic expansion goes to the top 10%, while in the last three years 2009-2012, the average top incomes more than doubled, while the bottom 90% actually lost in absolute terms.

Figure D2-3. The Distribution of Average Income during Expansions in the US.

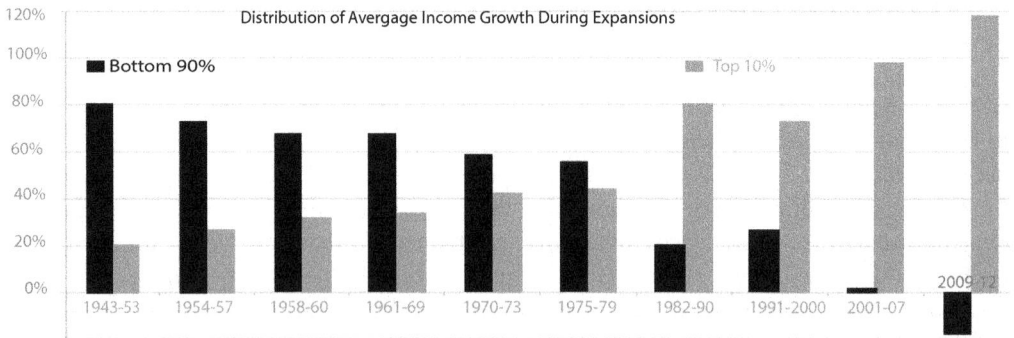

Source: Pavlina R. Tcherneva's calculations based on Piketty/Saez data and NBER.

Income inequality in the US is beginning to be a very ugly picture. A solution to what should be a grossly embarrassing political phenomenon is urgently needed, and at least some progressive solutions are proposed. In fact, economic evidence shows no generalizable relationship between rising inequality and faster growth, something which the political Right has been arguing. On the contrary, some argue that an agenda based on progressive redistribution can unambiguously raise living standards for the bottom 90 percent and even likely be better for overall growth. A recent report by Josh Bivens, published by the Economic Policy Institute, under the title "Progressive redistribution without guilt: Using policy to shift economic power and make US incomes grow fairer and faster," addresses this topic in more depth [17].

If, instead, income inequality stays high and if the saving rate of the bottom 90 percent of families remains low, then wealth disparity will keep increasing. While the rich would be extremely rich, ordinary families would own next to nothing, with debts almost as high as their assets. Thomas Piketty warns that *"inherited wealth could become the defining line between the haves and the have-nots in the 21st century."* This provocative prediction hit a nerve in the US in 2014 when Piketty's book, *Capital in the 21st Century,* became a national best seller, because it outlined a direct threat to the cherished American ideals of meritocracy and opportunity.

Arguments in favor of taxing wealth have important implications, and not only for America. A study in Ireland showed that putting the threshold of taxable income as high as one million euro and the tax rate as low as 0.6% could still produce a revenue gain of 0.6% of GDP [18]. With Ireland spending only 8.1% of GDP for health in 2012, this would be important in terms of increasing the welfare of society at a negligible cost to the super wealthy. The same could probably be said for America. America clearly needs policies that reduce the concentration of wealth, prevent the transformation of self-made wealth into inherited fortunes, and encourage savings among the middle class. First, current preferential tax rates on capital income compared to wage income are hard to defend in light of the rise of wealth inequality and the very high savings rate of the wealthy. Second, estate taxation is the most direct tool to prevent self-made fortunes from becoming inherited wealth—the least justifiable form of inequality in the American meritocratic ideal. Progressive estate and income taxation were the key tools that reduced the concentration of wealth after the Great Depression. The same proven tools are obviously needed again today.

There are, of course, arguments against the wisdom of a wealth tax. Some are based on narrow ideological and political grounds; others are silly, although popular. For example, an influential model by Gary Becker and Nigel Tomes, both of the University of Chicago,[7] predicts that accumulated wealth actually reduces income inequality because parents, who naturally love all their children equally, allocate their bequests to compensate for their stupid children's likely lower earnings potential in the labor market. According to the two authors, families redistribute from the smart to the dumb, and therefore, by implication, governments don't have to redistribute from the rich to the poor [19]. There are no reports whether the authors had their own children, or anything about them if they did.

The Concern over Competitiveness

US health-care costs have outpaced inflation, and some policy experts argue these costs impede competiveness. This goes far beyond the burden on competitiveness that we discussed

---

7 No surprise, I presume.

in the previous section, D-1. A March 2009 study from the Business Roundtable, an association of top CEOs, found that US employers and employees received 23% less value in health-care spending than most other countries within the G-8, including Japan, France, England, Canada, and Germany. "*When our health care system fails to deliver value, it does not just affect individual companies and their workers, it harms our nation's ability to compete in the global economy. This raises the cost of our products and services and diverts resources from needed investments,*" said Ivan Seidenberg, Chairman and CEO of Verizon, following the study. Others dispute the competiveness angle. "*When health costs rise, firms don't become less competitive as if insurance were lopped out of profits. Instead, non-health compensation drops. Or, wages rise more slowly than they otherwise would,*" argues a June 2009 editorial in *The Wall Street Journal* [20]. A similar argument is included in a December 2008 Congressional Budget Office report on US health-care reform [21].

One of the ways Europeans lower labor costs is to hire more part-time workers at a lower cost. This is something their US competitors cannot do, mainly because of the way health insurance works for historical reasons. One of the main reasons employers are reluctant to add more workers and reduce the hours of the current workforce is the overhead cost of hiring a worker, most importantly health-care costs. Typically, health care is a per-worker expense: employers pay a fixed amount for a worker's health insurance policy regardless of how many hours he or she actually works. This structure of health-care provision in the United States was not determined by accident. It dates back to World War II, when employer-provided health insurance became a mechanism for raising compensation, evading wartime wage-price controls. The policy of exempting employer-provided insurance from income tax (along with most other employer-provided benefits) gave firms an incentive to provide a substantial portion of workers' compensation in health care and other non-wage benefits [22]. Neither of these two reasons apply in our times, and the reverse is probably true, as Hillary Clinton discovered back in 1993.

The Public vs Private debate

Countries instituting health-care reforms in the last two decades have employed mixtures of public and private health care that build on existing health systems. The issue of public versus private insurance can often be contentious. For example, the US private insurance industry is protesting a proposed government-run health plan that individuals and small businesses could buy into on the grounds that they could not compete. Michael Tanner, a fellow at the libertarian Cato Institute, disputes that government-run models do any better than the current US system. One of his main arguments is indicative: "*To a large degree, America spends money on health care because it is a wealthy nation and chooses to do so*" [23]. He says the biggest lesson the US can learn from countries such as France, Britain, Japan, and Canada is to avoid government participation in systems.

Meanwhile, Jacob Funk Kirkegaard, a fellow at the Peterson Institute for International Economics, argues that countries with socialized medicine are better than America at containing costs and that US health care is, in fact, more socialized than in many other developed countries. According to his research, "*the share of health expenditures paid OOP by Americans declined from about 50 percent to 12.8 percent between 1960 and 2008*" [24]. He obviously neglects that in 1960 there was neither Medicare nor Medicaid and that now Americans pay more than anyone else in the world to a not so "nationalized" private insurance industry just to avoid exorbitant OOP expenditure. It is arguments such as these that make our book even more useful.

Universal Health Care Models

In creating a universal health model, governments must decide how health care should be administered and financed. Health journalist T.R. Reid divides the world's health funding models into four basic categories: a government service, similar to a police force or library, paid through tax revenue; government-run national insurance paid into by employers and workers via a payroll tax; mandated or voluntary private insurance; and out-of-pocket-only payments [25]. Many governments with universal health care pay for some portion using payroll taxes. Whether to follow suit is now one of the biggest debates in the United States.

Another issue is what to do about skyrocketing health-care costs. Other governments employ a number of methods to control costs once a universal program is in place. In countries such as Taiwan, which adopted a UHC program in the early 1990s, efficiency has been a major component of reform. Other methods for reducing costs range from ceilings on drug prices to controlling fees for services to limiting medical tests. For instance, in 2002 Japan cut payments for Magnetic Resonance Imaging (MRI) tests, which in turn encouraged manufacturers to make less expensive machines [26]. The United States also has a shortage of primary-care doctors, and, in fact, of almost all medical specialties. The implications of this will be discussed in Chapter D-4.

Another final issue for extending UHC coverage, say experts, may be health infrastructure. Michael S. Chen, Vice President and Chief Financial Officer of Taiwan's Bureau of National Health Insurance, recommends building up health-care infrastructure before embarking on UHC. Notably, many of the countries with majority government participation in health insurance rely on both public and private health services. In Japan, 80 percent of all hospitals are private, says Japanese health economist Naoki Ikegami [27]. This is in tune with ideological or political beliefs in the US and is a useful model. Public insurance does not necessarily mean "socialized medicine."

How to Finance UHC and NHI in America

Obviously a radical change in health coverage and health financing cannot be undertaken without greater public involvement. And this greater public involvement will certainly need more public revenue which normally means more taxation or more mandatory insurance contributions, or both. It is important, therefore, to give a picture of what public or government revenue collection looks like in America, compared to other rich countries. We have used data from the OECD Revenue Statistics database for all 34 OECD countries on average, for the US, and for three wealthy countries with different social protection systems, but also having many similarities with the US.

Table D2-1 below is rather revealing. The OECD countries, on average, as well as Canada, the UK, and Germany tax their citizens to the tune of one quarter of their Gross Domestic Product (GDP). The US, on the contrary, collects from its citizens less than one-fifth of GDP.

Table D2-1. Revenue Statistics-Tax Structure, OECD, US, Canada, the UK, and Germany, % of GDP, 2014 [27].

REVENUE SOURCES % GDP	OECD	US	CANADA	UK	GERMANY
Personal income tax	8.77	9.83	11.27	9.12	9.53
Corporate profits tax	2.88	2.15	2.96	2.54	1.79

REVENUE SOURCES % GDP	OECD	US	CANADA	UK	GERMANY
Property taxes	1.874	2.834	3.219	4.056	0.923
Tax on goods and services	10.848	4.344	7.428	10.855	10.241
Total Tax Revenue	**24.372**	**19.158**	**24.877**	**26.571**	**22.484**
Social Security contributions	9.015	6.156	4.856	6.223	13.98
Consumption Tax % Total Taxes	**30.9**	**15.0**	**22.8**	**31.6**	**27.3**

Source: OECD Revenue Statistics–Tax Structure.

The US collects considerably less revenue from the four main sources of public revenue and has the smallest reliance on consumption taxes, less than half of what other countries collect. Compared to the OECD, but also to Canada, the UK, and Germany, the US relies less on Social Security contributions, mostly for pensions and health care for the elderly. The conclusion from the data is that the US has a substantial margin for expansion of health insurance to the rest of the population. Sources of financing can be mainly an increase in consumption and other taxes, on income from all sources, property, and wealth. Although the VAT is considered by some to be the most regressive form of taxation, others have an opposite opinion [28]. Here, we should remind the reader of the already extremely regressive nature of income taxes in the US, especially those of the top 1% or top one-tenth of 1%, as shown previously.

Three Indicative Health Systems to Choose From

A number of countries, some emerging economies but competitors for US businesses, have achieved near universal health coverage in the last two decades. Such countries, each with a separate type of health system, are Brazil, Taiwan, and the Netherlands—the last one a true case-study for the US. Each has useful lessons to teach, as their government structures are sometimes similar to that of the US.

Brazil: The Government Service Model.

The current model was established after a "right to free health care" was codified in the country's constitution in 1988. A country of roughly 191 million, Brazil spends about 8% of GDP on health. According to a 2008 WHO paper, about 70% of Brazilians got government health services, with about 30% supplementing these services with additional private insurance [29]. The program is financed through federal tax revenues but is largely administered by state and local governments. Experts give the health system a mixed review, noting that it has improved immensely since its inception but continues to face challenges, particularly in health infrastructure and cost. A 2002 Inter-American Development Bank report also found instances of people with private insurance turning to public health services for costly procedures, which contributed to the overall scarcity of resources for those relying solely on the public health system [30]. This system may have some useful ideas for certain American states who appear unhappy with the federal government's approach and, perhaps, want to do more than just adopt the ACA.

Taiwan: The National Insurance Model.

Taiwan (population: 23 million) managed to increase health coverage from 57 percent of its population to about 99 percent between 1995 and 2000 [31]. The country now spends about 6% of GDP on health, one-third of what the US spends. Its compulsory system is financed largely through shared deductions by employers and employees on a sliding income-based scale, with the government funding a portion of services through the general budget. It has one useful lesson for the US.

The system has one of the lowest administrative costs in the world. The director of the National Health Institute notes Taiwan's health system applies "information technology to the maximum" with its smart-card system, which enables everything from making payments to disease monitoring to abuse detection to instant medical histories. He argues one of the biggest lessons for US policy reform is that single-payer systems provide the best protection for the sick and the elderly because everyone is in the same risk pool. Despite its achievements, the long-term financial viability of Taiwan's system is a concern. As of 2008 the program was running a $30 million deficit per month, according to Chu Tzer-ming, President of the Bureau of National Health Insurance [32]. A much more successful health system than the American at one-third the cost is not something to pass over lightly. And even if it now runs a deficit, increasing its cost from 6% of GDP to 7% will probably not bankrupt the country, a risk the US is running even now.

The Netherlands: A Private-Insurance/Managed-Competition Model.

The alter-ego of the US system works, and much better. Prior to 2006, the health system of the Netherlands (population: over 16 million) was similar to US health care, with social insurance schemes for the elderly and the poor and private insurance for the more affluent. Its problems included inequities of service based on income status, rising costs, and rationed health services. In 2006, the country created a mandatory scheme requiring the purchase of health insurance from private insurers [33]. Adults pay a set premium to the insurer of their choice for a basic package of services and the government collects about 6.5 percent in payroll taxes from all employees to fund health services—such as those for children, which are covered by the state. The government also subsidizes low wage earners and insurance companies for taking on high-risk individuals. In 2012, the Netherlands spent 11 percent of GDP on health. In 2008, the Dutch system was rated the best in Europe for consumers by Health Consumer Powerhouse, a Swedish policy institute [34]. It is incredible to many students of international health policy that the US is not "rushing" to copy the Dutch health system which, in terms of ideology and politics, resembles the American system, except more successful and only two-thirds as expensive.

Each one of the health systems sketched above hides important lessons for the American body politic. It seems that Bernie Sanders got the message. As this book is written, he doesn't appear as the probable Democratic candidate, but I do hope his ideas on health care eventually prevail. So should my American friends, for their sake and the sake of their children.

References

[1]   Relman A. Health Care: The Disquieting Truth; *The New York Review of Books* [webpage on the Internet]. 30th September 2010 [cited: 7th June 2016]. Available from: http://www.nybooks.com/articles/2010/09/30/health-care-disquieting-truth/

[2]   Health Care Cost Institute [webpage on the Internet]. [cited: 7th June 2016]. Available from: http://www.healthcostinstitute.org/

[3]   Kliff S. This study is forcing economists to rethink high-deductible health insurance; VOX Policy and Politics [webpage on the Internet]. 14th October 2015 [cited: 7th June 2016]. Available from: http://www.vox.com/2015/10/14/9528441/high-deductible-insurance-kolstad

[4]   Abelson R. 4 Insurers Will Supply Health Data; *The New York Times* [newspaper on the Internet]. 19th September 2011 [cited: 7th June 2016]. Available from: http://www.nytimes.com/2011/09/20/health/policy/20health.html

[5]   *The Economist* [magazine on the Internet]. Business in America: Too much of a good thing. 26th March 2016 [cited: 17th June 2016]. Available from: http://www.economist.com/news/briefing/21695385-profits-are-too-high-america-needs-giant-dose-competition-too-much-good-thing

[6]   Nolte E, McKee CM. Measuring the health of nations: Updating an earlier analysis. *Health Affairs.* 2008; 27(1):58–71.

[7]   Rudiger A. Why Universal Health Care Is Essential for a More Equitable Society; *The Huffington Post* [webpage on the Internet]. 31st March 2015 [cited: 7th June 2016]. Available from: http://www.huffingtonpost.com/anja-rudiger/universal-health-care_b_6973164.html

[8]   Gupta V, Kerry VB, Goosby E, Yates R. Politics and Universal Health Coverage—the Post-2015 Global Health Agenda. *New England Journal of Medicine.* 2015; 373(13):1189–92.

[9]   Krugman P. Golden State Gamble; *The New York Times* [newspaper on the Internet]. 12th January 2007 [cited: 7th June 2016]. Available from: http://www.nytimes.com/2007/01/12/opinion/12krugman.html

[10]   Jowett M. Health Financing Policy Brief N[o] 1 *Raising Revenues for Health in Support of UHC: Strategic issues for policy makers.* World Health Organization, Department of Health Systems Governance and Financing, Health Systems and Innovation; 2015.

[11]   US Government Spending [homepage on the Internet]. *Federal Deficit Analysis: What is the Deficit as Percent of GDP?.* US Government Spending; c2016 [cited: 17th June 2016]. Available from: http://www.usgovernmentspending.com/federal_deficit_percent_gdp

[12]   Patton M. US Government Deficit Is Rising Again; *Forbes* [magazine on the Internet]. 28th April 2016 [cited: 7th June 2016]. Available from: http://www.forbes.com/sites/mikepatton/2016/04/28/u-s-government-deficit-is-rising-again/#78fa9a97146f

[13]   Bankrate.com [homepage on the Internet]. Mortgage: Gross Domestic Product (billions). California: Bankrate, Inc.; c2016 [cited: 17th June 2016]. Available from: http://www.bankrate.com/rates/economic-indicators/gdp-gross-domestic-product.aspx?ec_id=m1117906&s_kwcid=AL!1325!3!68171479928!b!!g!!gross+national+product&ef_id=ViJgcwAAAPLx7SfC%3a20160324113633%3as

[14]   Healy T. *Inequality and Budget 2015*; Nevin Economic Research Institute (NERI) [webpage on the Internet]. 20th September 2015 [cited: 7th June 2016]. Available from: http://www.nerinstitute.net/blog/2015/09/20/inequality-and-budget-2016/

[15]   Williams-Grut O. *3 of the world's 10 largest employers are replacing workers with robots*. World Economic Forum [website on the Internet]. 2016 [cited: 7th June 2016]. Available from: https://www.weforum.org/agenda/2016/06/3-of-the-worlds-10-largest-employers-are-replacing-workers-with-robots?utm_content=bufferb63f0&utm_medium=social&utm_source=twitter.com&utm_campaign=buffer

[16]   Crook C. *Piketty's Wealth Tax Isn't a Joke*. Bloomberg View [webpage on the Internet]. 2014 [cited: 7th June 2016]. Available from: http://www.bloomberg.com/view/articles/2014-05-11/picketty-s-wealth-tax-isn-t-a-joke

[17]   Bivens J. *Progressive redistribution without guilt: Using policy to shift economic power and make US incomes grow fairer and faster*; Economic Policy Institute [webpage on the Internet]. 9th June 2016 [cited: 7th June 2016]. Available from: http://www.epi.org/publication/progressive-redistribution-without-guilt-using-policy-to-shift-economic-power-and-make-u-s-incomes-grow-fairer-and-faster/

[18]   McDonnell TA. Wealth Tax: Options for its Implementation in the Republic of Ireland. NERI working paper series; Dublin, Northern Ireland: Nevin Economic Research Institute; 2013.

[19]   Becker GS, Tomes N. Child Endowments and the Quantity and Quality of Children. *Journal of Political Economy*. 1976; 84(4, Part 2):S143–62.

[20]   *The Wall Street Journal* [newspaper on the Internet]. REVIEW & OUTLOOK: Health Reform and Competitiveness. USA: Dow Jones & Company, Inc.; c2016 [cited: 17th June 2016]. Available from: http://www.wsj.com/articles/SB124520327436821723

[21]   Congressional Budget Office. Key issues in analyzing Major Health insurance proposals. USA: Congress of the United States Congressional Budget Office; 2008.

[22]   Baker D. *The End of Loser Liberalism: Making Markets Progressive*. United States: Center for Economic and Policy Research 2011; p. 81.

[23]   Tanner M. *The Grass Is Not Always Greener: A Look at National Health Care Systems Around the World*. Policy Analysis, 2008. Available from: http://object.cato.org/sites/cato.org/files/pubs/pdf/pa-613.pdf cited: 17th June 2016].

[24]   Kirkegaard JF. *Europe and the US: Whose Health Care is More Socialist?*. The Peterson Institute for International Economics [webpage on the Internet]. 2009 [cited: 7th June 2016]. Available from: https://piie.com/blogs/realtime-economic-issues-watch/europe-and-us-whose-health-care-more-socialist

[25]   PBS-Frontline [webpage on the Internet]. Five Countries – Health Care Systems -- The Four Basic Models. USA: WGBH educational foundation; c1995-2014 [cited: 17th June 2016]. Available from: http://www.pbs.org/wgbh/pages/frontline/sickaroundtheworld/countries/models.html

[26]   OECD [homepage on the Internet]. *Tax policy analysis: Revenue Statistics - tax structures*. France: Organisation for Economic Co-operation and Development; c2016 [cited: 17th June 2016]. Available from: http://www.oecd.org/tax/tax-policy/revenue-statistics-tax-structures.htm

[27]   PBS-Frontline [webpage on the Internet]. Interview: Naoki Ikegami. USA: WGBH educational foundation; c1995-2014 [cited: 17th June 2016]. Available from: http://www.pbs.org/wgbh/pages/frontline/sickaroundtheworld/interviews/ikegami.html

[28]   Confessions of a supply-side liberal: a partisan nonpartisan blog [webpage on the Internet]. *Scrooge and the Ethical Case for Consumption Taxation*; c2016 [cited: 17th June 2016]. Available from: http://blog.supplysideliberal.com/post/38740379428/scrooge-and-the-ethical-case-for-onsumption

[29]   Bulletin of the World Health Organization [webpage on the Internet]. *Flawed but fair: Brazil's health system reaches out to the poor*; 2008 [cited: 17th June 2016]. Available from: http://www.who.int/bulletin/volumes/86/4/08-030408.pdf

[30]   Inter-American Development Bank [webpage on the Internet]. Topics. USA: Inter-American Development Bank; c2015 [cited: 17th June 2016]. Available from: http://www.iadb.org/en/topics/topics-in-latin-america-and-the-caribbean,1125.html

[31]   Lu JR, Hsiao WC. Does universal health insurance make health care unaffordable? Lessons from Taiwan. *Health Affairs*. 2003; 22(3):77–88.

[32]   GAO P. *Taiwan Review: Healthcare for All*. Taiwan Today [webpage on the Internet]. 2008 [cited: 7th June 2016]. Available from: http://taiwantoday.tw/ct.asp?xItem=25614&ctNode=2198&mp=9

[33]   Reinhard B, Klazinga N. *Descriptions of Health Care Systems: Germany and The Netherlands*. The Commonwealth Fund; 2008. Available from: http://www.allhealth.org/BriefingMaterials/CountryProfiles-FINAL-1163.pdf [cited: 7th June 2016].

[34]   Health Consumer Powerhouse [webpage on the Internet]. Euro Health Consumer Index 2008 Report; 2008. Available from: http://www.healthpowerhouse.com/files/2008-EHCI/EHCI-2008-report.pdf [cited: 7th June 2016].

D-3: LESS "MARKET" AND MORE "E's" IN THE HEALTH SYSTEM

The health system could benefit by adopting successful practices that are already in use, that are informed by good management, even if they don't conform to caricatures of "competitive" and "businesslike."

—*Henry Mintzberg*

Regardless of the way the US chooses to finance its health system, it must first be transformed into a "system," as described in the Introduction to Part A. As analyzed there, the main characteristics of a sound health system are efficiency, effectiveness, equity, and sustainability. In order to achieve high scores in each of these dimensions, a health system must do much more than choose a fair financing system. It must decide on the rest of its core elements, namely the ideological and political underpinnings on which the health system works. First and foremost among these is the role of the free market, most venerable in the US but unsuited as the mechanism with which health care is produced and allocated. Throughout this book we have maintained that health is not something "bought and sold on the market." On the other hand, the health system is monetized in the sense that it does not consist of free goods. It costs to produce and someone has to pay the cost, except that the prices and the cost must obey a logic acceptable to society.

We maintain that the market and all its elements—such as competition among the providers, scarcity of resources, and the profit motive—are all operational but not predominant in the health system. In other words, if competition is to work, we must rethink the way drug patents are granted and their duration, the role of for-profit hospitals, restrictions to entry of new doctors by the AMA, the position of private for-profit health insurance *vis-à-vis* social insurance, or a single payer in the form of NHI for a basic package of services. From then on, private insurance definitely has a role, as well as private provision of services, but also public infrastructure as a public choice for state and local governments, the church, or other philanthropic non-profit interests.

There are, however, problems with private insurance that the market cannot fix. Nobel Laureate Joseph Stiglitz examines them in a recent article in CBS *Moneywatch* [1]. He mentions the two main problems of private insurance: *Moral hazard,* the fact that many will go without health insurance because they know most of their health problems will be taken care of anyway, and *adverse selection,* the fact that insurance companies know less about their customers' health than they themselves do.

Far be it from me to disagree with a Nobel Laureate, but the proof he offers is rather flimsy. First, the answer to the moral hazard problem is definitely not, as he says, to "*buy health insurance,*" when I cannot afford it, even if the government chips in. The 25-30 million people still not covered under the ACA testifies to this. Second, the adverse selection problem is equally not solved by forcing insurance companies to "*cover everyone*" (with preexisting conditions or not). Stiglitz acknowledges market imperfection in the health market, but he finds that "*Obamacare deals with the problems successfully.*" He, in fact, eventually concludes that "*government regulations or, as in most other developed countries, government-managed health care systems, can help to make these markets work better.*" The failure of HMOs in the past offers no convincing evidence of this either. However, there may be some light at the end of the tunnel.

A major step in the direction of fixing the problem with the market in health is to use its strong point, namely price and quality competition. In order for competition to work, however, a set of rules and standards must be set by some type of public authority in health care. Public health-care networks such as primary health care (PHC) centers, public and other non-profit hospitals, and other forms of health care can then "compete" with for-profit providers on the basis of common quality criteria independently of the financial ability of the user. Local, state, and federal governments must see their role as in other public goods, such as education, national security, law and order, etc. Health care must be seen as a field in which government must be "measured" in terms of its achievements and health care as a public responsibility, in terms of affordability, quality, and adequacy of service. It would be the sign of a great nation if health were to become a matter of political responsibility and not a political battleground for campaign contributions.

Increasing government expenditure is expected in the next few years, as the data from the US Medicare-Medicaid Office of the Actuary indicate, but this is not the only key to a good health system. If private providers operating in a market system produce expensive health care, the end result of higher government expenditure may be private profits and a higher public deficit. If, on the other hand, health care is produced efficiently, any increase in public funding is accompanied by a gain in welfare in terms of the quantity and quality of health services produced.

Henry Mintzberg is the Faculty Director of the International Masters for Health Leadership Program at McGill University. In his October 2011 column in the *Harvard Business Review*, he offers some advice. Under the title "How to Fix Health Care, Ask the Right Questions," he lists some ways to use "less market" in health care with better results. The four points in the Box below are Mintzberg's guide to a better health system [2]:

- **Look to the people on the ground, not outside experts for ideas for real improvement.** One dramatic improvement in recent times which not only cut costs, but also improved care, was the introduction of outpatient surgeries. This innovation came from practicing physicians who saw a better way to organize their work, not from administrators trying to cut costs.

- **Build communities that engage people rather than conventional hierarchies that control them.** Recognize that health care at its best is a calling, not a business. Consider the Mayo Clinic, where for many years physicians have been paid straight salaries rather than fees for individual services. This practice lowers costs since it eliminates incentives to over treat, creates a sense of shared purpose and commitment to the institution, and supports a culture that puts patients' needs rather than doctors' convenience at the core.

- **Stop debating the merits of public versus private governance.** This debate pits the efficiency of the private sector against the equality of the public sector. What country can ignore either? But why try to choose? A full 70% of American hospitals, including the most renowned, are neither private nor public. They're part of the Social Sector, owned by no one.

- **Encourage greater collaboration.** We need to build genuine systems that both promote health and treat illness. To do that, we need more cooperation, not more competition.

The example of European countries, such as the UK, is a useful guide if America wanted to adopt a new model for organizing its health system. But for Americans, practically addicted to private health insurance, Uwe Reinhardt, economics professor at Princeton University, has an alternative. "*If you want a health care system where you don't have to worry that you could go broke, where you could lose your health insurance or get off-the-charts doctors bills, look at the German model,*" he says. He believes that German and Swiss systems, which offer near-universal care without rationing services, come closest to something that Americans, long used to a private system, could stomach [3].

The Era of Delivery System Reform Begins?

Besides "fixing" the health insurance issue and re-defining the importance of the market in health care, one needs to think again in terms of what would give Americans more "bang for their dollars." For this, what is needed is to find acceptable methods to introduce a new search for improvements in the three E's, namely efficiency, effectiveness, and equity. The key, in other words, is efficiency in the production of effective health services and their equitable delivery and distribution without an income constraint. Healthy competition between public and private providers, reimbursed by a single payer utilizing all available cost control and other reimbursement techniques is a good bet. Some progress on this front is showing. The Commonwealth Fund organized a special event on June 1, 2016 to address the issue. In the announcement of the event, we read [4]:

> "*Every day, physicians make complex decisions that directly affect the cost and quality of health care. But payment reform efforts, including 2015's Medicare Access and CHIP Re-authorization Act (MACRA), are creating new incentives and promoting new models for care delivery. The question, therefore, is how will attempts to drive quality improvement and reward providers for better outcomes change the American health care system?*"

Health care reform evolves in distinct phases. Insurance reform, the critical first step, gained a foothold through the 2010 Affordable Care Act. The nation is now in the midst of payment reform, a second chapter motivated by the need to slow health-care spending. Payers across the country are increasingly putting health care on a budget, moving from fee-for-service to lump-sum payments for bundles of services or populations of patients. Hospitals, health-care centers, and physicians in turn are consolidating into Accountable Care Organizations (ACOs) to address these new payment contracts, which reward lower spending and higher quality. In July 2016, 89 new ACOs were launched in Medicare. Combined with 59 Medicare ACOs started in January, these organizations bring more than 130,000 physicians and 2.2 million beneficiaries into an emerging model of organization-based health care [5]. Global budget contracts from private insurers are doing the same for millions more working-age adults, their families, and their physicians.

Interest in Accountable Care Organizations has increased dramatically with the passage of the Affordable Care Act, which establishes ACOs as a new payment model under Medicare and fosters pilot programs to extend the model to private payers and Medicaid. Proponents hope that ACOs will allow physicians, hospitals, and other clinicians and health care organizations to work more effectively together to both improve quality and slow spending growth. Skeptics are concerned that ACOs will focus narrowly on their bottom line and either stint on needed care or use the leverage they achieve through local integration to demand unreasonable prices from payers.

During the push to pass federal health reform legislation, considerable attention focused on the possibility that medical liability reforms could "bend the health care cost curve." Conservatives in Congress and others argued that liability reform would address two drivers of health-care costs: (1) providers' need to offset rising malpractice insurance premiums by charging higher prices, and (2) defensive medicine, clinicians' intentional overuse of health services to reduce their liability risk. President Barack Obama elevated the profile of liability reform by acknowledging that "*defensive medicine may be contributing to unnecessary costs*" and by authorizing demonstration projects to test reforms [6].

The era of health-care-delivery reform seems to be here, and it may take the form of integrated systems. Health systems across the nation are exploring the benefits of vertical integration, and an increasing number of systems are choosing to offer their own health plans, according to a report by McKinsey & Company. "*Health systems, if they are to benefit from offering a health plan, will need to be able to understand how they can use consumerism to their advantage and where the best opportunities for growth exist,*" wrote the authors of the report. "*In addition, they must be willing to rethink the administrative infrastructure they want to use and take advantage of the integrated claims and clinical data at their disposal.*" Here are five things to know about provider-led health plans, according to the report [7]:

1. Between 2010 and 2014, the most recent year for which data is available, the number of providers offering health plans has steadily increased from 94 to 106.

2. Enrollment in provider-led plans grew to 15.3 million in 2014, up from 12.4 million in 2010. However, most provider-led health plans remain comparatively small in terms of enrollment. Only five healthcare providers owned plans that covered more than 500,000 lives in 2014.

3. Financial performance of provider-led plans remains mixed. Of the 89 plans analyzed for the report, more than 40 had negative margins in some or all of the past three years.

4. Like other insurance carriers, most provider-led health plans have struggled to achieve profitability in the individual market on the public exchanges.

5. Based on the study's findings, the authors concluded that although offering a health plan may be an attractive opportunity for some systems, it is not without risk.

The Centers for Medicare and Medicaid Services, in May 2016, introduced a final Medicaid managed-care rule establishing a new regulatory framework for the next generation of managed care. A policy watershed, the rule ultimately will touch the lives of tens of millions of low-income children and adults, and individuals with disabilities. Estimates suggest that a majority of today's 72 million Medicaid beneficiaries are enrolled in managed care plans in 40 states (including the District of Columbia), and the number is expected to increase over the next decade [8].

The rule places states in the driver's seat of an undertaking that may prove a watershed. As explained in a still-relevant 1997 landmark study [9], states have been working toward creating entire health care delivery systems for their Medicaid managed care beneficiaries. As they tackle everything from marketing and enrollment to quality improvement in service delivery and creating relationships with social service programs, states face unique challenges because of whom they serve and the level of coverage and service integration that managed care must be structured to achieve. These challenges must be met and serve as a model or paradigm for the transformation of the whole health-care delivery system in the new NHI environment.

References

[1]   Thoma M. *When markets aren't perfect, government can help*; CBS News [webpage on the Internet]. 2016 [cited: 7th June 2016]. Available from: http://www.cbsnews.com/news/when-markets-arent-perfect-government-can-help/

[2]   Mintzberg, H. To fix health care, ask the right questions. *Harvard Business Review* 89.10 (2011): 44.

[3]   Raghavan A. Beyond Hysterics: The Health Care Model That Works; *Forbes* [magazine on the Internet]. 21st September 2009 [cited: 7th June 2016]. Available from: http://www.forbes.com/forbes/2009/0921/health-obama-germany-health-care-model-that-works.html

[4]   Eventbrite [homepage on the Internet]. *Nudging Physicians Toward Value: Incentives in the Era of MACRA-Economics*; 2016 [cited: 7th June 2016]. Available from: https://www.eventbrite.com/e/macra-economics-nudging-physicians-for-value-tickets-24626880663

[5]   Song Z, Lee TH. The era of delivery system reform begins. *Journal of the American Medical Association*. 2013; 309(1):35.

[6]   Mello MM, Chandra A, Gawande AA, Studdert DM. National costs of the medical liability system. *Health Affairs*. 2010; 29(9):1569–77.

[7]   Sutaria S. *The post-reform health system: Meeting the challenges ahead*. McKinsey & Company [webpage on the Internet]. 2013 [cited: 7th June 2016]. Available from: http://healthcare.mckinsey.com/post-reform-health-system-meeting-challenges-ahead

[8]   Rosenbaum S. *The Medicaid Managed Care Rule: The Major Challenges States Face*. The Commonwealth Fund [webpage on the Internet]. 2016 [cited: 7th June 2016]. Available from: http://www.commonwealthfund.org/publications/blog/2016/may/the-medicaid-managed-care-rule?omnicid=EALERT1032982&mid=lliaropo@nurs.uoa.gr

[9]   Rosenbaum S. A look inside Medicaid managed care. *Health Affairs*. 1997; 16(4):266–71.

D-4: CHANGES IN THE MEDICAL PROFESSION

The fourth major driver of change has to do with the central role of the medical profession in the health system. It is not just the number of doctors, or their remuneration, but also their role in the health-care system. It is reasonable to assume that doctors have a lot to do with the cost of health care. They prescribe drugs, they decide the appropriate diagnostics, they recommend care, including the need for invasive or non-invasive therapies, and, in general, they determine the kind and amount of resources which are necessary for the treatment of illness, the prevention of disease, and the course of rehabilitation in case of need. An interesting variable in the analysis of health expenditure, therefore, is the influence of doctors on total health expenditure (THE).

The Numbers of Doctors and their Command on Health Resources

America has an extreme shortage of doctors. In fact, among OECD countries for which a complete set of data for the number of doctors per 1000 population were available for 2012, the US is in almost the last position (Table D4-1). Only Canada, Japan, Poland, Mexico, and Korea have fewer practicing doctors/1000 population. With an average of 2.5 doctors/1000 population, the US is well below the average of 3.2 for the 34 OECD countries [1]. Doctors' services by themselves are important cost centers for the health system, and also revenue centers not only for themselves, but also for the many economic entities involved in the course of treatment, private and public. Hospitals, HMOs, insurance companies, health-care delivery associations and, in fact, public health expenditure, all depend on doctors who organize and manage health care and determine the two variables normally used to measure health expenditure, namely total health expenditure per capita and the percent of GDP spent on health.

In addition to their numbers and their pay-scale, however, the influence of doctors on health expenditure is shown by the amount or the value of health resources or of the total health expenditure over which doctors, at least theoretically, exercise some kind of control. At the end of the day, in other words, it is the doctor who has "command" over the use of health resources and, therefore, the total cost of health care in a given country. We have named this the Health$ (H$) per doctor, and to measure the extent and the size of this "health dollar" (H$), we constructed an interesting statistic showing the total health expenditure that corresponds to each doctor (licensed or professionally active). This is shown in the last column of Table D4-1 and in a more graphic form in Figure D4-1.

Table D4-1. Doctors and Health Expenditure, Selected OECD Countries, 2012 Data.

OECD COUNTRIES	(1) Physician (density per 1000 population)	(2) Total Health Expenditure (THE) per capita	(3) Total Health Expenditure (THE) % GDP	(4) Health$/doctor
United States	2.5	8454	16.42	3,381,763
Japan	2.29	3592	10.09	1,568,475
Germany	3.96	4693	10.78	1,185,169
France	3.08	4045	10.8	1,313,356

OECD COUNTRIES	(1) Physician (density per 1000 population)	(2) Total Health Expenditure (THE) per capita	(3) Total Health Expenditure (THE) % GDP	(4) Health$/doctor
United Kingdom	2.75	3175	8.49	1,154,721
Italy	3.87	3137	8.83	810,719
Mexico	2.12	1026	6.11	484,083
Korea	2.08	2142	6.69	1,029,854
Spain	3.82	2928	8.93	766,388
Canada	2.48	4304	10.22	1,735,659
Australia	3.31	3866	8.79	1,167,893
Poland	2.23	1448	6.25	649,186
Netherlands	3.25	5081	11.03	1,563,478
Belgium	2.93	4225	10.21	1,441,880
Switzerland	3.92	6140	10.98	1,566,437
Sweden	4.01	4743	10.81	1,182,848
Austria	4.9	4528	10.09	924,092
Norway	4.23	5823	8.77	1,376,595
Czech Republic	3.67	2021	7.06	550,806
Portugal	4.1	2502	9.27	610,338
Greece	6.27	2329	9.1	371,408
Denmark	3.62	4512	10.36	1,246,498
Finland	3.01	3403	8.46	1,130,469
Ireland	2.71	3663	8.1	1,351,649
New Zealand	2.7	3214	9.81	1,190,265

Source: OECD Health Database, 2015.

Figure D4-1. Health$ per Doctor, OECD Countries, 2012.

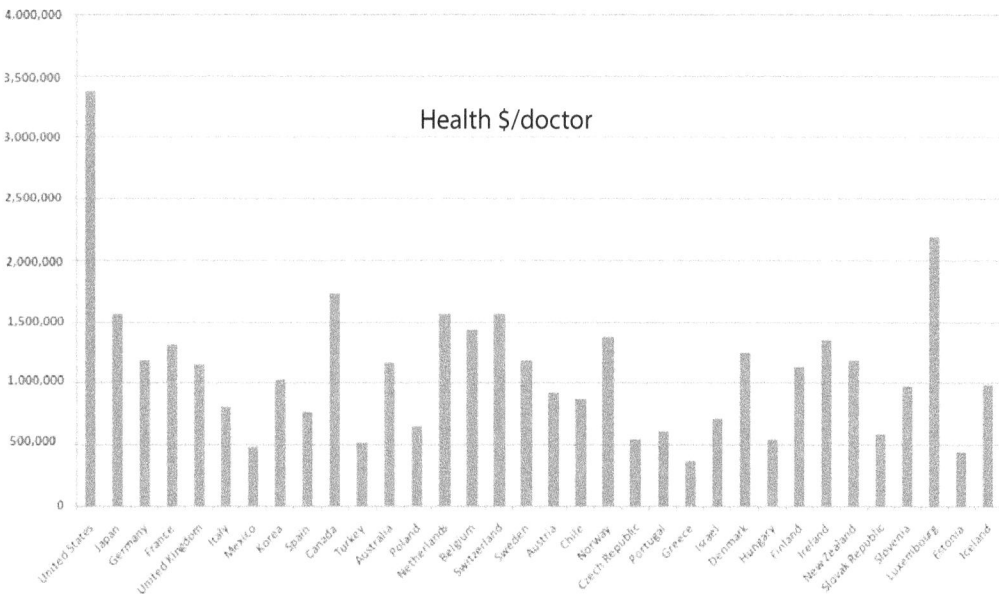

With more than 3.3 million health dollars per doctor, the US is by far the leader. No other country comes close, including countries with GDP per capita equal to or even higher than the US. What is really interesting is the comparison with Canada, a country which shows almost identical physician density, and Japan and the UK also close to the US. The difference in total health expenditure per doctor is immense, demonstrating the effect of better health system organization. It is evident that the scarcity of doctors in the US leads not only to their high remuneration, as we will see below, but also to overuse of health resources. In an effort to investigate this relationship further, we attempted some simple correlation analyses.

First, we see a strong positive correlation[1] between GDP per capita and Health$/doctor (Diagram 1). GDP per capita in rich countries is associated with more Health$/doctor. It is to be expected that the richer the country, the more resources are put at the disposal of medical decisions. The US, however, is a clear outlier with doctors commanding many more health resources than what the US GDP per capita would justify.

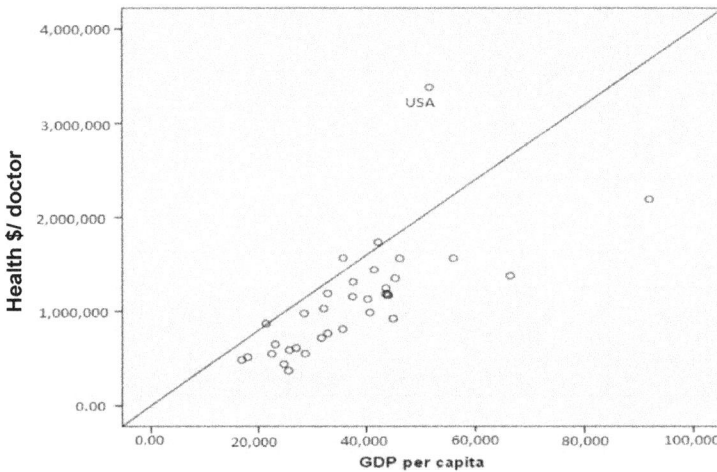

Diagram 1. Correlation between GDP per capita and Health$/doctor.

Second, in Diagram 2 we see a low negative correlation[2] between physician density and Health$/doctor. Although barely significant, high physician density is associated with lower Health$/doctor. The US is again an outlier, since doctors, although few in number, command the most health resources by far.

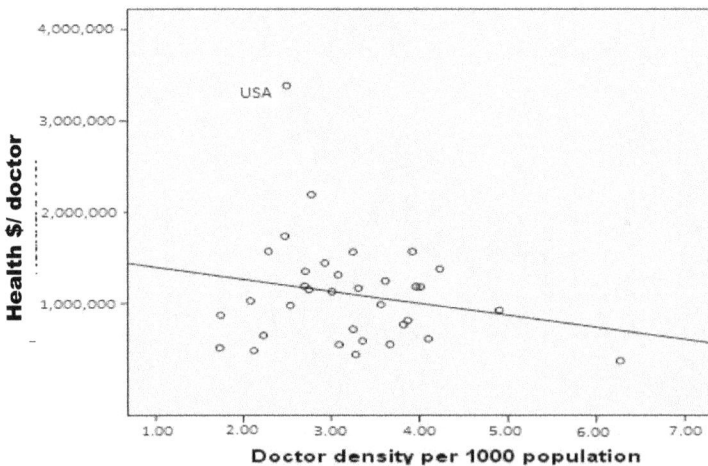

Diagram 2. Doctor density per 1000 population and Health$/doctor.

1   Spearman's correlation coefficient = 0.84, p<0.001
2   Spearman's correlation coefficient =-0.12, p=0.51

Third, there is a moderate positive correlation[3] between doctor density per 1000 population and total health expenditure per capita. High doctor density is associated with increased total health expenditure per capita. High physician density (many doctors) is loosely associated with lower health expenditure/1000 population. There are two major outliers: the US with the highest, by far, total health expenditure per capita and Greece, where the highest doctor density is associated with fairly low per capita expenditure.

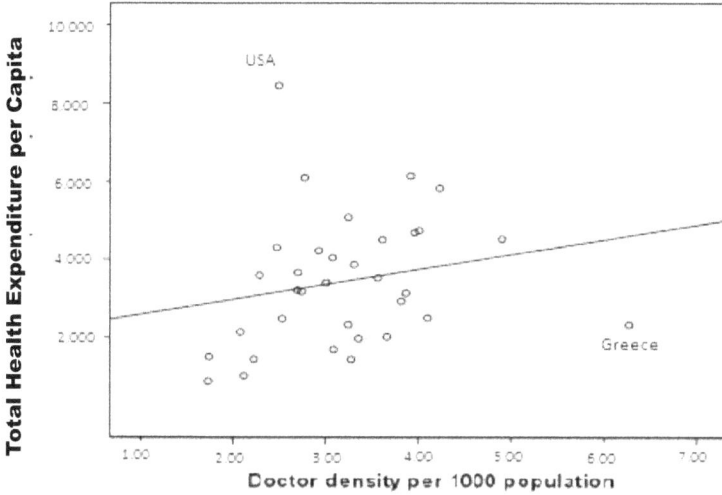

Diagram 3. Correlation between physician density and health expenditure per capita.

The overall conclusion from the simple correlation analysis shows a clear disconnect in the market for physician services in America. The fact that the number of doctors is kept artificially low enables them to command an extremely high value of health resources (Diagram 2). In this way they cause extremely high per capita health expenditure (Diagram 3), in total disagreement with the already high GDP per capita. In other words, doctors in the US are in a much more central role in terms of their command of health resources than the country's GDP would justify. We should look into this in further detail.

The Remuneration of Doctors

Physician/doctor salaries as reported by PayScale, a company specializing in human resources, may be in the range between $174,000 and $240,000 [2]. However, in an article in *The Atlantic* we see figures ranging at much higher levels [3]. The data are from Doximity [4], a fast-growing social network for physicians, now claiming more than 400,000 members and best described as "a LinkedIn for doctors." According to Doximity, "*these data show average salary numbers by specialty and are valuable almost exclusively in a relative way, showing what the US healthcare model tends to value most, and partly explain why there is an ongoing shortage of primary-care doctors.*" According to *The Atlantic*, "*while similar salary breakdowns have been published by Forbes, Medscape, and Merritt Hawkins, among others, Doximity's numbers are based on the most comprehensive approach yet.*" The top and bottom five specialties are listed below in Table D4-2:

---

3   Spearman's correlation coefficient 0.34, p=0.05

Table D4-2. Top and Bottom Five Medical Specialties According to Doximity.

TOP EARNING SPECIALTIES ($)		BOTTOM EARNING SPECIALTIES ($)	
Neurosurgery	609,639	Pediatric Gastroenterology	196,708
Orthopedic Surgery	535,668	Pediatric Hematology & Oncology	192,855
Thoracic Surgery	471,137	Pediatric Infectious Diseases	163,658
Cardiology	436,849	Medical Genetics	158,597
Vascular Surgery	428,944	Pediatric Endocrinology	157,394

Table D4-3, below, shows the average physician earnings for a number of countries with which the US can compare in terms of per capita GDP. With the exception of the Netherlands, another country heavily dependent on private insurance financing, in all other countries physician earnings are considerably lower than in America, not only in absolute terms, but also relative to GDP per capita. However, when compared to other high earners, namely those in the 95th to 99th percentile of the income distribution, doctors in America lag behind those in Canada and Australia, and are close to those in France, Germany, New Zealand, the Netherlands, and the non-US Average.

Table D4-3. Comparison of Physician Earnings across Countries.

Country	Specialists			General practitioners: Ratio to high earners
	Average earnings (1,000s)	Ratio of earnings to:		
		GDP per capita	High earners	
United States	$230	5.8	1.37	0.92
Australia	$173	5.3	2.54	0.98
Canada	$161	5.0	2.11	1.41
France	$131	4.4	1.47	0.92
Germany	$155	5.4	1.45	1.06
Italy	$84	3.0	1.31	
Netherlands	$286	8.7	2.56	1.06
New Zealand	$87	3.5	1.47	0.86
Norway	79	1.9	0.78	0.68
Portugal	79	4.3	1.11	0.69
Sweden	71	2.3	0.98	0.86
Switzerland	130	3.7	0.87	0.77
United Kingdom	114	3.7	0.8	1.02
Non-US Average	$129	4.3	1.45	0.94
Ratio: US/Non-US Average	1.78	1.35	0.94	0.98

Sources: Data on physician earnings are from the OECD (2010). Average incomes for high earners are based on data in Alvardo, Atkinson, Piketty, and Saez (2011).

Notes: Data on physician earnings are adjusted to 2004 as described in the US Congressional Research Service (2007). High earners are people in the 95th to 99th percentile of the earnings distribution. Primary care and specialist incomes are reported combined for Norway and Portugal. They are distributed to general practice and specially based on the general practitioner-specialist differential in Sweden (for Norway) and the differential in France (for Portugal).

The Role of the Doctor

The doctor is a central figure in all health systems. However, the role doctors play depends to a large extent on the way the health system is organized and funded. In highly centralized systems where doctors are mostly salaried, as in the UK, and health care is paid for by the central government budget, the doctor commands less influence in the way the system works and the way resources are used. On the other hand, facing a certain career as a public servant, the doctor is not actually concerned about competition from other doctors. In a system such as the American, where decisions are in fact made by non-medical business people and concerns, with no central organizational authority, decisions are more heavily influenced by doctors who have monopoly power on "medical knowledge." They, therefore, tend to organize around their specialties and exercise oligopolistic power on major decisions, including their reproduction rate. To safeguard this position, they naturally tend to keep their numbers low, through their influence on medical education. In order for this to change, America must do a certain amount of soul-searching.

References

[1]   OECD [webpage on the Internet]. OECD Health Data; 2012 [cited: 7th June 2016]. Available from: http://stats.oecd.org/index.aspx?DataSetCode=HEALTH_STAT

[2]   PayScale [webpage on the Internet]. People with Jobs as Physicians/Doctors Salary: Average Salary for People with Jobs as Physicians/Doctors. USA: PayScale, Inc.; c 2016 [cited: 14th October 2015]. Available from: http://www.payscale.com/research/US/People_with_Jobs_as_Physicians_%2F_Doctors/Salary

[3]   Hamblin J. What Doctors Make: Variations in salary are drastic and opaque. *The Atlantic* [magazine on the Internet]. 27th January 2015 [cited: 7th June 2016]. Available from: http://www.theatlantic.com/health/archive/2015/01/physician-salaries/384846/

[4]   Doximity [webpage on the Internet]. The professional network for healthcare professionals. USA: Doximity, Inc.; c 2016 [cited: 14th October 2015]. Available from: https://www.doximity.com/about/company

PART E

THE MAJOR DRIVERS
FOR CHANGE

INTRODUCTION

WHY CHANGE MATTERS

"If change cannot take place gradually and peacefully, it is likely to erupt suddenly and violently."

—Hubert H.
Humphrey, 1966

In Part D we explained what a new health-care system in America should look like and we talked about the necessity for a new social and economic paradigm. Describing heaven, however, is no guarantee that one will get there. There are powers at work that make the transition easier and others that work against it. Societies grow and change because of internal forces, as with the 2008 recession which started in the US, but also by interaction with global phenomena, such as the slowdown of the Chinese economy, the energy price crisis which appeared in 2015, or, more important, and much more threatening, climate change and global warming. This is true even for countries who play major roles in shaping world events. It is especially true when the world environment develops tensions and powers that can influence the domestic environment. In this last Part E, we will try to search for major drivers for change which may favor, deter, or direct change specifically in health care in the US. The aim should always be a health system which is more effective, efficient, equitable, and durable. If this sounds like heaven, the road to it is paved with *good* intentions.[1] I firmly believe that America not only needs, but also deserves, a better health system and, in fact, why not the best? [1].

The forces that can, and probably will, bring about fundamental change in health-care belong in two major categories. Forces *external* to the health-system, such as the world economy and globalization, and *internal* forces directly related to health care. External forces are political, economic, and societal, related to the American value system and the structure of society or even other global developments. Internal forces are related to the structure of the health-care industry itself, such as the medical profession and the insurance industry. In many cases the two categories are intertwined, as in the drug market, where local conditions are influenced by world market developments. This makes fundamental change in the health system an especially difficult political undertaking. It also raises the question of whether change should be slow and gradual or quick and radical. The evidence on the success of reforms is scant and difficult to apply from country to country. My inclination is to side with what Hubert Humphrey said 60 years ago about the need for change (the by-line at the top of the page). After all, in the long-run we are all dead, as another pundit said a century ago.[2] The American health system is so sick that no time can be wasted in curing it now.

---

1 Somebody has said that *"the road to hell is paved with good intentions."*
2 John Maynard Keynes, eminent British economist, first half of 20th century. That was said well before the threat of climate change became apparent.

Our previous analysis showed why health-care is a problematic aspect of American society and the economy. There are forces at work which may either hamper and delay reform, or foster change within the health system and help rid it of problems we identified in earlier chapters, especially in Part A. The main external forces are related to world politics and the world economy. More specifically, we refer to the process and the effects of globalization on the American economy with emphasis on income distribution as a result of America's value system. The forces internal to the health system are the insurance industry, the medical profession with its control over the production of professionals, the lack of competitiveness in the drug industry, and all other factors affecting the production and distribution of health services in a "market system."

More than anything else, the way to fix health care in America is to change the mentality and the set of values that shaped the present situation. It is important that society realizes that the pioneering spirit, the energy, the inventiveness, and the voluntarism, which made America a great world political and economic power in the last century, are no longer enough to fix American health care. In fact, they may be part of the problem, as selfish individualism seems to prevail over concern about the common fate. A new sense of commitment to the public good may be now needed. More important perhaps, is adherence to the 1948 United Nations Universal Declaration of Human Rights, accepted by now well beyond the boundaries of "the West," as representing progress in a society. The UN Universal Declaration of Human Rights includes among other rights, the *"right to adequate medical care and necessary social services"* [2].

This human right is essentially denied to those who cannot afford insurance and, hence, health care, simply because of partisan politics. Even the majority of Americans who can afford it, however, spend exorbitant amounts to cover the unnecessarily huge cost of health care. In any case, it is important to realize that a new world dynamic is developing towards the 5-75-20 society, a phenomenon already apparent in the US and in Europe, after the Great Recession of 2008 [3]. This new social divide is among the 5%, the "new elite" who gain as asset prices and wealth soar, the net gainers from globalization; the 75% who are at work or in retirement but in a constant struggle to keep up as the "new insecure"; and the 20% who have "lost out" and struggle in a vicious cycle of low-wage, irregular work, unemployment, and limited access to welfare including health care [4]. It is with this social paradigm in mind that the new health system must evolve in a manner that will try to heal, protect, and preserve social welfare.

Any way one looks at it, the 20% of GDP spent for health comes out of peoples' pockets. The failure of society and politicians to recognize the need for universal health-care coverage for essential care and the separation of health care from the market is a serious flaw in the American value set. Even if private health insurance remains a "sacred cow" in American politics, there is nothing to prohibit the public sector, including federal, state, or local government, from ensuring that essential health services are available to those that cannot afford the "market solution." The domain of these essential services must include at least life threatening situations, catastrophic illness, and essential preventive services. The key-words to achieve this are universal health coverage, and national health insurance.

The US, especially after WWII, has been a world leader in many aspects. There is an interesting collection of statistics by the OECD [5] which, in a way, reflect the relative country achievements in a great number of indicators. The latest data are for 2013 and in most the US ranks near or much better than the OECD average. It is rather telling, however, that it lags behind in most if not all the indicators which have to do with the health status and the overall social conditions faced by parts of the population and especially of the young. These indicators are: US vs OECD average life expectancy at birth [78.7 vs 80.1], infant mortality at birth [6.10

vs 3.97], low birth weight [8.0 vs 6.65], obesity rate [9.02 vs 2.65], self-reported[3] health status, adolescent (aged 15-19) suicide rates [7.4 vs 6.4], teenage birth rates [31.00 vs 13.54], NEET[4] [8.42 vs 7.10], educational deprivation[5] [8.36 vs 4.34], and child homicide rate[6] [4.02 vs 1.18].

The statistics mentioned above paint the picture of a society that leaves part of the people, and especially the young, with neither health care nor many of the other services which can help them keep their "heads above the water." At least, it seems that the US is doing worse than the OECD average—worse than countries which in most instances are not as rich as the US. There is something in this that America must address if she wants to maintain a leading position in what matters most—the well-being of her people. Health care might be a good start, and in the next three chapters we will say more on that.

References

[1]   McCarthy D, How SKH, Fryer AK, Radley DC, Schoen C, Eds. *Why Not the Best? Results from the National Scorecard on U.S. Health System Performance*, 2011 [monograph on the Internet]. Washington: The Commonwealth Fund 2014 [cited: 7th June 2016]. Available from: http://www. commonwealthfund.org/Publications/Fund-Reports/2011/Oct/Why-Not-the-Best-2011.aspx

[2]   Harrison LE. *The Central Liberal Truth: How Politics Can Change a Culture and Save It from Itself.* United States of America: Oxford University Press 2008.

[3]   Policy network [webpage on the Internet]. *How social democracy can triumph in the 5-75-20 society.* 24th April 2014 [cited: 7th June 2016]. Available from: http://www.policy-network.net/pno_detail.aspx?ID=4627

[4]   Pratschke J, Morlicchio E. *Social Polarisation, the Labour Market and Economic Restructuring in Europe: An Urban Perspective.* Urban Studies 2012; 49(9):1891-907.

---

3   Percentage of 11, 13, and 15-year-old children with self-perceived fair or poor health.
4   Youth Neither in Employment nor Training.
5   Number of 15-year-olds reporting having less than the four essential educational items (a desk, a place to study, etc.) per 1000 15-year-olds in the school population.
6   Death rate by intentional injury per 100,000 children.

E-1: AMERICA IN THE NEW WORLD ENVIRONMENT

"The distribution of income and wealth is one of today's most controversial issues. The good news is that there are several possible futures. History tells us that there are powerful economic forces pushing in every direction. Which one will prevail depends on the institutions and policies that we will collectively adopt."

—*Thomas Picketty [1].*

Ten years ago, Tony Judt, a prolific and renowned British historian, presented his seminal work "*Postwar: A History of Europe since 1945*" at a forum of the Open Society Institute in New York. When asked to sum up the essence of his 831-page story, he acknowledged his high but hesitant hopes for Europe and, at the same time, of a festering subtle disillusionment with America. His tale points to a Europe that "*has learned the value of trying to provide for the common welfare, health and happiness of most of its citizens,*" a Europe that, with him, sees an America "*overburdened by military missions and shamed by doctrinal individualism, unfair social policies, and often violent tendencies*" [2]. The most important of Judt's themes is that Europe's welfare states were not constructed for ideological, socialistic reasons, but rather as a "prophylactic" against the disasters that had befallen the Continent throughout the 20th century. This is not widely understood in the United States, and perhaps even Europe is beginning to forget. As the rationale of a United Europe as protection from the evil of war and communism wanes, 60-70 years after the end of WWII, and 30 years from the fall of the Iron Curtain, the impulse for new "national" solutions rears its ugly head again. In what follows, we will take the reader on a journey that may at times be a little discomfiting. It is simply an attempt to put an international perspective to social and economic problems that are common to all, but appear different in the way various nations deal with them, not for moral but for political reasons.

Adam Smith, the father of the economic science, and inventor of the "invisible hand," said that to increase national wealth "*profits should be low and wages high . . . land should be distributed widely and evenly, inheritance law should partition fortunes, taxation can be high if it is equitable, and the science of the legislator is necessary to thwart rentiers and manipulators.*" This paints a picture of capitalism quite different from the way it has evolved in the era of globalization, especially after the disappearance of socialism and communism as "competing paradigms." A lot has been written about the "new economic order" during the last twenty years. The globalization of the world economy is a fact of life not likely to change in the foreseeable (distant) future.[1] Moreover, it is spreading into other areas such as the arts, lifestyles, and social models. Resistance is high in some areas, and it remains to be seen whether the recent emergence of a (new) cultural-religious divide is a once-on affair or a more permanent rift.[2]

The global economic, political, and social architecture in the 21st century is changing in a rapid and accelerating manner. In thirty years, the world went from bi-polar US-Soviet domi-

---

1 Although some manufacturing recently seems to be returning to America from China.
2 See the disturbing earlier work by Samuel Huntington and the recent developments with the Islamic State (IS).

nance, to the US dominated world at the end of the 20th century. The New Millennium brought a third transition to the poly-polar world, where the US, the EU, the BRICs, Japan, the Asian "Tigers," and an emerging Islamist world vie for dominance. Each has strengths and weaknesses on which the ability of each player to survive depends. This is a difficult exercise in geopolitical prognosis, where the underlying theory is nebulous, and statistics *"are like bikinis: what they show is interesting, but what they hide is vital."*[3]

Globalization, which we also discuss in the next chapter, is a potent force which affects all aspects of economic, political, and cultural developments globally. In many respects, it is a phenomenon that goes well beyond the power of individual governments, or even of groups of countries such as the European Union. Although likely to influence the way societies respond to obligations in crucial sectors such as health, pensions, and income protection, the effect of globalization on the social sector has not been thoroughly examined, the main interest focusing on the economy. For some years the conventional wisdom was that globalization, with its emphasis on competitiveness, will be the doom of the European social model. A fat welfare state, low or zero population growth, and a passé economy gorging on state subsidies were doomed to failure. A globalized economy, where production takes place and goods and services are sold anywhere, insures that countries with wide social care safety nets will lag behind. Welfare programs are thought to increase the cost of production, dull incentives for work, and protect redundant jobs (or whole industries) at a loss of total welfare. The theory goes that competitiveness is the *sine qua non* of social welfare, or even happiness. A simple but naïve theory, which life (or sound theory)—at least in most of Europe—proves faulty, or at least certainly of dubious value.

The connection is not, of course, made in a direct way, but using a conceptual "bridge," that competitiveness leads to economic prosperity, which, of course, leads to happiness. Thus, the argument goes—less government intervention with welfare programs means a more competitive economy, and, therefore, more economic growth. It is then simply taken for granted that higher economic growth is tantamount to more happiness. If only happiness were so easy! The fallacy of this argument is not what this book wants to investigate. After all, Europeans know—and many Americans are increasingly finding out—what academics such as Richard Easterlin from the University of Southern California and Claudia Senik of the Sorbonne have argued, that *"material wealth alone does not (necessarily) bring happiness"* [3].

In this book we take issue with the "neo-liberal" connection between the social welfare state and the competitiveness of the economy. The argument that growth and wealth gained through a competitive economy is enough to make a society successful and happy falls flat when we introduce the concepts of *equity* and *social cohesion*. In fact, we suggest that social cohesion and a modicum of equity through a publicly financed health system is good for the competitiveness of the economy. Moreover, we hold that dependence on the market to meet needs, such as for health care, is inefficient, costly, and, in fact, bad for the economy. Social cohesion and a degree of equity is possible in a caring society where all citizens carry the burden according to their ability. The practical implication for the health sector is for universal health care, not only because it is socially fair, but because it is economically prudent in a globalized economy.

Societies may change their culture in response to major trauma [4]. Many examples in human history show that a new set of values may prove superior to long-held beliefs [5]. While the

---

3   A famous phrase by Aaron Levenstein, Associate Professor Emeritus of Business at Baruch College, from 1961 to 1981.

American tradition of individualism with its emphasis on entrepreneurship and innovation has been instrumental in producing an economic miracle, its continuing application in all spheres of human endeavour may prove counter-productive. We believe that this realization will soon occur in the US with respect to health care. We will try to show that a major change in the "politics of health" is essential, if not inevitable, as the current political status quo proves inadequate in the new world economic environment. This change of politics will bring about an ideological shift with important ramifications.[4]

Ideology, or the set of values that shape American culture, can change if the liberal paradigm becomes the driving force. When culture fails to meet some of the essential needs of society, the liberal truth holds that it is time for politics to play a creative role. In order for this to happen, a society must be either convinced of the benefits of a paradigm change, or in despair with the predicament upon which the current paradigm has brought it. A major crisis in health care may do precisely that. When the stark reality of the vulnerability to the double risk of bad health and/or financial ruin hits home, the American people may decide that health care is not the right setting for the application of rigid free market principles and for rugged individualism. America is already falling behind in many respects, although the signs are not always seen by all. The world is becoming more competitive, more complex, but not necessarily better for all. I am not sure there are common standards of well-being by which we may measure success or failure, but a healthy life still holds some allure and is worth striving for. It is time for America to join the race, but there are hurdles to overcome.

An Empire in Retreat? Or Just a Lost Decade?

The economic decline in the US has been persistent in the last few years. It was especially painful for the poor, according to the US Census Bureau. The 2010 results, released on September 13, 2011, show that in 2010 another 2.6 million people slipped into poverty, bringing the number of Americans who lived below the official poverty line ($22,314 for a family of four) to 46.2 million. This number is the largest in the 52-year history of this statistic. The number of the poor rose for the fourth consecutive year, and as a percent of the population it rose to 15.1%, the highest since 1993, and considerably higher than the 14.3% of 2009. A lack of jobs, rather than a drop in wages, was the main problem. At the same time, the median family disposable income for 2010 was $49,445 or 2.3% lower than in 2009, and very near the 1997 figure. It was the first time since the Great Depression that median household income adjusted for inflation had not risen over such a long period, said Lawrence Katz, an economics professor at Harvard. *"This is truly a lost decade. We think of America as a place where every generation is doing better, but we're looking at a period when the median family is in worse shape than it was in the late 1990s"* [6].

Living Standards: A Society in Decay?

On August 30, 2011, *The Economist* Intelligence Unit published its listing of "the best cities in the world to live in." The criteria used were political and social stability, crime, access to medical care, cultural events, the environment, schools, and general infrastructure. After 10 years,

---

4 The "Sanders phenomenon" in the 2016 Democratic primaries is indicative.

Vancouver lost the first position to Melbourne. With the exception of Vienna and Helsinki in Europe, eight out of the ten top countries were from Australia, New Zealand, and Canada. The best US city is Honolulu, in 26th place, with New York in the 56th position. Considering the general cultural proximity of Canada and Australia to the US, one must ponder as to the reasons that make American cities relatively "unliveable." The main reason for this may lie in the economic decline apparent more than anywhere else in American cities.

The Economic Risk

Is the United States bankrupt? Many would scoff at this notion. Others would argue that financial implosion is just around the corner. A provoking paper ten years ago explored these views and concluded that countries can indeed go broke, and that the United States is, actually, going broke. The paper offered three policies to eliminate the nation's enormous fiscal gap and avert bankruptcy: a retail sales tax, personalized Social Security, and a globally budgeted universal healthcare system [7]. The rate of 33% for a retail sales tax, which Kotlikoff suggests, may seem high compared to the VAT in other countries, but it must cover a huge deficit in terms of total revenue collected just to meet the 20% of GDP health expenditure. The US collects only 4% of GDP from taxes on goods and services, compared to 10% for other major countries and the OECD on average (Table D2-1). The retail tax is among the measures proposed in this book (see Chapter D-2).

Regardless of whether the US is going broke, which I do not believe, it is interesting that health care is one of the three main reasons for such a dismal prognosis. I am not convinced about the author's proposal for Social Security reform, but I find his proposal for universal health insurance, with government-provided yearly vouchers based on the person's age and "expected" health expenditures over the year, quite interesting.

Throughout the book, I have pointed out the reasons why the exorbitant health costs in the US and the dependence on private health insurance for health care financing will cause a serious loss of competitiveness and a general weakening of the American economy both in relative and in absolute terms. This will have far-reaching repercussions in many aspects of life, beginning with unemployment, further deterioration in income distribution, the prevalence of poverty, and the decline of living conditions, especially in big urban areas.

America as an Economic, Political, and Military Power

George Soros, the legendary financier, when referring to the US current economic position in his 2008 book says: "*A sixty-year period of credit expansion based on the US exploiting its position at the center of the global financial system and its control over the international reserve currency has come to an end.*" He goes on assessing the political position of the US, "*During the Bush Administration, the US failed to exercise full political leadership. As a result, the US has suffered a precipitous decline in its power and influence in the world*" [8].

America is no longer the richest country in the world [9]. More importantly, the growth in median income in the first decade of this century is below the average rate of increase in the OECD countries [10]. From a historical perspective, the median income in America is back to where it was in 1973. In order to understand the situation, one must realize that the "average" American family—103 million Americans or 34 percent of the population—is struggling in the area between the poverty line and its double ($44,000 for a family of four), essentially trying to keep their heads above water, in an environment of increasing job insecurity. It is well known that the unemployment figures don't always tell the full story. The qualitative statistics are the most disheartening. Between 2007, the start of the Great Recession, and 2011, a full 9.4 million permanent jobs were lost. These are the type of jobs permitting job security and upward mobility. The loss of jobs like that is what makes the discussion of health care and health insurance, as important factors in the economy, so vital.

On the other hand, the ability of a society to absorb shocks, accept the need for change, and move on to necessary reforms depends on the cultural and educational level of the majority of the population. I must say I was not surprised when, in the spring of 2011, I saw a picture in *The New York Times* showing a half dozen citizens in one of the sun-belt states, holding hands, heads bowed, in a semi-circle, praying for (. . .wait for it. . .) the gasoline price to fall! It is extremely difficult to pass economic and social reforms—which may seem to go against widely held beliefs—as faulty, unjust, and even dangerous to such citizenry. An "informed elite" is not enough. It is not surprising that it has been almost ten years since the ACA was introduced in the public agenda for discussion, and it still has not captured the imagination of the majority of Americans. It will be even more difficult for them to accept it as a first step towards an even bolder but essential move to UHC and NHI. We will say more on this in the next chapter.

References

[1]   McTernan M, Ed. *Making Progressive Politics Work. A Handbook of Ideas.* London: Policy Network, 2014.

[2]   Lucey B. *The New York Times: A Chronology: 1851-2010.* New York State Library [webpage on the Internet]. 23rd May 2010 [cited: 7th June 2016]. Available from: http://www.nysl.nysed.gov/nysnp/nytlucey.htm

[3]   Dunleavey MP. Finding Happiness in the Pursuit. *The New York Times* [newspaper on the Internet]. 8th April 2006 [cited: 7th June 2016]. Available from: http://www.nytimes.com/2006/04/08/business/finding-happiness-in-the-pursuit.html

[4]   Harrison LE, Huntington SP, Eds. *Culture Matters: How Values Shape Human Progress.* New York: Basic Books 2001.

[5]   Rifkin J, Ed. *The European Dream: How Europe's Vision of the Future is Quietly Eclipsing the American Dream.* New York: Penguin Group Inc. 2014.

[6]   Tavernise S. Soaring Poverty Casts Spotlight on "Lost Decade". *The New York Times* [newspaper on the Internet]. 13th September 2011 [cited: 7th June 2016]. Available from: http://www.nytimes.com/2011/09/14/us/14census.html

[7]   Kotlikoff LJ. *Is the United States Bankrupt?* Federal Reserve Bank of St. Louis Review 2006; 88(4):235-49.

[8]   Soros G. *The New Paradigm for Financial Markets. The Credit Crisis of 2008 and What it Means.* New York: Public Affairs 2008.

[9]   Wikimedia Foundation [webpage on the Internet]. San Francisco: List of OECD countries by GDP per capita [cited: 7th June 2016]. Available from: https://en.wikipedia.org/wiki/List_of_OECD_countries_by_GDP_per_capita

[10]   The Organisation for Economic Co-operation and Development (OECD) [webpage on the Internet]. *Paris: Society at a Glance 2011: OECD Social Indicators* [cited: 7th June 2016]. Available from: http://www.oecd-ilibrary.org/sites/soc_glance-2011-en/04/01/g4_ge1-02.html?itemId=/content/chapter/soc_glance-2011-6-en&_csp_=048bf5a4e0cb098ff846908f382f63e1

E-2: GLOBALIZATION AND THE SOCIAL SECTOR: A NEW WORLD ORDER?

"The economic crisis of 2008-10 and the rise in unemployment that accompanied it were associated with more than 260,000 excess cancer-related deaths--including many considered treatable--within the OECD, according to a study from Harvard T.H. Chan School of Public Health, Imperial College London, and Oxford University. The researchers found that excess cancer burden was mitigated in countries that had universal health coverage (UHC) and in those that increased public spending on health care during the study period" [1].

In 2006, in a book titled *Globalization and the Welfare State: Europe and the US* I claimed that globalization and its implications in the economic and social sphere put the US at a disadvantage *vis-à-vis* Europe in the foreseeable future [2]. The gist of the argument was as follows: Free capital movement favours profits, income from interest, and capital gains at the expense of labour.[1] As the financing basis of health insurance based on employment shrinks, health care becomes inaccessible to an ever larger share of the population. Therefore, I argued at the time, this *"will reach crisis proportions as more people are added to the ranks of the 50 million already without health insurance."* I, therefore, concluded that the American health system should be fundamentally overhauled with universal health care and national health insurance financed out of taxes on income from all sources, property, and wealth. My somewhat pessimistic comment then was that such a major shift runs contrary to the American DNA. A society nurtured with *"Freedmanite Chicago School Economics"* bred in the tradition of the *"Go West, young man"*[2] and *"be your own man,"* where *"poverty is sin"* must make quite an about-face to deal with new realities. To some small extent, Obamacare fixed this, but the real problem remains, as we discussed in Part A. UHC and NHI did, however, make it to the central political scene with Bernie Sanders in the 2016 election campaign.

It is exactly with the discouraging conclusion of my 2006 book that this book begins. If globalization proceeds on its current course, large segments of the population stand to lose in relative and, perhaps, in absolute terms. The American middle class, let alone the part of the population below the poverty line, will look for a different social model, especially in health care. The prospect of devoting an increasing share of GDP without meeting the health needs of the population will soon prove politically untenable. Comparing the prospects for the social sector of the two main "Western" players, the US and the EU, I still claim that, contrary to conventional wisdom, the US will need to transform the foundation on which its economic and social models are based. Obamacare in 2010 was but a hint of change in the American DNA.

---

1 A position convincingly argued seven years later in the seminal work of Tomas Picketty, *Capital in the Twenty-First Century*, in 2013.

2 Although this phrase is often credited to Horace Greeley concerning America's westward expansion (related to the concept of Manifest Destiny), John B.L. Soule actually wrote "Go West, young man, and grow up with the country" in an editorial in an Indiana newspaper in 1851. Greeley used the phrase in 1865.

The resistance posed, not only by neo-conservatives, shows that major change in the national paradigm, although essential, will prove difficult. Globalization, not just as an economic phenomenon, but as a widely shared and successful political paradigm, can prove useful. This book is written with this in mind.

A New "Happiness Model" for America

Let us imagine an equation with a dependent variable (Y) and five independent variables. The independent variables are understood to contribute to the value of Y by the values taken by the coefficients X_1, X_2.. X_n. In classical economics this would be the "utility function" of the American society.

$$Y = X_1W + X_2H + X_3E + X_4F + X_5S$$

If Y is the "level of happiness" in a society, it is reasonable to say that it is "explained" or depends on variables such as **W**ealth, **H**ealth, **E**quity, **F**reedom, and **S**ecurity. I suppose few would dispute that these (one may add, of course) are important building blocks for a "happy society." If we "solved" the equation in an American context, Wealth would show the highest "coefficient estimate," meaning that Wealth is the most important factor for happiness. This, however, was probably before 9/11, or the emergence of the Islamic State (IS). After that, Security may be the first, or, at least a close second factor "producing" happiness. On the other hand, Americans may even object to "Equity" being among the variables, whereas in Europe, Equity along with Health, would probably play the most important roles.

The problem with choosing the best solution is with the "hidden relationships." In America, Health may be less important, since Wealth (theoretically) "buys" Health. At society's level, the low priority value of Health is compensated for by high (national) Wealth. For the 30 million still without insurance in 2016, however, the model simply fails. Society maximizes (or tries to) national happiness by maximizing variables such as GDP, albeit with little impact on the happiness of many Americans because of the extremely unequal income distribution. In other words, both Health and Equity receive low values in the Happiness equation. In Europe, on the other hand, the high value placed on Equity is simply because Europeans realized many years ago that only when the whole of society bears the burden in an equitable way, health care, the value of which they hold high, can be available to all. So, to maximize happiness, Europeans value Equity in order to have Health for all.

An example may be useful. We have already seen in Part A that the American GDP includes a huge but inefficient health-care sector with inefficient health insurance, a monstrous claims management infrastructure, and a huge pharmaceuticals market—all of which waste resources and reduce health outcomes. In July 2011, the United Nations passed Resolution 65/309, adopted unanimously by the General Assembly in July 2011, placing "happiness" on the global development agenda. If we were to construct some sort of "National Happiness Index," it is doubtful that a higher GDP would compensate for the negative effects of bad health and income insecurity. By the same token, it seems that the huge military and national security (including police departments) expenditure in the US has limited impact on the feeling of the American people concerning personal security.[3] Why, then, are, Americans so fixated on wealth as a major

---

3   One of the least "talked about" but most disgraceful realities in America is the huge number of people

determinant of happiness? How much can globalization change this perception (if at all)? Can American society adapt to new realities, if change is shown to be imperative? These are questions we raise and tackle in this book in the hope that America will find the suitable answers.

Globalization or Americanization?

The dilemma is new but it has already been addressed in the American literature. For John Updike, globalization was used as a virtual synonym to cover the negative connotations associated with Americanization.[4] The power of economics is, indeed, all pervasive in what we call Americanization. For a long time, especially in the 20th century, the success of the American model promoted the adoption of cultural stereotypes, popular art forms, and even social models. For example, the blatant failure of the American health-care system was overlooked, as ex-communist countries rushed to study the American HMO [3]. Some of us in Europe scratched our heads in disbelief back in the early 1990s as American consultants "advised" governments about health care.[5] As with all "bubbles," this did not last very long.

According to an increasingly popular school of thought, Americanization, even to the American mind, has come to mean "*a setting aside of the social order in ruthless pursuit of profit, a jury-rigged class system based on money, a rootless and dislocated population, a random disordering of priorities*" [4]. The reckless American foreign policy adventurism in the last decade did not reverse this perception. Neither did the "political scene" in 2016. Unfortunately, even the 2016 presidential primaries revealed a rapidly declining public value system, in which political correctness was replaced by vulgarity, and the Presidency seemed something which could be "bought." Hardly an enviable paradigm, one would say. It is not flattering that, as we saw in Chapter C-3, of all the presidential candidates in the primaries, in both parties, only Bernie Sanders made serious health-care reform part of his agenda. It is especially heartening that most of his strength seemed to come from young people. This is a good omen for the future.

Intergenerational Income Mobility Waning

Another source of "American pride" is beginning to prove a myth. Comparative studies of socio-economic mobility have long challenged the notion of "American Exceptionalism," a term invoked by Tocqueville and Marx to describe what was in the 19th century thought of as an exceptionally high rate of social mobility in the United States [5]. An important study, ten years ago, examined intergenerational earnings mobility in the Nordic countries, the UK, and the US [6]. The results suggest that all countries exhibit substantial earnings persistence across generations, but with statistically significant differences across countries. Mobility is lower in the US than in the UK, where it is lower compared to the Nordic countries. Persistence is greatest in the tails of the income distributions and tends to be particularly high in the upper tails. In the US this is reversed with a particularly high likelihood that the children of the poorest fathers will remain in the lowest earnings quintile. This is a grave challenge to the popular notion of Amer-

---

currently jailed or imprisoned.

4 In his disturbing novel *Terrorist*, in 2006.

5 Especially in Latin America or the ex-socialist countries of Eastern Europe.

ican social mobility. In this, the UK is more similar to the US. Low social mobility in the US in the new century, given the rapid rise of income inequality, has huge implications for equity and social justice and is probably the most potent argument in favor of NHI and UHC.

Fortress America: The Myth of Self-Sufficiency

America is, indeed, a huge country, but the European Union is also very big. The idea that the American economy is self-sufficient because of its size holds for Europe as well. Its population is 50% bigger than that of the US (but aging more rapidly) and its economy, at 25.4% of global GDP, is slightly larger than that of the US [7]. Obviously, this does not mean much without a "national" economic policy.[6] Since 2006, a European economic policy has been appearing, and in the Euro area the European Central Bank (ECB) regulates the money supply through interest rates, much as the Federal Reserve (the Fed) does in the US. There is a loose fiscal policy, which may, in fact, be more effective than it is in America, given the ease with which America reached a budget deficit of 6.5% of GDP in the first decade of this century. This was more than twice the limit of 3% set by the Maastricht Treaty for the EU. For many years, warnings about budget deficits, as well as external trade imbalances, were scoffed at in the US as foreigners were more than happy to hold debt in the world's largest economy. Ten years ago, this notion was challenged by the cover story in *The Economist* [8], but the "falling dollar" was not a permanent disease. Instead, it is Europe that is now shaken by BREXIT[7] and other problems that come with maintaining a union of nations in troubled times.

Europe, on the other hand, is not complacent about its market size or its scientific and technological prowess, and realizes weaknesses, such as energy dependence, demographic decline and, above all, climate change. The difference with the US is that Europe often tries to do something about it. Most European countries have signed the Kyoto Treaty, and the EU is talking about a European Fiscal and Economic Policy.[8] Above all, Europe maintains its commitment to humanitarian and social values, supporting superior social support and health systems at half the cost compared to the US.

The Competitiveness Retreat: Is America (still) More Competitive?

"With a low savings rate, a record high current account deficit – well in excess of US$800 billion in 2006, equivalent to some 6.5% of GDP, an all time record – and a worsening of the US net debtor position, there is significant risk to both the country's overall competitiveness and, given the relative size of the United States, the future of the global economy."

The words above are not from an obscure academic exercise, but a direct quote from pages 30-31 of the (2006) World Economic Forum "Global Competitiveness Report." The report, which "demoted" the US from the number 1 position on the world competitiveness scale to number 6, behind Switzerland, three Scandinavian countries and Singapore, comes to the same

---

6 Slowly and hesitantly, however, monetary unification will lead to further economic unification.
7 BREXIT is the exit of Britain from the European Union.
8 See Tomas Picketty: http://www.nybooks.com/articles/2016/02/25/a-new-deal-for-europe/

very disquieting conclusion as the one we predicted in our 2006 book. A year later the American economy caused the Great Recession of 2007. That it also was the first to come out of it and had recovered completely by 2014, shows the dynamism of the American economy. It also showed the sound economic "damage control" by President Obama and the Fed. In any case, it came as a cure to an underlying disease, namely, "unfettered capitalism."

An economy is more competitive if it can produce (and sell) goods and services of comparable quality at a lower price and sustain this mode of production for a considerable period of time—enough, at least, to pay back the necessary investment. In a macro-economic sense, the competitiveness of the economy must take into account the cost of maintaining a workforce and of providing an overall climate amenable to doing business in the manner chosen by the social paradigm of society. In other words, the French economy cannot claim to be competitive in the long run if the society in which it operates suffers unrest such as that experienced in the urban suburbs in the Spring of 2006 and again by labor union strikes in 2016. The question here is whether the American paradigm of rampant individualism, distrust of central government, and unbridled market economics is one in which a productive and competitive society can be sustained in the new environment of a poly-polar globalized world economy.

Obviously Walmart can prevail in its competition with local rivals, as long as its labor policies are less generous than theirs. The question is whether Walmart or any other American company with a cost structure developed in the American social "test tube" can survive in an environment where certain labor policies are simply not acceptable. The ignominious retreat of Walmart from the German market in 2006, after 10 years of efforts and a loss of $1 billion, proves otherwise. It is not surprising that a few months later Walmart was planning to invest another $1 billion to enter into the Chinese market, where labor policies resemble those of the US. However, even in China recent labor legislation allowed increased union activity [9].

Competitiveness, therefore, is not all that matters. According to *Fortune* magazine, *"The fact that the American economy is the world's most competitive comes as cold comfort to the nation's unemployed and to those who have not experienced real wage increases in a generation"* [10]. Michael Porter, professor and lead researcher of the Harvard Business School's 2013-2014 survey on competitiveness says [11]:

> *"The big message here is that if the economy is going to grow and thrive in the long run, you have to be competitive. We define competitiveness as consisting of two things: You have to provide an environment in which firms operating in the US can win in the marketplace, but at the same time we have to do that in a way that allows income and the standard of living of the average citizen to go up. Fundamentally, competitiveness depends on doing those things together. If you're doing one but not the other, it's unsustainable."*

It is precisely on this second criterion of success where the competitiveness of the US economy fails the test. The economy may have recovered fully by 2014, but the standard of living experienced only one positive effect, and this was not from the economy. It was the drop in the number of uninsured Americans because of Obamacare, vilified as nothing less than the "death of the American economy."

References

[1]   Maruthappu M, Watkins J, Noor AM, et al. Economic downturns, universal health coverage, and cancer mortality in high-income and middle-income countries, 1990–2010: A longitudinal analysis. *The Lancet*. 25th May 2016.

[2]   Liaropoulos L. *Globalization and the Welfare State: Europe and the US* Eds. Papazisis. Athens 2006 [in Greek].

[3]   Kleinke JDD. *Oxymorons: The myth of a US Health care system*. United States: Jossey-Bass Inc., US; 2001 Sep 27. ISBN: 9780787959708.

[4]   Stone R. 'Americanization,' real and imagined. *The New York Times* [newspaper on the Internet] 16th Jun 2006 [cited: 7th June 2016]. Available from: http://www.nytimes.com/2006/06/16/arts/16i-ht-idlede17.html

[5]   Jäntti M, Bratsberg B, Røed K, et al. American exceptionalism in a new light: A comparison of intergenerational earnings mobility in the Nordic countries, the United Kingdom and the United States. Warwick Economic Research Papers. 2007.

[6]   Aaberge R, Wennemo T, Bjorklund A, Jantti M, Pedersen PJ, Smith N. Unemployment shocks and income distribution: How did the Nordic countries fare during their crises? *Scandinavian Journal of Economics*. 2000 Mar;102(1):77–99.

[7]   Bryan B. Europe is bigger than the US. *Business Insider* [magazine on the Internet]. 30th Jun 2015 [cited: 7th June 2016]. Available from: http://www.businessinsider.com/charts-eu-economy-is-bigger-than-the-us-2015-6

[8]   *The Economist* [magazine on the Internet] The falling dollar. 30th November 2006 [cited cited: 7th June 2016]. Available from: http://www.economist.com/node/8353179

[9]   NYU Law. The NYU Law School. *The Chinese labor problem: Cynthia Estlund studies how the Communist government is responding to demands for reform from the world's largest workforce.* 28th Jan 2015 [cited cited: 7th June 2016]. Available from: http://www.law.nyu.edu/news/ideas/cynthia-estlund-china-labor-law

[10]   Matthews C. The US has the world's most competitive economy. So what?; *Fortune* [magazine on the Internet] 23rd May 2014 [cited: 7th June 2016]. Available from: http://fortune.com/2014/05/23/the-u-s-has-the-worlds-most-competitive-economy-so-what/

[11]   Matthews C. The slow decay of American economic competitiveness; *Fortune* [magazine on the Internet]. 8th September 2014 [cited: 7th June 2016]. Available from: http://fortune.com/2014/09/08/us-economic-competitiveness/

E-3: THE NEED FOR A NEW SOCIAL VALUE SYSTEM

"My reading of the evidence suggested that 'national interest' was in reality nothing but that of veto points: small but tightly-organized interest groups able to capture public policy precisely because they are few in number and organized effectively. In contrast, the public at large (i.e., the legal and philosophical origin of the national interest) was sidelined owing to its inherent weakness in resolving collective action problems."

—Mehmet Ugur, British-Turkish writer, on the occasion of the European-Turkey Summit
on Turkey's accession to the EU, on March 15, 2016.

Can American Values Cope?

Although on an entirely different subject, the caption above referring to Turkey summarizes the true problem with health-care reform in America. The national interest, which should be a reflection of a country's value system, is seen instead as *"veto points: small but tightly-organized interest groups able to capture public policy. . . ."* It is easy to imagine what these *"veto points"* are in America, and how they have managed to misguide the public discussion on health-care reform. In this book we mentioned a few. The day when this realization dawns on American society, health reform will become a major issue on the political agenda. At that time, if it ever comes, the names of a few presidents will be cited, Barack Obama's is last but not least among them.

Beginning in 1864, during the Civil War, American coins said it: *"In God We Trust"* (later this phrase was added to most American coinage and paper currency). Americans may follow many sects or even religions, but for them, there is "one more god," money. A major question, however, begs for an answer: "Does money alone make people happy?" Perhaps not, Angus Deaton, a British-American economist, would say. He received the 2014 Nobel Prize for his work on this question, and even more on the conventional wisdom in Western cultures, namely that high income brings happiness. This is not true [1], at least not above $75,000 per year, says the evidence by another Nobel Prize winner [2].

Anecdotal evidence does not provide scientific proof, but sometimes it helps when approaching complex issues. An interesting study among UN diplomats gives a rare picture of how people from different cultures perform under new cultural norms. The authors studied the incidence of unpaid parking tickets racked up by diplomats at the UN Mission in New York. Although diplomatic immunity enjoyed by all diplomats means that there was essentially zero legal enforcement of diplomatic parking violations, the authors found that the incidence of unpaid tickets by county correlated highly with the relative corruption index published by "Transparency International" for their respective countries of origin [3]. The conclusion was that a culture of corruption will create corrupt behavior, even when no direct gains from corrupt behavior are to be made [4]. What this means is that culture determines how we behave, but it does not always point us in the right direction.

It is our contention that the American cultural, political, and philosophical DNA will make it hard for America to face many of the challenges posed by the restructuring of the world economic order as discussed in the previous Chapter E-2. On the other hand, there are enough elements in the American culture that may allow, and in fact enable, her to rise to the challenges posed by the new economic environment. America is still a young nation, compared to "old" Europe, and, in a way, even younger compared to its Asian competitors. The great task ahead for America, therefore, is to learn from the rest of the world and adjust its value set in a way that maximizes its comparative advantages, while participating in the new planetary family. After all, as Darwin aptly showed a long time ago, the ability to adjust is the best guarantee for a species to survive and thrive.[1]

The Power of Culture in Shaping Behavior

All cultures need values, because they provide coherence and continuity, but that is where similarities stop. Some cultures foster development, others resist, retard, or inhibit progress. Some cultures check and fight corruption, while others tolerate and permit, if not promote, it.[2] Some focus on the future, while others look back, often with nostalgia. Finally, some cultures encourage the belief that individuals can control their own destinies, while others take a more fatalistic view. In an important study, Harrison [5] presents twenty-five factors that operate very differently in cultures prone to progress than in those that resist it. These factors include our influence over our destiny, the importance we attach to education, the extent to which people identify with and trust others, and the role of women in society. There is some evidence from a meta-analysis of 100 comparative values studies that values important to the Western world are not equally important worldwide [6]. US Muslims, for example, find it hard to accept that, as elders, they may "end up" in an assisted living setup instead of at home with their children [7].

There is another aspect to the relationship between societal values and progress, which has to do with the external environment and the ability of a culture to adjust to major challenges. It is simply the realization that when you are alone at home you can do as you wish, but if you live in a society of people, certain things have to change. If you do not live in harmony with your environment, it will eventually cast you aside, and this usually costs. America is finding out now that unilateralism in major world affairs is a costly business. The war in Iraq probably would not have happened without an administration that chose to bring out the worst in its people's value set. And this is precisely what it did. It exploited the fear instilled in Americans after 9/11 to promote a course of action that proved ruinous to the country.[3] At a cost that some put as high as one trillion dollars, the Iraq war will probably prove to be the single most serious blow to the US international economic standing. Former President Clinton then spoke to the Congress against the invasion of Iraq saying that no matter how accurate the bombs and missiles were, innocent civilians would be killed. This view was shared by many, but the national attitude towards war, as shown by the war in Vietnam half a century before, takes long to be formalized and heard, and often this has consequences. As Richard Reeves wrote in the summer of 2006, after the war in Iraq had already "gone sour" [8]:

---

1 In a country where Darwin was disputed so vehemently, not long ago, this argument may not be very convincing.

2 One cannot help but think of Sicily and the Mafia, but the examples are many.

3 The number of analysts putting the origins of the Islamic State (IS) at the Iraq War is growing.

"Being American seems to mean being alone. It has been more than a couple of years now since the White House was pushing unilateralism. Now President Bush wants friends again. But people in other places remember. America is alone, ready to take on the world – and maybe its own people, too."

America's individualistic value set was ideal when the job of society was to expand in its own backyard, developing the national potential to its fullest extent. The well documented dynamism of American society owes a lot to this spirit of "go it alone" which allowed a rush of innovation and an economic expansion rarely experienced to a comparable degree in scale and duration.[4] It is easy, on the other hand, to see how, in an increasingly complex and interdependent world, the notion of a country's supremacy when coupled with arrogance may eventually produce negative results. Donald Trump is one of the most out-spoken in this way. While formally accepting the presidential nomination at the 2016 Republican National Convention, Trump declared that "Americanism, not globalism, will be our credo." A related article in *The Economist* remarked that "[a] world of wall-builders would be poorer and more dangerous. If Europe splits into squabbling pieces and America retreats into an isolationist crouch, less benign powers will fill the vacuum" [9].

The American value-set includes, and probably in a prominent position, the "love of country." On many occasions this has been demonstrated, as in the two World Wars, when the basic principles on which the country was founded were defended on a world scale. But at times, the pride of the American people and their individualistic spirit can be abused by ruthless populists. The way Donald Trump, for example, treats the real, and indeed horrifying, threat of global warming while remaining the presidential candidate, as this book is written, is not encouraging. After all, it was a previous Republican president, only 16 years ago, who ignored all the available evidence, won the presidency, but harmed the world climate. Equally horrifying is Trump's stated intent to dismantle NATO, the country's and the world's most important international defense coalition.

After this rather long digression to national and international politics, we should return to our main topic. The question is the extent to which the "American exceptionalism" includes, against all evidence, the obviously erroneous conviction that the American health system is "the best in the world." It is bizarre that the notion of individualism or self-reliance in America has been used in a politically immoral way even in health care. The Americans most likely to support Republican opposition to health-care reform are also the ones more likely to benefit from it. As *The New York Times* wrote on Nov. 2, 2015:

"Something startling is happening to middle-aged white Americans. Unlike every other age group, unlike every other racial and ethnic group, unlike their counterparts in other rich countries, death rates in this group have been rising, not falling." [10]

---

4 American individualism can be seen in other facets of life as well. It is not surprising, for example, that America rarely excels at world levels in team sports, other than basketball, which allows personal achievement to shine. Soccer, for example, developed only recently—mainly as a result of Latin American and Balkan immigration. Instead, the major American sports are track and field, swimming, boxing, golf, or tennis. Of course, America would probably excel in a "World Championship" in American football or baseball. That no such championship exists is, again, testimony to "National Individualism" if such a concept exists, or of "American Exceptionalism."

the Next 10 Years."[1] In 2025, says the author, in accordance with Moore's Law, we'll see acceleration in the rate of change as we move closer to a world of true abundance. Among eight areas where we'll see extraordinary transformation in the next decade, the fifth is "Disruption of Healthcare." I would very much like to see the American society take these predictions to heart when choosing the direction that a change in health care should take.

> *"Existing healthcare institutions will be crushed as new business models with better and more efficient care emerge. Thousands of startups, as well as today's data giants (Google, Apple, Microsoft, SAP, IBM, etc.) will all enter this lucrative $3.8 trillion healthcare industry with new business models that dematerialize, demonetize and democratize today's bureaucratic and inefficient system. Biometric sensing (wearables) and AI will make each of us the CEOs of our own health. Large-scale genomic sequencing and machine learning will allow us to understand the root cause of cancer, heart disease and neurodegenerative disease and what to do about it. Robotic surgeons can carry out an autonomous surgical procedure perfectly (every time) for pennies on the dollar. Each of us will be able to regrow a heart, liver, lung or kidney when we need it, instead of waiting for the donor to die."*

Such an apocalyptic view of what is coming in health care is certainly impressive. It is also not compatible with the way the health system in America is currently organized and funded. It is difficult to even imagine what a market-driven, for-profit health system can do when the structure to which it is addressed undergoes such fundamental changes. Without a central governing, regulatory, and financing mechanism, the market alone will create a chaos where the have's will survive for longer and age successfully, while the have-nots will lose ground and probably die much younger. Health may prove the leading force in this major transformation of a caring society to a "privileged" majority and a forgotten, left-behind minority. What a retrogression this would be and what a pity for a would-be world leader. It is for this reason we believe that Americans must abandon the nonchalant attitude that theirs is the best health system in the world, as theirs is the best country in the world. Change is imperative, and it must be, quick, radical, wise, and based on universal values.

---

1   http://singularityhub.com/2015/05/11/the-world-in-2025-8-predictions-for-the-next-10-years/?utm_content=buffercb9af&utm_medium=social&utm_source=facebook.com&utm_campaign=buffer

More middle-aged white Americans are dying, and earlier, because they include more Americans who are poor, less educated, more prone to substance abuse, and more likely to lack health insurance. I may be wrong, but the description of the specific population group, most in need of a sound health system, fits more the stereotype of Republicans in certain states than of Democrats. Ironically, Republicans are the most vociferous opponents of Obamacare. Bogus ideological claims have been used by special interests in the health industry, as discussed in previous chapters, to motivate poor and uninformed people and usurp their vote to promote their own agenda. This is immorality in politics on a large scale.

The Demographic Effect

It is well-known that life expectancy has been increasing steadily in the last decades. The share of the US population over the age of 65 was 8.1% in 1950, 12.4% in 2000, and is projected to reach 20.9% by 2050. The percent over age 85 is projected to more than double from current levels, reaching 4.2% by mid-century [11]. For many, ageing populations threaten the sustainability of fiscal policies. With people retiring at 65, increasing the years of life remaining are not only an increasing burden for the public purse, but also an increasing need for higher savings during the work-life. Even so, some more fundamental questions remain, together with uncertainties, particularly due to the long horizons involved. For many, the increase in life expectancy is thought to increase health care costs, although the years people live in good health increase as well. The combined effect of higher pension expenditure and higher health expenditure due to aging is thought to be a threat to fiscal stability.

Since the thrust of our proposal is for health-care financing to move closer to a model used in Europe, we refer to research results concerning policy-making in countries where social protection is the job of the government, not of the market. In 2005 the Netherlands Bureau for Economic Policy Analysis conducted a study with the title "Can we afford to live longer in better health?" [12]. The study analysed the effects of ageing populations upon public finances, focusing on the implications of population ageing for acute health care, long-term care, and public pension expenditures for 15 EU countries. It paid particular attention to three novel insights: i) a large proportion of health-care spending relates to time to mortality rather than to age; ii) life expectancy may increase much faster than current demographic projections suggest; and, iii) average health status may continue to improve in the future.

The projections show that gains in life expectancy increase age-related expenditure, while improved health, due to the progress in medicine, has the opposite effect. Combined, these trends reduce health-care costs, something we also find in US studies [13], and increase pension expenditures. Their joint effect upon public finances in Europe is rather modest, but the assessment of public finances does not change: The EU study concludes that even if a rapid increase in life expectancy is combined with an improvement in health, current fiscal and social security institutions will be unsustainable, basically because of pension expenditures.

We believe that these results concerning ageing societies and future fiscal developments in the EU hold for the US as well. The aging of the US population makes issues of retirement security increasingly important. Elderly individuals exhibit wide disparities in their sources of income. For those in the bottom half of the income distribution, Social Security is the most important source of support, and program changes—should health care become unaffordable—would directly affect their well-being. Income from private pensions, financial and other assets, and savings from life-time earnings are relatively more important for higher-income elderly individuals, who have more diverse income sources. The trend from private-sector defined benefits to defined contribution pension plans has shifted a greater share of the responsibility for retirement security to individuals, and made that security more dependent on the choices they make before they retire. A significant subset of the population is unlikely to sustain their standard of living in retirement without higher pre-retirement saving. We maintain that part of these savings may come from a reduction in health-care insurance and OOP health costs. The more America contains health costs, the easier it will be for the government to finance the growing retirement cost of a successfully aging population.

In every case, America's value system must come to terms with these unavoidable and largely desirable long-term developments. Society must start to think more in terms of "we" rather than in the extremely individualistic manner of the past, in the time they, and their country, were always young and active, rather than older and dependent. In this book we have tried to show that reducing unnecessary health expenditure will and should be the most preferable course of action in the future. If Americans want to continue to live healthy lives and age successfully, they should do it at a cost they can afford—collectively, and as individuals. It all comes with the maturity and prudence the American society must show, as it comes to terms with an increasingly more complex and less secure future.

References

[1] Fottrell Q. *7 reasons Americans are unhappy*. MarketWatch [website on the Internet]. 17th March 2016 [cited: 7th June 2016]. Available from: http://www.marketwatch.com/story/5-reasons-americans-are-unhappy-2015-10-12?mod=MW_story_latest_news

[2] Kahneman D, Deaton A. High income improves evaluation of life but not emotional well-being. Proceedings of the National Academy of Sciences. 7th September 2010; 107(38):16489–93.

[3] Transparency International. Corruption Perceptions Index 2015 [cited: 7th June 2016]. Available from: http://www.transparency.org/cpi2015?gclid=Cj0KEQjw-YO7BRDwi6Stp7T296ABEiQAD-6iWMXy84bWZcY2wdRv3dULtURoz-cRCdomF-wgA1T7eI00aAlp-8P8HAQ

[4] Fisman R, Miguel E. Nber Working Paper Series, Cultures of Corruption: Evidence from Diplomatic Parking Tickets. Cambridge, USA: National Bureau of Economic Research; 2006.

[5] Harrison LE. *The Central Liberal Truth: How Politics Can Change a Culture and Save It from Itself*. United States: Oxford University Press, USA; 2008 Jun 5. ISBN: 9780195331806.

[6] Triandis HC. The self and social behavior in differing cultural contexts. *Psychological Review*. 1989; 96(3):506–20.

[7] Clemetson L. U.S. Muslims confront taboo on nursing homes. *The New York Times* [newspaper on the Internet]. 18th Feb 2006 [cited: 7th June 2016]. Available from: http://www.nytimes.com/2006/06/13/us/13muslim.html

[8] Reeves R. The dangerous Americans - Editorials & Commentary - International Herald Tribune. *The New York Times* [newspaper on the Internet]. 7th Jun 2006 [cited: 7th June 2016]. Available from: http://www.nytimes.com/2006/06/07/opinion/07iht-edreeves.1914874.html?_r=0

[9] *The Economist* [magazine on the Internet]. The new political divide. 30th July 2016 [cited: 30th July 2016]. Available from: http://www.economist.com/news/leaders/21702750-farewell-left-versus-right-contest-matters-now-open-against-closed-new

[10] Kolata G. Death rates rising for middle-aged white Americans, study finds. *The New York Times* [newspaper on the Internet] 4th Nov 2015 [cited: 7th June 2016]. Available from: http://www.nytimes.com/2015/11/03/health/death-rates-rising-for-middle-aged-white-americans-study-finds.html?emc=edit_th_20151103&nl=todaysheadlines&nlid=12129446&_r=0

[11] Poterba JM. Nber Working Paper Series, Retirement Security in an Aging Society. Cambridge, USA: National Bureau of Economic Research; 2014.

[12] Westerhout E, Pellikaan F. CPB Document no 85: *Can we afford to live longer in better health?* Netherlands: CPB Netherlands Bureau for Economic Policy Analysis; 2005 Jun 6.

[13] Lubitz J, Cai L, Kramarow E, Lentzner H. Health, Life Expectancy, and Health Care Spending among the Elderly. *New England Journal of Medicine*. 11th September 2003; 349(11):1048–55.

AFTERWORD

On January 17, 1961, Dwight D. Eisenhower ended his presidential term by warning the nation about the increasing power of the military-industrial complex. His remarks, issued during a televised farewell address to the American people, were particularly significant since "Ike" had served the nation as military commander of the Allied forces during WWII. Eisenhower urged his successors to strike a balance between a strong national defense and diplomacy in dealing with the Soviet Union. He did not suggest arms reduction and in fact acknowledged that the bomb was an effective deterrent to nuclear war. However, cognizant that America's peacetime defense policy had changed drastically since his military career, Eisenhower expressed concerns about the growing influence of what he termed the military-industrial complex. At that time expenditure on defense was 50.8% of federal spending and 33.8% of public spending or 9.1% of GDP.

Since then, defense spending in the US, although rising in nominal terms, was down to 3.3% of GDP in 2015.[1] In January 2017, President Obama will address the nation concluding a rather successful presidency, the first in a very long time which produced a major change in the health-care system. I believe he will not be far off track if he coins another term, that of the medical-insurance complex. At the time of Eisenhower, total health expenditure was 5% of GDP. Obama will leave his presidency with the nation already looking at health expenditure at almost 20% of GDP. Almost half of the $3 trillion in 2017 will be public expenditure. I do think that the American health system must be reformed, but not simply because it is unjust. I use the same argument in the heart of the main philosophy in America. Its value system and the basis on which most political arguments are founded are self-interest and the pursuit of individual happiness. The health system must change because it is dangerous for the economic health not only of the country, but of each individual separately. It costs too much in health insurance, out-of-pocket expenditure, and in waste of resources. It offers too little, and it increases the public debt. In that sense, it is "bad business," something to which the American DNA must show little tolerance. On top of this, the American health system, although capable of offering the best in health care, it is also a heaven for the "cleptocracy" of special interests, be they in private insurance, drugs, health-care management, or even among the medical profession.

American health care must strive to retain its excellence in scientific achievement, health education, technology, infrastructure, and quality of human resources. At the same time, it must introduce new methods of professional and public oversight in the quest for greater efficiency, effectiveness, and equity. The central direction should be towards greater public stewardship and more accountability. The way forward should be the reduction of the role of the market and the enlargement of the public domain. In other words, the health-care system must add to the welfare of all the people living in America and not only to individual wealth.

I will close this book with a prediction taken from "The World in 2025: 8 Predictions for

---

1 http://comptroller.defense.gov/Portals/45/Documents/defbudget/fy2016/FY16_Green_Book.pdf